SEA
DEVILS

SEA DEVILS

PIONEER SUBMARINERS

JOHN SWINFIELD

For Bridgit and my late mother and father.

It is the greatest art of the devil to convince us he does not exist.

Charles Baudelaire (1821–67)

First published 2014
by Spellmount, an imprint of

The History Press
The Mill, Brimscombe Port
Stroud, Gloucestershire, GL5 2QG
www.thehistorypress.co.uk

© John Swinfield, 2014

The right of John Swinfield to be identified as the Author
of this work has been asserted in accordance with the
Copyright, Designs and Patents Act 1988.

British Library Cataloguing in Publication Data.
A catalogue record for this book is available from the British Library.

ISBN 978 0 7509 5356 6

Typesetting and origination by The History Press
Printed in Great Britain

Contents

Acknowledgements

I would like to thank the staffs of the National Maritime Museum; Royal Navy Museum; Greenwich Maritime Institute (University of Greenwich); George Malcolmson, Royal Navy Submarine Museum; Andrew Choong, Brass Foundry (NMM); Imperial War Museum; Barrow-in-Furness Submariners Association; Cambridge University Library; Churchill Archives. Special thanks go to: Anna, Luis, Dominic and Helen; Dick Richards; Shaun Barrington, Rebecca Newton and Paul Baillie-Lane at The History Press; a legion more who so generously offered their time, patience, reassurance and constant encouragement. Inundation would have been certain without Bridgit. To all the submariners past and present, whose ceaseless courage and fortitude still astonish: distant sentries in sunless depths, their silent vigil offers security to all those who lead more sheltered lives.

Author's Note: Quixotic Machines

After a lengthy period writing a history of the military and commercial airship, I learned that dirigibles were one of the most fickle forms of transport yet devised. I have not changed my view, though I now appreciate that, in its caprice, coquettishness and complexity, the early submarine matched that of the airship. The distinct parallels between the two are touched upon in this volume: while the airship flew without wings, the submarine, curious in many ways, is a ship that travels not on but beneath the water. I wanted this work to appeal to a lay as well as a scholarly audience: consequently, there is as much emphasis on the politics, culture and personalities, the scheming, shenanigans and skirmishing, as there is on the technicalities and hardware. I have included a list of participants, which serves as a brief guide to who did what where and sometimes when, and extensive appendices to amplify and illuminate if the reader seeks further clarification. There is a comprehensive guide to other submarine books, some of them first class, to whet the appetite of those caught in the thrall of the submarine; some I have shamelessly mined for nuggets of wisdom, as credited in the text, and to whose authors I am appreciative and indebted. The title of this work is taken from a quote in 1900 by the architect of the modern submarine: the rebellious and captivating Irish–American John Philip Holland (1840–1914). The submarine has a long, eventful history, rich in eccentricity. It made its mark, however, only comparatively recently. It was during the second half of the nineteenth century, with the developed world growing molten with invention, that the submarine benefited from a diversity of more general industrial breakthroughs. Metal replaced wood, and petrol and electric engines made previous forms of propulsion obsolete. Finally, the gradual refinement of the torpedo guaranteed that the submarine would become one of the world's deadliest weapons. The potential of the submarine would be seen in the First World War when the Victoria Cross, Britain's highest military decoration, was awarded to no less than five commanders. Twenty years later, on the eve of the Second World War, the presence of the submarine had become cardinal to victory. As is so often the case, it was conflict which quickened development. *Sea Devils* traces the submarine's evolution from embryo, a period haphazardly recorded and subject to fable, to the conclusion of the First World War, as, by this time, its principal characteristics had been established.

By 1918, it had become convention that the submarine required underwater propulsion that did not depend on air; thus batteries came into their own. The physics of buoyancy had been largely mastered: a submarine needed ballast tanks filled with water to make it dive and from which water could be expelled; the tanks were then replenished with air to ensure that it surfaced. Craft were fitted with tanks that could be partially filled, enabling it to be balanced or 'trimmed' − kept level, or at an angle required by its commander. Other fixtures were also developed: a rudder for steerage was positioned at the stern, as on surface vessels; horizontal rudders on either side of the craft facilitated diving and surfacing in a way not entirely dissimilar to the manner in which ailerons work on aeroplanes' wings; a conning tower on the upper deck incorporated a periscope for a commander to take bearings and study surface activity without imperilling craft and crew, nor negating its axial advantage, that of stealth, by having to surface and reveal his presence. Such fundamentals had been established by the end of the Great War, but their achievement had taken 400 years of costly trial and considerable error.

Prologue

Errors like straws upon the surface flow;
He who would search for pearls must dive below.
John Dryden (1631–1700)
Prologues and Epilogues: Prologue, All For Love.

In his desire to fly man has not been unduly inhibited by being devoid of wings. Nor has his ambition to swim with the fishes, not on but *beneath* the sea, been thwarted by an absence of gills, fins or tail. If one *really* could fly like a bird or swim like a whale, such compulsions might be more easily fathomed. While most would think of journeying in a submarine as the human equivalent of being a sardine trapped in a can, others have been beguiled. This is the story of those not content to go down to the sea in ships, but who yearned to voyage beneath it, performing astonishing feats to achieve their goal. The submarine began with a quirky carnival of hobbyists, engineers and scientists: obsessive, gifted, eccentric, and sometimes mad. As decades turned to centuries, bizarre craft metamorphosed into more practical vessels: fantasy slowly becoming reality. The starry-eyed were elbowed aside as businessmen moved in, driven more by profit than the unalloyed joy of virgin science. In its tortoise-like progress the submarine would become the dangerous plaything of the military, the novelty of its presence resented by navies hidebound by tradition, steeped in the belief that grandeur equalled might and that submariners were the wrong sort and their trade underhand. The chronicle of those besotted by getting underway underwater is one of fortitude and fantasy, imagination and innovation; it is a salute to the forgotten legions of long-dead from whose daring, ingenuity and tenacity would eventually emerge an extraordinary machine that was destined to change the course of maritime history and military thinking forever.

Dramatis Personae

ACKROYD-STEWART, HERBERT (1864–1927). Yorkshire-born creator of heavy oil engine, made by Richard Hornsby, Grantham, Lincolnsnhire.

ARNOLD-FORSTER, LIEUTENANT (later Rear Admiral) Delafield Frank (1828–59). Captain of the first British-built, American-designed *Holland* submarine, launched by Vickers of Barrow-in-Furness in 1901.

BACON, REGINALD (1863–1947). First British submarine chief. Cerebral, cautious and technically gifted.

BAUER, WILHELM (1822–75). German submarine creator, who took a band aboard which played music underwater to entertain a Russia tsar on his wedding day.

BLISS, ELIPHALET (1836–1903). American businessman. Leading New York-based maker of torpedoes, which transformed the war at sea when allied to the submarine.

BOURGEOIS, SIMEON (1815–87). French designer, with Charles Brun, of the steam-driven *Le Plongeur* submarine.

BOURNE, WILLIAM (*c.* 1535–82). Englishman and former innkeeper, who produced Britain's first submarine design. Brilliant, self-taught and prescient.

BORELLI, GIOVANNI (1608–79). Italian priest and submarine designer. Used leather pouches as buoyancy bags.

BOYLE, Lieutenant Commander (later Rear Admiral) **EDWARD COURTNEY** (1883–1967). Intrepid commander of the submarine *E-14* in the Sea of Marmara during the Gallipoli Campaign. He was later awarded the VC.

BRUN, CHARLES (1821–97). French naval builder of *Le Plongeur* submarine.

BUSHNELL, DAVID (1740–1824). American builder of barrel-shaped *Turtle* submarine, which made the first attack on a warship.

CABLE, FRANK (1863–1945). Crucial in John Holland's coterie. Captained first *Holland* submarine on American trials and tutored crews in England on British *Hollands*.

CALDWELL, HARRY (1873–1938). Distinguished US Navy officer. Captained the first *Holland* submarine and helped to establish its credentials.

DAY, JOHN. Eighteenth-century woodworker drowned in his sinking boat.

DE SON. Frenchman and creator of the spear-pointed *Rotterdam* submarine with clockwork motor.

DIESEL, RUDOLPH (1858–1913). German inventor of diesel engine modified and used eventually in submarines. Its fitment transformed utility.

DREBBEL, CORNELIUS (1572–1633). Dutch alchemist influenced by Bourne. Built underwater rowing boat smeared in grease to make it waterproof.

DURSTON, SIR JOHN (1846–1917). Royal Navy Chief Engineer, 1889–1907. Critical and suspicious of petrol engines being used in submarines.

FISHER, JOHN ARBUTHNOT (1841–1920). Mercurial reforming British admiral and champion of submarines.

FORSTMANN, *Kapitanleutnant* **WALTHER** (1883–1973). Successful German U-boat commander. With Perière, he made test voyages using U-boats as aircraft carriers.

FOURNIER, GEORGES (1595–1652). French priest, writer and philosopher, who designed the wheeled submarine.

FROST, ELIHU (1860–1925). US lawyer. Promoted and helped fund John Holland. Formed Holland Torpedo Boat Company, which was taken over by Isaac Rice's Electric Boat Company.

FULTON, ROBERT (1765–1815). American engineer who built *Nautilus* for the French to attack the Royal Navy. He later developed a commercially successful steamboat service.

GARRETT, the Reverend **GEORGE** (1826–1902). English clergyman and inventor of *Resurgam* (*I will rise again*) submarine. One version, however, did not rise again, and he and his crew drowned.

GOUBET, CLAUDE (1870–1914). French civil engineer who built battery-driven submarine with the novelty of two helmsmen sitting back to back.

GRUBB, SIR HOWARD (1844–1931). Dublin optical inventor of the periscope used by First World War soldiers and submariners; perfected in submarines by Lake in US and Bacon in Britain.

HOLBROOK, Lieutenant **NORMAN DOUGLAS** (1888–1976). Commander of submarine *B11* in the Dardanelles, and won the first VC of the Great War and submarine service. An Australian town was later named after him.

HOLLAND, JOHN PHILIP (1841–1914). Brilliant Irish–American inventor of *Holland* submarines, forerunner of contemporary boats, which were bought by US and British navies.

HORNSBY, RICHARD (1790–1864). Englishman and founder of Lincolnshire-based firm that made steam units and Ackroyd-Stewart heavy oil engines bought by the Admiralty for submarine trials.

HORTON, Lieutenant Commander (later Admiral) **SIR MAX KENNEDY** (1883–1951). Heroic commander of the submarine *E9* during the Heligoland and Baltic campaigns. Also a submariner during the Second World War.

HOWELL, JOHN ADAMS (1840–1918). US Navy officer who developed the self-steering torpedo guided by gyroscope.

HUNLEY, HORACE LAWSON (1823–63). Revered American builder of *Hunley* hand-powered Confederate submarine in American Civil War. First submarine to sink a warship.

KEYES, ROGER (1872–1945). Inspecting Captain Submarines, later Admiral of the Fleet. Valiant and popular, though criticised for ordering steam submarines and buying foreign designs.

KIMBALL, WILLIAM (1848–1930). Ex-US Navy officer, torpedo expert, influential friend and supporter of John Holland.

LAKE, SIMON (1866–1945). Highly influential and successful American submarine builder, and main competitor to John Holland. Launched *Argonaut*.

LAUBEUF, MAXIME (1864–1939). Talented French builder of influential, twin-hulled, dual propulsion, steam reciprocating and battery-driven submarine *Narval*.

LITTLE, Lieutenant **CHARLES** 'Tiny' (1882–1973). An early submarine captain and, later, commander of the Grand Fleet Submarine Flotilla during the Great War, 1916–18.

LUPPIS, GIOVANNI (1813–75). Austrian Navy officer who initiated the idea of a torpedo. His idea was taken over and developed by Robert Whitehead.

MAHAN, ALFRED THAYER (1840–1914). American naval strategist who influenced Tirpitz, the Kaiser and others. Writings led, in part, to arms-navy building race before the Great War.

MAXIM, HIRAM Sir (1840–1916). American-born naturalised British businessman: submarine innovator and inventor of the Maxim gun, the mousetrap, fairground rides and aircraft.

MERSENNE, MARIN (1588–1648). French priest who worked with Father Georges Fournier on the wheeled submarine.

MORRIS, CHARLES (1853–1914). Far-seeing American engineer. Important and gifted supporter of submarines and the endeavours of John Holland.

McCLINTOCK, JAMES and **BAXTER, WILSON**. American businessmen in consortium with Hunley, which built *Pioneer* and *American Diver* submarines in the American Civil War.

MOFFETT, Admiral **WILLIAM** (1869–1933). Father of US naval aviation. Much-loved, influential, a friend of President Franklin D. Roosevelt, and a powerful submarine advocate.

NASMITH, Lieutenant Commander (later Admiral, Sir) **MARTIN DUNBAR** (1883–1965). Daring British officer who served in both World Wars. Won the VC as commander of submarine *E-11* at Gallipoli.

NIMITZ, Admiral **CHESTER W.** (1885–1966). Legendary US Navy chief. Captained early submarines and led US submarine fleet. Highly respected strategist and commander.

NIXON, LEWIS (1861–1940). Graduate of the US Naval Academy and respected naval architect who founded Crescent Shipyard, New Jersey. Built illustrious ships and submarines.

NORDENFELT, THORSTEN (1842–1920). Swedish industrialist, engineer and gun-maker who worked with the English submarine cleric George Garrett.

OTTO, AUGUST (1832–91). German inventor of internal combustion engine in 1876. Represented crucial progression for submarines.

PAPIN, DENIS (1647–*c.* 1712). French physicist and mathematician whose submarine looked like a watering can.

PARSONS, CHARLES ALGERNON (1854–1931). British inventor of the steam turbine engine for marine propulsion. Built sleek-hulled, super-fast yacht *Turbinia*.

PERAL, ISAAC (1851–95). Gifted Spanish Navy officer who built the innovative and advanced *Peral* submarine. This highly talented engineer was frustrated in his career and died prematurely.

PERIÈRE, LOTHAR VON ARNAULD DE LA (1886–1941). Formidable German U-boat commander and Chief of the German Naval Air Service. He later conducted U-boat aeroplane-carrying trials.

RICE, ISAAC (1850–1915). An astute businessman who formed the Electric Boat Company and sold British Admiralty *Holland* designs. He also produced *Holland* and *Plunger* submarines for the US Navy.

SANDFORD, Lieutenant Commander **RICHARD DOUGLAS** (1891–1918). Captain of the submarine *C3* during the Great War. He was killed on a mission to blow up a viaduct in the raid on Zeebrugge, Belgium, and was awarded a posthumous VC.

SCHWIEGER, *Kapitanleutnant* **WALTHER** (1885–1917). German U-Boat commander who sank forty-nine ships, including the *Lusitania*, which helped bring the United States into the Great War.

SPEAR, LAWRENCE (1870–1950). American naval architect with the Electric Boat Company; one of those who forced Holland to quit the company. Spear went on to forge a powerful corporate career.

SYMONS, NATHANIEL. Eighteenth-century English carpenter who built a sinking and surfacing boat.

TIRPITZ, ALFRED VON (1849–1930). German Navy chief, arch exponent of powerful U-boat fleet and the driving force behind German fleet restructure pre-1914.

TUCK, Professor **HORACE** (1825–1900). American inventor of *Peacemaker* submarine powered by fireless steam engine. Relatives had him locked up in a lunatic asylum.

VILLEROI, BRUTUS DE (1794–1874). French inventor of the first US Navy submarine, *Alligator*, in 1862.

WEDDIGEN, *Kapitanleutnant* **OTTO EDUARD** (1882–1915). German U-boat commander who sank three elderly British warships in an hour in 1915, killing 1,459 officers and men.

WHITE, Lieutenant Commander **GEOFFREY SAXTON** (1886–1918). Followed Boyle as commander of submarine *E-14* in the Gallipoli Campaign. Killed by gunfire and awarded a posthumous VC.

WHITEHEAD, ROBERT (1823–1905). English engineer who invented the first properly effective naval torpedo.

ZÉDÉ, GUSTAVE (1825–1891). French naval architect who launched the technically advanced submarine *Gymnote*, and the larger and more ambitious *Gustave Zédé*.

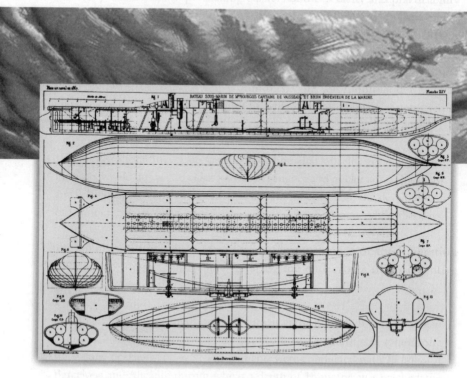

'Bateau sous-marin de M Bourg[e]ois Capitaine de Vaisseau et Brun Ingenieur de la Marine.' See pages 39-40.

1

To Take the Plunge

A monk builds a toy duck, watching it waddle, dive and swim back to the surface, his devotions rudely interrupted by thoughts of carnage and destruction. A submariner throws a switch, accidentally killing himself and others in a deafening explosion. A man pedals a glorified barrel with clever fitments through a harsh sea to fix explosives to a warship's hull. A Frenchman builds a submarine disguised as a watering can. An American is committed to a lunatic asylum after spending his fortune on a steam-driven submarine. A British commander surfaces his boat to perch on its stern rail and answer the call of nature while a German Zeppelin drops bombs on him. Submariners are locked in a bread oven to see if any suffocate. Another departs his craft and swims after a torpedo which has failed to detonate, and, not wishing to see it wasted, chaperones it back to his boat. Three armoured cruisers are sunk in one hour. A liner is attacked and 1,200 drown. A submarine sinks without warning; its commander and crew are never seen again. Forty submariners gasp for oxygen trapped in a hulk on a seabed; fighting for breath, chests heaving, lungs imploding, they last fifty-seven hours, while thirty more are already dead. The saga of the submarine is one of tragedy and triumph, heroism and hardship, its inventors and operators as daring as their exploits.

Across the globe and down the centuries, a diversity of personalities would come to be recognised as central to the advancement of the submarine. They were from different backgrounds and spurred on by a galaxy of motives: some wanted money; others sought maritime supremacy; some were caught in the thrall of new technology; and others strove to go where nobody had gone before. With its powerful navy it was inevitable that Britain would play a central role, though the initial response of its Admiralty was tardy and steeped with suspicion. In the British and American navies, two names stand out in the annals of submarine progress. The first was the mercurial British admiral John Arbuthnot Fisher, who booted Britain's obsolete, class-ridden Victorian

21

navy into a modern fighting fleet. The second was an Irish–American, John Philip Holland, who was a persistent, steel-willed religious schoolteacher and Irish liberationist whose facility for engineering was honed by an animosity towards the British. Holland invented what is now generally accepted as the world's first submarine, though others might claim the distinction. In Britain, Fisher's endorsement ensured its evolution. From designer and believer came a weapon to force eventual obsolescence on the thinking and hardware which had preceded it; an instrument to transform all prevailing strategic and political opinion forever. However, the curious, tragic and sometimes farcical saga of the pioneer submarine pre-dates Fisher and Holland by nearly four centuries.

Though its history brims with sporadic interludes of lunacy, once the template of the contemporary submarine had been achieved then the changes it wrought laid waste to aeons of nautical convention. Before its inception, naval might had been gauged by simple arithmetic: numbers of ships in a fleet, their size, power and range; fortification in terms of thickness of hull and superstructure; numbers of guns, strength of arsenal, capabilities of commanders; and the sagacity of the armchair admirals who directed their deployment. This was a sensible, if prosaic, way of assessing naval potency, though the submarine, and swift ascendancy of the aeroplane, rendered such measurements largely redundant.

The early response from officers in the Royal Navy was imperious: submarines were small, silly and scruffy; their captains and crews the wrong sort. Naval intransigence to the novel was customary, though it would have taken a seer to imagine little 'tin-fish' would at some distant date usurp traditional maritime power, disproving entrenched notions about scale and firepower being immutable guarantees of security and effectiveness. Battleships had ruled supreme: oceanic colossi, their command unchallenged; a daunting invincibility exemplified by the density of their plating; each in its pomp and ceremony a personification of imperial glory. The submarine would eventually reduce the battleship to a state of wretched fragility.

It has become convention that, in charting the heritage of the submarine, the endeavours of a British former naval gunner and mathematician, William Bourne (c. 1535–82) of Gravesend, Kent, are taken as a starting point.[1] Bourne produced what is considered one of the earliest designs for a submersible, though it is no surprise that Bourne was, in fact, pipped by the scientific prophet Leonardo da Vinci (1452–1519). Not content with sketching falling leaves envisaged as helicopters, da Vinci imagined diving suits and diving machines which, in all essentials, were submarines.[2] The self-educated Bourne, a former innkeeper, served as a gunner under Admiral Sir William Monson (1569–1643) and it can be assumed he was greatly influenced by Monson, who was judged among the more enlightened and educated naval officers, as evidenced by his Naval Tracts penned during his final years. The Tracts, though arcane, assured Monson of his place in seafaring history, offering a lucid, if still esoteric insight into naval minutiae.

Bourne, too, wrote maritime articles designed to supplement a meagre living which he forged by addressing numerous technical and natural conundrums. He also researched and wrote navigational critiques which advanced the way sailors might plot and navigate their voyages. The story of the submarine and its lengthy creation is awash with inventive, courageous, largely forgotten souls: Bourne deserves his recognition for refining the navigational principles which enhanced the axioms of good seamanship which prevailed at the time. In 1574 he wrote an approachable, less academic treatise, which challenged those precepts defined in the *Arte de Navegar*, published in 1551 by the brilliant Spanish royal cosmographer, Martin Cortes de Albacar (1510–81). *Arte de Navegar* was one of the most important books on navigation in the sixteenth century; it was carried by the English adventurer and explorer Sir Francis Drake (1540–96), an indication of its central position in nautical thinking of the period.[3] Bourne's work, *A Regiment of the Sea*[4] scrutinised de Albacar's peregrinations and explored, drawing on his own mathematical prowess, the way in which mariners could take bearings using triangulation and, by the use of a cross-staff, determine their own position by plotting that of the stars and the sun.

In 1578, in his book *Inventions or Devises, Very Necessary for all Generalles and Captaines, as well by Sea as by Land* (usually called *Inventions or Devises*), Bourne described a submersible wooden-framed craft encased in leather and made waterproof by being smeared in a greased potion. It was to be rowed by its crew, though sadly it was never built. Almost fifty years would elapse before his underwater rowing boat was finally made flesh by an alchemist from the Netherlands, Cornelius Drebbel (1572–1633). Drebbel's fame owed much to the patronage of James I (1566–1625), the first Stuart king. King James I had an inquiring mind and a penchant for filling his court with writers, philosophers, explorers and theologians. The king's pursuit of those he felt could see beyond the accepted led to Drebbel, at the age of 32, being invited to England. Born at Alkmaar in the Netherlands, he had been apprenticed to the painter and engraver Hendrick Goltzius (1558–1617) who might have introduced him to alchemy.

Drebbel was ingenious and prolific. His most renowned innovation was a perpetual motion device in the form of a globe. He also invented a machine that recorded the season, year, day and hour, a contrivance which bewitched the king and his court and won the Dutchman international plaudits. It also caused him trouble. Its fame saw him twice invited to Prague in 1610 and 1619 by the Holy Roman Emperor Rudolf II (1552–1612), who had a keen interest in scientific development, immersing himself in alchemy, astrology and the occult. On each occasion Drebbel was thrown into jail, becoming ensnared in the volatile politics of the time. It was only royal intervention from England that secured his release.[5]

Drebbel had a cornucopia of amazing inventions: some were wizardly, with one supposedly able to magic up thunderstorms. Coupling his vivid imagination to innate technical flair, he turned his considerable intellect to nautical matters, and his subsequent craft would echo Bourne's earlier ideas. Details about Drebbel's submersible are absent: how he delivered an air supply is a mystery. Such gaps are a bane and apply to numerous aspects of submarine history. It was recorded, however, that he built three submarines, each larger and more capable than its predecessor, and that it is probable they were powered by rowing, with a crew of three or four labouring at their oars. Within the craft, pigskin bladders were tied at the throat by a length of rope. A web of pipes joined the bladders to the exterior of the craft. For it to submerge the ropes were untied, permitting the bladders to fill with water, creating sufficient weight for the vessel to sink. To raise the craft the crew squeezed the water from the bladders, leaving only air, lightening the boat and increasing its buoyancy. The use of animal organs, mixing the archaic with the advanced, played its part in aviation as well as maritime progress.*

Much of the thinking in airship technology is in early submarines. An airship's hydrogen gas was held in impervious bags of goldbeaters' skin scrupulously crafted from the intestine of cattle; a voluminous hydrogen bag comprised hundreds of skins sewn together. Large herds of cattle were bred

---

* More than three centuries after Drebbel, one of the few highly placed supporters of submarines in Britain, Admiral Fisher, was an advocate of the unjustly derided military airship, naval chiefs being among the most sardonic. Fisher's admirers claim his support of such contraptions was because he was far-seeing; detractors allege that, being himself combustible and eccentric, he had a propensity for oddball causes; the theory may have an arguable basis in truth with regards to the airship, but of the submarine is luculently untrue. In the opening years of the twentieth century, there was a crossover in thinking, technology and personnel between submarines and airships. Small dirigibles such as the Sea Scout Zero class served with commendable distinction as reconnaissance craft, submarine spotters and convoy patrols in the Great War, thanks partly to Jacky Fisher's insistence on their construction and deployment. Scouting airships, introduced in 1916 under the auspices of the Royal Naval Air Service, had a three-man crew of sky-sailors and could stay aloft for seventeen hours, making them effective for submarine reconnaissance and having a superior field of vision to surface craft.

specifically as the source of goldbeaters' skin. Had Drebbel's pigskin diving bladder caught on, doubtless the demand for home-reared swine would have rocketed.[6]

Drebbel's third submarine caused a sensation. It carried a handful of passengers, inarguably intrepid though some questioned their sanity, with a crew of six frenziedly working the oars (others insist it was twelve). As with its two forerunners, the wooden frame of the boat had been encased in a leather shell and coated with layers of grease to make it impervious to water, though in initial tests it leaked like a sieve. It was fitted with a watertight hatch – though in the context of pioneer submarines such reassuring adjectives should be treated with caution – and a primitive rudder for some semblance of steering. In *c.* 1622, King James I, accompanied by the perfumed elite which comprised his court and thousands of excited Londoners, thronged the Thames to see Drebbel's submersible disappear and, to much babbling and widespread astonishment, reappear. Supposedly it could stay submerged for three hours at 15 feet (ft) below the surface; it seems the problem of getting air to its occupants had been solved by the installation of two pipes which floated above the surface. This might have worked if the machine were to maintain a constant depth, but it would have been catastrophic had it dived more deeply. While the craft remained at a stable level it is feasible that one pipe could have supplied the vessel with fresh air, while used air would have been expelled through the other.

Maritime historians ponder if it was a true submarine capable of total or only partial submersion. There is also discussion about the breathing pipes: were they the first snorkels? It is an entertaining proposition, with the first snorkel not being seen until late in the Second World War, three centuries after the Drebbel's invention. The premise is further clouded by reports that he had found a way of purifying contaminated air by heating salt petre to make oxygen, referred to as the magical distillation of a mysterious chemical. There is also speculation about the amount of oxygen which would have been consumed by a crew of six panting oarsmen – let alone twelve – plus the passengers, who would have been breathing heavily if only out of sheer terror; it seems unlikely a solitary pipe would have sufficed in preventing the voyagers being overcome by foul air.

It is usual for maritime historians to dwell on such arcane matters. Even if the detail has become hazy with the passing of centuries, Drebbel seems to have achieved some sort of amazing feat. All this could be wrong: a well-spun yarn romanticised over the years.[7] Perhaps Drebbel's craft was only a partially submerged rowing boat, sloped at the front so that when rowed it became partly awash, driven a few inches beneath the water by the forward motion as the rowers got into their stride. And if the oarsmen ceased at their labours it would have risen as any sodden log might do. We may never know.

Divine Intervention

In Drebbel's wake came men of the cloth, with French and Italian priests producing designs. Though why the Church wished to swim with the fishes is an enigma; it would have been a miracle. Two centuries later, a technically minded English vicar, the Reverend (Rev.) George Garrett, made a significant contribution, but more of him later. Submersible history is rich with references to God and the Devil, the submarine being miraculous and unearthly.*

In the 1630s the French priests, thinkers and writers, Georges Fournier (1595–1652) and Marin Mersenne (1588–1648), designed an armed submarine made largely of copper, pointed at the stern and bow, and having wheels with which to trundle along the seabed; an arresting notion if not entirely practical, though wheeled submarines were still being explored two centuries later and are dealt with here. An Italian priest, Abbé Giovanni Alfonso Borelli (1608–79), another submarine hopeful, addressed the eternal problem, that of buoyancy, by squeezing out water from leather containers. While airships used the intestine of cattle and Drebbel employed his pig bladders, Borelli favoured goatskin. He would have made his submarine dive by filling a large quantity of goatskin bags with water and then squeezing them dry to make the craft rise, hopefully; there is no certainty it would have done. He had a knowledge of physics, and understood the theory of displacement and the conundrum of weight versus volume with which designers had to contend. Though strong on the academic and theoretical side, there is little evidence that Borelli ever built a submarine; to further confuse matters there is a well-known diagram of his creation. If in reality it is a work of fiction, nobody knows.

Bishop John Wilkins of Chester (1614–72), England, was another influential figure who recognised the possibilities of the submarine in his work *Mathematicall Magick* of 1648.[10] Wilkins was a polymath, his book in part influenced by the writings of Marin Mersenne, with Fournier the designer

---

* Phrases common in the surface marine were used in submarines. When steam ousted muscle power in submarines, references were heard to the Devil and slice: long, unwieldy tools that stokers in surface ships used to break up clinker.[8] A Second World War submarine veteran said: 'We were between the devil and the deep. If we were down they dropped depth-charges. If we came up we got shot at, bombed or rammed. Best to stay under and keep praying.'[9]

of the wheeled submarine. His tome was concerned with engineering, mechanical and scientific breakthroughs, with some based on achievements of the time and others parts more speculative. If some references to submarines appear optimistic today – with the benefit of over 360 years of hindsight – his prophecies about the submarines' strategic strengths were unerringly accurate. He wrote of the submarine:

> Tis private: a man may thus go to any coast in the world invisibly, without discovery or prevented in his journey.
>
> Tis safe, from the uncertainty of Tides, and the violence of Tempests, which do never move the sea above five or six paces deep. From Pirates and Robbers which do so infest other voyages; from ice and great frost, which do so much endanger the passages towards the Poles.
>
> It may be of great advantages against a Navy of enemies, who by this may be undermined in the water and blown up.
>
> It may be of special use for the relief of any place besieged by water, to convey unto them invisible supplies; and so likewise for the surprisal of any place that is accessible by water.
>
> It may be of unspeakable benefit for submarine experiments.

Clockwork Motors and Kettle-like Submarines

Another seventeenth-century submarine was designed in 1653 by the Frenchman De Son. Driven by a clockwork motor, the *Rotterdam* was spear-shaped at either end in order to ram the English. With its pointed bow and stern, *Rotterdam*, its sponsors claimed, could punch holes in the hulls of British warships; an alarming strategy had it worked, which it did not. One of many drawbacks was fundamental: its clockwork motor was so limp that it was hardly capable of propulsion. *Rotterdam*'s designer, not famed for modesty, claimed that his clockwork ram, which was more a clockwork nudge, could race to and fro the English Channel in a day and sink a hundred ships en route.[11]

The French physicist and gifted mathematician Denis Papin (1647–*c.* 1712), who like others who dabbled in submersibles had at one time studied medicine – the link between killing and curing seems inexplicable – designed a submarine which from its drawings looked oddly like a kettle crossed with a watering can. In 1679 he invented the pressure cooker, its creation offering a clue as to why his submarine had something of the domestic in its profile. Papin is also credited with inventing the world's first paddle steamer, another large claim which invites challenge.

In 1698 the English military inventor and engineer Thomas Savery (1650–1715), inspired by Papin's pressure cooker, made the world's first steam engine, less crude versions being used to power submarines.*

Papin was no slouch: a Calvinist moulded by a Jesuit education he was a renowned mathematician who mastered a clutch of disciplines. The creator of manifold inventions he was an authority on steam power and steam pumps, and their application in industry. There is speculation that his submarine bore little resemblance to existing drawings: concerned about plagiarism, as rife then as it is today, he perhaps camouflaged his submarine as a kettle; he may also have had a pronounced sense of humour. His solution to the problems of ballast in his culinary-reminiscent craft was far-seeing: a pump balanced the external water pressure with the pressure which existed in the craft. By engaging the pump he could achieve a level of buoyancy using water which would then flow unhindered in and out of his boat.[13]

Diving Carpenters

Nathaniel Symons, a carpenter from Devon in England, caused amazement in 1729 by creating a craft that utilised an idea which had been central to Bourne's thinking. Bourne's boat had been intended to shrink and sink. It was envisaged that the sides of his craft would close in, allowing water to enter and exit, with the watertight compartment of the operator diminishing in size as the walls contracted; thus the vessel would sink, becoming heavier than the water it displaced. It would surface as the sides of the craft were pushed out to expel the water, thus increasing buoyancy. However, Symons would rate as more showman than submariner. His boat was a device which dived and, with luck, surfaced again, while no attempt was made to propel it through the water. The Devonian performed sinking and, after several minutes, surfacing his vessel as a trick rather than any form of scientific endeavour. Spectators showed their appreciation by filling a hat with coins.

---

* Savery left a significant maritime impression, also inventing the ships' odometer for measuring travelled distances. Refining Savery's breakthrough, the Englishman Thomas Newcomen (1663–1729) produced the first practical steam engine in 1712, modified by the English civil engineer John Smeaton (1724–92). It was then brought to practical utility by the mechanical engineer James Watt (1736–1819).[12] Their creations were central to the Industrial Revolution, the catalyst in the long half-century of change from sail to steam in shipping, and in the slow, though inexorable, advance of the submarine.

The story of the submarine is a medley of courage, tragedy and dark humour: in the 1770s, John Day, also a Devon woodworker, acquired the sloop *Maria*, a 50ft sailing boat which he refurbished as a diving ship. His incentive was the rash acceptance of a wager. He had made a previous dive, though not in the *Maria*, and its success had whetted his appetite for a more ambitious plunge. He secured and waterproofed an area amidships, the centre of the *Maria* being by his calculations the safest location: it would serve as his cabin which he furnished with books, bed, a candle to light the darkness of the depths, and provisions for what he anticipated would be a lengthy submersion.

Day's nostrum for solving the riddle of buoyancy comprised a collection of large barrels attached to the hull, estimated at some seventy-five in number. To make the ship sink, two 10-ton weights were suspended from the keel. While submerged the weights could be detached by removing bolts and permitting the craft to rise to the surface. A signalling system would inform the curious on the surface about his progress: if he released a white buoy, it would indicate he was in fine fettle; a red buoy meant that his health was indifferent; and a black buoy would be symbolic of danger. In June 1774, John Day clambered aboard the *Maria* and sank like a stone in 170ft of water in Plymouth harbour. He was never seen again, and neither were his buoys.

The American Revolutionary War and Bushnell's *Turtle*

Day's folly and God's disciples wanting to take a spin around the seabed lend colour to the submarine legend. Of a greater significance were the endeavours of the Americans David Bushnell and Robert Fulton; the first swathed in antagonism towards the British, the second driven by the zeal of the pacifist, though his fervour seems to have mellowed in later years. Bushnell, a science-minded citizen of Westbrook, Connecticut, wrote an influential chapter in submarine history. A Yale graduate, he had studied engineering, medicine and, somewhat contrarily, explosives; to heal or harm, death or doctoring, a dichotomy common to pioneer submariners, and one which rarely hindered them, if at all. He began building a submersible which he hoped would help vanquish the British oppressor, this being the time of the American Revolutionary War (1775–83). Variously described as egg-like, a barrel and by Bushnell himself as tortoise-shaped, it would be christened the *Turtle*, looking as if two turtle shells had been conjoined. Conflict quickens innovation and the war in America would bolster the submarine cause.[14]

The *Turtle* was accomplished and left its smudge on posterity as the first submarine (well, *nearly* a submarine) to attack an enemy ship, even though it ultimately failed. Its action obliged a legion of doubters, as well as a tiny band of believers, to recognise that the submarine, or in the case of the *Turtle*, a semi-submarine, could adopt an attack as well as a defensive posture. Made of wood, waterproofed by tarring as one would caulk the planking of a boat or barrel, the whole contraption held together with iron bands, the *Turtle* bobbed along with marginal buoyancy, a few inches of its shell revealed, which poked above the surface. From even close range in a placid sea it would have been difficult to identify from a target ship; in a heavy sea with cross currents and a swell it would have been well hidden, though difficult to control; on a starless night it would have been virtually impossible to detect from the deck of a ship bobbing quietly at its anchor. Though a significant advance, the *Turtle* was still alarmingly perilous, demanding in its operator a compendium of qualities: guile, strong nerves and Herculean exertion. It played well to the submarine's greatest attribute, stealth, though its ingenuity went far beyond that of mere concealment.[15]

At a minuscule 7ft, with a diameter of 6ft, the *Turtle* could claim a pioneering first: it was driven by screw-propulsion, a marked progression on its predecessors which, in essence, casting aside romantic stories embroidered over the centuries, were underwater rowing boats, and which, most likely, achieved only partial submersion.

The *Turtle* had two propellers: one set horizontally from its side for lateral propulsion, activated by a foot pedal from within its restricted confines; and the second poked from its top and was controlled by an interior handle. Attached to it was an augur, at the end of which was a charge of 150 lb of gunpowder in the form of a limpet mine. The idea was that the augur could be screwed up into the wooden hull of an enemy ship and the mine attached. Once fixed, the explosive could be detonated by a primitive clockwork timer: a spectacularly dangerous procedure which threatened assailant as well as assailed. On the part of the *Turtle*'s commander, such an assault demanded a distinct madness and manic endeavour. He had to perform an array of monumentally difficult tasks in a very short space of time: pedalling furiously to achieve lateral propulsion, sometimes against tide and wind; steering by rudimentary rudder; attempting to screw the explosive into the enemies' hull; and all this whilst maintaining an absolute quietness and discretion to avoid alerting sentries on the deck. Its captaincy would demand a Titan: enter Ezra Lee, an army sergeant.

The *Turtle* was towed by three whaling boats along the Hudson River to a point as close as was dared, at which juncture Lee scrambled aboard his floating egg. In his sights was the 64-gun HMS *Eagle*, the regal flagship of Admiral

Richard 'Black Dog' Howe, which on the night of 7 September 1776 lay temptingly in New York harbour, a haughty reminder to the Patriot army of the despised British presence and its loathed, but successful, blockade of the thirteen rebellious colonies. The attack by Lee (1749–1821) was sanctioned by General George Washington (1732–99) – affirmation of his uncertain faith in Bushnell's bizarre weapon.

Lee paddled along the Hudson to what is today called Governors Island, south of Manhattan, where the Hudson and the East rivers meet. He reached the *Eagle*, but fought in vain to attach the explosive to its hull, his efforts frustrated by the swirl of currents at the confluence of the waters. A minuscule glass porthole in the brass conning tower of his vessel allowed him only limited vision; were he to pedal with Olympian endeavour his craft had a top speed of 3 miles an hour. Ezra Lee's inexperience played its part in the botched attack: Bushnell's brother, also called Ezra, rather confusingly, had trained for a year on the machine, but illness forbade his presence as commander on the night. Why he failed to attach the charge is puzzling. Perhaps something simple had been overlooked: the ordinary curvature of the *Eagle*'s hull, for instance, which rendered the use of the augur impossible. Capricious tides would have hindered him. It is feasible he was rank unlucky: instead of screwing into wood, comprising the bulk of the hull, he hit iron banding which broke the augur. Another hypothesis is that the hull of the *Eagle* was sheathed in copper which the augur could not penetrate; coppering became common practice to counter the growth of weed which lessened speed and impaired manoeuvrability; coppering also inhibited infestations of worm and rot which, if left untended, made hulls friable, reducing them to dust. The explanation stood for two centuries, but recent research shows the *Eagle*'s hull had not been coppered until years after Lee's fruitless attack. There could be other explanations: the cramped *Turtle* afforded limited breathing time; it is suggested Lee struggled for two hours trying to ready his assault. Though indisputably courageous and lion-hearted, his lungs were as others: if fighting for air he would have become lethargic, succumbing to an irresistible fatigue. Nevertheless, though forced to abandon his quarry, against all the odds he somehow managed to paddle himself and the *Turtle* to safety. The *Turtle* made two more attacks on British ships, neither of which were successful. Ironically, after its exploits, the craft met its end while being transported on a frigate which foundered.

A year after Lee's attack on the *Eagle*, Bushnell tried a different approach in an attempt to sink the British frigate HMS *Cerberus*, moored off Connecticut, its name derived from the triple-headed dog with a snake's tail which guarded the gates of Hell. A warship of the Coventry class, the sister ship of HMS *Active*, *Cerberus* was cruelly symbolic to Patriots, it being the first British vessel to enter North America after the revolutionary hostilities had erupted in 1775. Its commander carried the inflammatory Parliamentary Acts, certain to heighten tensions between the British and the Patriots, or rebels as the British insisted. His passengers included three figures destined to play crucial roles in the campaign to quell the American uprising: John Burgoyne, William Howe and Henry Clinton. In 1777, helped by the currents rather than being disadvantaged by them, Bushnell floated two barrels of gunpowder towards the *Cerberus* as she lay at anchor. The crew of a yacht moored close to her stern saw one of the barrels and pulled it aboard for a closer inspection. On its retrieval it blew up, killing three and injuring a fourth. This incident was logged by the *Cerberus* and listed by the Admiralty as an early example of mine warfare, a prophecy of things to come; unlike Cassandra, never to be believed, an inkling that submersibles and mines might be effective weapons had begun to register, though such impressions would not be wholly accepted for decades, and not until the submersible proved more deadly to an enemy than to its operators.[16]

European Conflict and the American Robert Fulton

The one-time pacifist Robert Fulton (1765–1815) from Little Britain, Lancaster County, Pennsylvania, earned his place in maritime, not just submarine, history. His celebrity was assured through his later attainments as a steamboat pioneer, plying the rivers of New York. Earlier, around 1796, he had built a 21ft submarine, the *Nautilus*, its hull made of copper sheets stretched across iron ribs. Seventy-three years later, the name would acquire glory in *Twenty Thousand Leagues under the Sea*, written in 1870 by the French writer Jules Verne (1828–1905) with its legendary hero, Captain Nemo of the *Nautilus*.[17]

Fulton's first ambition was to be an artist and, in pursuit of a painting career, he had travelled to Paris to advance his studies. Later his passion would turn from canvas to engineering. Ingenious, if idealistic, Fulton had at one time wished to build a submarine to destroy all the weaponry in the entire world, including the totality of ships in the all-conquering British fleet. The historian George Isles recognised Fulton's abilities:

> As he sketched new engines of battle, he believed that he was making engines of war so terrible so that soon it should wholly cease. He was a many-sided man and as he took up tasks widely diverse, each of his talents lent aid to the other. He was a capital draftsman and painter, a mechanic and an engineer, and inventor and a researcher. With all this variety of accomplishment he

was a shrewd man of business and a warm friend. Now that fields of human action are divided, and sub-divided, minds of his inclusive horizon no longer appear, and, indeed, may no longer be possible.[18]

In trying to raise money and sponsorship, Fulton turned to France for support, which at the time was caught in revolutionary ferment. But his novel ideas were regarded as too costly; French coffers had been emptied by the incessant years of tumult. The Dutch, long reckoned to be a financially prudent nation, also considered his plans too grandiose and expensive for the carefully managed economy. He returned to France, modified his ideas and his budget, and finally secured financial backing: it was a highly intriguing union given the strength of his pacifism; he was working for Napoleon Bonaparte, who had emerged as Europe's foremost belligerent

One of Napoleon's several flaws, which would contribute to his eventual undoing, was his naive inability to appreciate naval strategy: the supremacy of whale over elephant. His instincts were those of a soldier, not a sailor, though one might wonder what he and his Minister of Marine had intended for Fulton's creation. The relationship between the French and Fulton soured when Napoleon dismissed him as a charlatan; Fulton's outré claims generally erred toward the fanciful. Nevertheless, the *Nautilus* was a significant achievement; with the blinding clarity lent by hindsight, Napoleon was perhaps peremptory in his abrupt discharge of machine and creator.

The elongated teardrop profile of the *Nautilus* – which would also become the name of the world's first nuclear submarine in the US Navy, USS *Nautilus* (1954) – resembled that of a contemporary submarine. With a three-man crew, she was powered by a hand-operated screw propeller, the design of which was subsequently improved with the addition of more vanes. Two horizontal fins on the rudder determined her angle of dive; an innovation with distinct echoes of the diving planes found on today's submarines.

Fulton designed a hollow keel which filled and emptied with water to control the buoyancy. On the surface, the vessel could be rowed or used as yacht; it had a collapsible sail which might be raised and utilised in appropriate airs. Its armaments were equally intriguing: Fulton devised a way in which his vessel could plunge a spiked metal eye into the hull of a target ship, through which a rope was looped dragging an explosive mine. The submarine would then attempt to make an exceedingly swift retreat from the target ship, pulling the line to its extremity, at which the mine would be hoisted up to the enemies' hull and detonate by means of a gunlock contrivance.

Nautilus was tested in the Rouen and Seine rivers – in the Seine River, Fulton initiated tests with two small steam-powered surface craft, the results of which were pertinent to his subsequent career as a steamboat operator. In Le Havre, *Nautilus* reputedly submerged for more than an hour, with Fulton and two others using candles to try and gauge the degree of available air.[19] The French were enthusiastic and envisaged Fulton building a larger version, but relations between the inventor and the French deteriorated and Fulton, coming full circle given his early idealism, found support in the British Admiralty, which would subsequently reveal itself more enamoured with his method of planting and detonating mines than in his construction of submarines.

Fulton and Early British Involvement

The British Prime Minister, William Pitt the Younger (1759–1806), showed some support for the submarine and Robert Fulton's endeavours. Pitt was confronted at the time by an assortment of economic and military problems: the submarine offered a novel solution to at least some of them. Assuming office in 1783 at the age of 24, Pitt was Britain's youngest prime minister, and his youth made him less prejudiced about the adoption of experimental weapons.[20] The decade-long turmoil of the French Revolution (1789–99) had cast an uncertain despair across Europe; and, too, the ceaseless struggles of Napoleon's France with Britain had financially and militarily drained both nations.

Britain's army had become depleted, with national security resting heavily on its navy. Among naval hindrances, however, was a shortage of sailors. To bolster the hated impressments (press gangs) – the strong-arm way the navy swelled its ranks – Pitt introduced the Quota System in 1795, in which each county in Britain offered a quota of men for naval service, with the number governed by the seaports and the size of population. Faced with such an array of difficulties, Pitt cast about for solutions. Building surface warships was forbiddingly expensive and took years, and, having built them, the next hurdle was in finding personnel to man them. The submarine offered an unconventional alternative, even if its technology was coarse and its capability limited. However, Pitt received scant support from naval chiefs for what they deemed his provocative interest in the submarine. His passing interest, for it was barely more than that, brought howls of opprobrium from stalwarts in the Royal Navy and Admiralty.

Leading the fray was the Staffordshire-born First Sea Lord, John Jervis, 1st Earl of St Vincent (1735–1823).[21] A veteran of the Seven Years War (1756–63), the American Revolutionary War (1775–83) and the Napoleonic Wars (1799–1815), his celebrity had been assured by his remarkable victory against all odds at the Battle of Cape St Vincent in 1797. His pronouncements had weight, and in 1800 Jervis was scathing about the submarine: 'Pitt was the greatest fool that ever existed to encourage a mode of warfare which those who command the sea did not want and which, if successful, would deprive them of it.'[22] With such illustrious foes the progress of the submarine would always be guaranteed a hostile passage.

There were plenty of other critics of the submarine, some of them being grandees of the American navy. Commodore John Rogers, a renowned figure in the US fleet, whose family became something of a US Navy dynasty, proved one of the most unsparing:

> I leave the reader to make his own conclusions and to judge whether such torpid, unwieldy, six-feet-sided, fifteenth-sixteenth-sunk-water dungeons, are calculated to supersede the necessity of a navy, particularly when the men who manage them are confined to the limits of their holds, which will be under water, and in as perfect darkness as if shut up in the Black Hole of Calcutta.[23]

Napoleon's rout and the British victory at Trafalgar in 1805 spelled the end for Fulton; Nelson's magisterial success eliminated previous continental dangers against which Fulton's boats may have featured. Though his ambitions for a more capable submarine with a six-man crew and armed with several mines would end in frustration, with Fulton packing his bags and returning to America a year after Trafalgar, fate had a further delight in store: he would burnish his reputation as a pioneer in the relatively new world of surface marine steam. In 1807 Fulton undercut the price of stagecoach fares with the first commercially viable passenger steamship service, which shuttled between Albany and New York on the Hudson River. His 142ft ship, the lithe and elegant paddle steamer the *Clermont*, has a special place in maritime affections. In 1812 he began building a steam-driven warship, *Fulton the First*, to help defend New York harbour. Sadly, he died before its completion; his memory is honoured in Statuary Hall, Washington DC. Fulton's pacifism appears to have mellowed over time, though his idealism and dislike of militarism stayed intact. To some he remains a controversial figure, his flamboyant claims for his contraptions sometimes exceeding their capability. There is veracity in the charge, but it is too unforgiving; few pioneer submariners succeeded without ornate blandishment of their creations. Fulton thoroughly merits his maritime accolades for being resolute, resourceful and as the first commercially successful steamboat operator.[24] Cadwallader Colden, Fulton's biographer, wrote:

Nature had made him a gentleman and bestowed upon him ease and gracefulness. He had too much good sense for the least affectation. He expressed himself with energy, fluency and correctness, and as he owed more to his own experiences and reflections than to books, his sentiments were often interesting from their originality.[25]

Wilhelm Bauer and Tsarist Russia

Among a roll call of pathfinders it would be remiss to omit Wilhelm Bauer, a soldier in the once mighty Prussian army. In his time, Bauer ran the gamut of submarine experience: he enjoyed success, had a hair-raising escape and dreamed up a novel way of celebrating tsarist accession in pre-revolution Russia. Midway through the nineteenth century, in his extraordinary *Brandtaucher* (*Fire Diver*) submarine, he made an accomplished dive, which appeared to pose such a threat to the Danes that they lifted their blockade of Kiel harbour, in north Germany, during the Prussia–Denmark conflict. His craft was of metal, oblong and tank-like. Propeller-driven, operated by a wheel set within the vessel, its control while submerged depended on the crew's movement of a sizeable weight, which slid from bow to stern and back, causing the craft to point up, or down, sometimes at an alarmingly sharper angle of incline than its operators intended.

Only days after his Danish offensive, Sergeant Bauer and two colleagues became the first to escape from a submarine when it sank in 200ft of water in Kiel harbour. On this there are two schools of thought: one insists that Bauer and his men waited coolly until their craft was inundated and blew apart, permitting them to shoot like corks out of a bottle in a bubble of air to the surface; this version is widely acknowledged, well chronicled and, with good fortune, even possible. There is, however, debate about the effects of divers' palsy, the bends, which can be extremely painful and utterly debilitating, even fatal. The condition is triggered by sudden decompression caused by surfacing too rapidly, as the air pressure must be consistent with the depth pressure; today a decompression chamber would be used to balance the pressure levels in the event of surfacing swiftly. An alternative and more prosaic view is that the men scrambled to safety in shallower waters before their craft sank to the harbour floor.

In addition to their daring, it was a sign of the persistence and single-mindedness of submarine inventors that they were not averse to hawking designs across borders in a ceaseless safari to enlist capital and support; their pursuit was uninhibited by national loyalty or concern at their immersion in other peoples' imbroglios. They were driven by one over-arching consideration:

come Hell or high water their creations should be made flesh. There were those in high command in the world's surface navies who thought an apt name for submarines, their creators and commanders, would be *Perfidy*.

Bauer tried to entertain the British and the Russians in submarine proposals, neither at the time being the closest of allies. However, he enjoyed a modicum of success with each. His involvement in Russian naval affairs led to one of the legends of the submarine chronicle: in a neoteric gesture he marked the coronation of Tsar Alexander II (1818–81) by persuading bandsmen in the seaport and naval hub of Kronshtadt, near St Petersburg, to take a dive (*c.* 1855–56) in his submarine, the ambitious 58ft *Seeteufel* (*Sea Devil*), which in all would make more than 130 successful dives. Beneath the water the musicians struck up a rousing version of the Russian national anthem, clearly audible on the surface and much to the merriment of Alexander II and his celebrants.*

Early Spanish and French Intervention

The Spanish and French were markedly innovative in the formative years of the submarine. An intriguing thread of utopianism runs throughout these early pioneers, a belief that the submarine could, by its potency, save the world from self-destruction. In its wash would be peace and harmony. The Spanish engineer, writer and intellectual, Narcis Monturiol i Estarriol (1819–85), was caught in the swirl of political and social movements gathering momentum at the time. Such bodies were seen as dangerous and a challenge to the state. Almost a century had elapsed since the French Revolution, but for some its spirit still threatened in authoritarian and rigidly Roman Catholic societies such as Spain. Membership of organisations which were dedicated to equality, egalitarianism and fraternity would inevitably make Monturiol enemies; such gatherings were condemned as heretic in their anti-establishment posturing.

Monturiol had at one time been forced to flee and find sanctuary in France, the Spanish authorities hard on his tail for what they interpreted as subversive

---

* It was a lighter interlude for the Tsar whose absolute rule, and that of his forebears, had brought Imperial Russia to Stygian plight; the nation a wasteland, its servile people humiliated after their heroic but failed defence of Sebastopol (1854–55), the home of the Tsar's Black Sea Fleet which had long menaced the Mediterranean. It was finally overwhelmed by combined British, Ottoman and French forces. The fall of Sebastopol, after a protracted siege which involved vast numbers of military personnel, including 20,000 Russian sailors, and the scuttling of fifteen Russian ships in an effort to blockade the harbour, would end in Russia's ruinous defeat in the Crimean War (1853–56).[26]

tendencies. Some might call Monturiol the Don Quixote of submarines; in his case tilting at lighthouses, supported by a coterie of well-intentioned, if largely woolly-headed dreamers. His politics were a species of utopian socialism fashionable in the second half of the nineteenth century, laced with a touch of Welsh co-operative thinking espoused by the likes of the guild socialist Robert Owen (1771–1858), an antidote to the unhindered surge of capitalism which had brought a mix of unparalleled squalor and style, despair and joy, misery and prosperity to its servants and beneficiaries. The ideas of Karl Marx (1818–83) would become widespread during this period, more red-blooded than Monturiol's fragile notions.

Monturiol had ideals and a charming manner. While at all times modest and self-deprecatory, he was determined and intellectually able. He was also alarmingly honest to those brave or rash enough to join him for a dive. His biographer Matthew Stuart states:

> He warned his fellow passengers that the enterprise could well be 'the tomb of the first explorers'. Yet, he assured his anxious comrades, he, at least, was eager 'to sacrifice everything' for the sake of underwater navigation. As in his days as a young revolutionary, Monturiol was strangely attracted to the prospect of martyrdom.[27]

A lawyer by training, though he never practised, he had seen a coral harvester lose his life in Cadaques, the coastal resort in Spain's Catalonia. The sensitive Monturiol had been moved by the occurrence; a native of Figueres in the province of Gerona, Catalonia (where the surrealist Salvador Dali lived), the incident was said to have been Monturiol's motive in building a submarine, the *Ictineo*, which he launched in 1859 in the harbour at Barcelona, which lies within striking distance of Cadaques. The wooden *Ictineo* looked as lithe as a fish and as roundly curved as a beached mammal, with oddly swollen portholes, giving it a demented air. (Today there is a model of it in the garden of the Barcelona Maritime Museum (*Musea Maritim*); the original was destroyed in an accident after making some fifty dives when a ship ran into it whilst docked.) Matthew Stuart describes the contraption thus:

> On the morning of 28 June 1859 the *Ictineo* stood poised on its dockside ramp, its polished olivewood skin shimmering in the morning sun, its spout-like hatch and bulbous portholes on each side giving it the look of a bug-eyed whale on dry land, gazing eagerly towards the life-giving sea. At around 9am this artificial leviathan slid down its guide-rails and splashed into the water.[28]

Monturiol had imagined his boat – 23ft long, 11ft high and 8ft wide – being used to gather coral, eliminating the dangers that had cost the life of the coral diver. He had equipped it with machinery for cutting and harvesting the coral crop. What he really strove for, though, was something more fundamental: he saw the creation of his submarine as a way to improve mankind, to better its lot. Precisely how he intended to do this is something of an enigma. Finding government enthusiasm scarce for his endeavours, he used his talents as a writer to compose a persuasive 'begging' letter to raise funds: the public donated some 300,000 pesetas. He began building a successor boat, *Ictineo II*. The first had been driven by muscle power, but Monturiol had decided that he would build a steam engine for his second boat; given that he was primarily a writer and publisher, it was no mean feat.

The task required a long period of experimentation before he found a suitable formula. What he finally came up with was astonishing: an anaerobic engine – one which did not need oxygen – the principle of which was centuries ahead of its time. The only real anaerobic engines are the nuclear plants used to propel today's gargantuan submarines. He had found a cocktail of chemicals that produced heat and oxygen, and the heat drove the little steam engine. He made a successful dive in 1867 but his company later went bust, meaning the cessation of his submarine endeavours. He was one of the most talented and innovative submarine engineers of the time, and his boat had been one of the most promising. The anaerobic engine was extraordinarily clever and the book *Tools of Violence* suggests how far ahead Monturiol was in his deliberations:

> Early submarines were air-breathing. They had to surface or raise a snorkel to feed oxygen to their propulsion plants – a nuclear reactor requires no air to function, nor fuel, until the more than 30-year-life of its radioactive core is exhausted. The only factor limiting the time they (nuclear subs) may remain submerged is the human crew itself, who must be resupplied and relieved at some point.[29]

Monturiol was highly inventive, and is credited with several creations, from a meat-pressing device to an advanced printing machine and a cigarette-maker.[30]

The French submarine *Le Plongeur* (*The Diver*) of 1863 gave another push to the technology. It was among the first to be powered by an engine, rather than human toil. Once more it was conflict, the ceaseless battles for supremacy between the French and the British – resumed with customary vigour after an uneasy alliance in the bizarre Crimean escapade – which provided the imperative for the development of the machine. *Le Plongeur* had a steam engine and took its constructors, the distinguished naval builder Charles Brun (1821–97) working to plans conceived by Captain Simeon Bourgeois (1815–87), four years to build the vessel at the Rochefort naval arsenal, at the mouth of the Charente River, in the Charente Maritime. After *Le Plongeur* both men went on to enjoy successful careers.*

At a length of 145ft and with a crew of twelve, *Le Plongeur* was sizeable and accomplished. Her armaments, though, remained coarse. She was propelled by an 80 horsepower (hp) steam engine powered by compressed air stored in extensive tanks; the air provided fresh air for the crew and 'blew' out her ballast tanks. The design was flawed: the tanks for the compressed air were incapable of holding sufficient pressure and the craft was unstable. The problems proved insoluble. Though a disappointment, *Le Plongeur*, despite her weaknesses, still represented noteworthy advance. The progress of the submarine would have been swifter had she fulfilled her promise. Her method of attack, however, like that of her predecessors, was unreliable and crude: an explosive attached to the end of a pole, a 'spar', to be driven into the hulls of enemy ships. Such assailment could be as lethal to the predator as to the prey; until realistic weapons were devised, and problems such as ballast and propulsion resolved, the submarine would have little import beyond the novel.

The American Civil War

The American Civil War (1861–65) saw more submarine developments; again, tumult heralded technical advance. Abraham Lincoln ordered that southern ports be blockaded to stop the sale of cotton and the importation of supplies. Consequently, the Union navy blockaded ports, though in the preliminary days of hostilities it was barely up to the task. Theoretically, the Union navy could muster 100 vessels; in reality, the figure was far fewer and the blockades, which

---

* Brun became director of French naval construction and, later, a politician and statesman. In 1883 he was made Minister of Marine and the Colonies (a peculiarly French title passed down and changed in accord with French civil society). Bourgeois was a progressive thinker; his metier was the submarine. La Jeune Ecole (Young School), to which he subscribed, lobbied for a new-look navy to utilise the latest, most agile technology. The way Bourgeois saw his navy was mirrored decades later in Britain by the reformist Admiral Jacky Fisher, the principal advocate of the 'new arsenal': mines, airships, submarines and torpedoes. Fisher garnered a cadre of officers in his 'fish-pond'; those within flourished, others beyond its confines were sometimes beached. Bourgeois rose from captain to a vice admiral. In 1872 he instigated a programme to design and construct torpedo craft. France's first Commissioner for Submarine Defence in 1888, he wrote a far-seeing treatise *Le Torpiller* (The Torpedo Boat).[31]

were expected to blanket a Confederate coastline of 3,500 miles, were being attempted by a handful of vessels. The Confederates regularly beat the blockades with 'runner' vessels camouflaged in grey to help evade detection. Nevertheless, though the Union navy was at full stretch, gloomy predictions by Confederate officers that the South was still vulnerable and might be stifled demanded fresh thinking and new weapons with which to strike at the enemy.*

Both the Confederate and Unionist forces built submarines.[32] The first to be deployed was purchased by the Union navy in 1862. It was innovative, cigar-shaped, and its green livery gave meaning to its name: the *Alligator*. At 47ft its initial role was as a defensive instrument to lay mines in Confederate harbours. A year later, in April 1863, it sank while under tow to take part in the attack on Charleston harbor; it was lost in a violent storm and cruel seas off Cape Hatteras on the north Carolina coast, known as the graveyard of the Atlantic. Its loss in military terms, and as a historical contrivance, was significant.

The *Alligator* had been designed by the French inventor, Brutus de Villeroi (*c.* 1797–1874), whose sagacity and determination warrant acknowledgement. *Alligator* was built in Philadelphia in 1861, Villeroi having immigrated to America five years earlier. He had a history of submarine experimentation which pre-dated the American Civil War: in 1832, in Nantes harbour on the Loire River in western France, he had demonstrated a type of submersible. The *Alligator* had a device which – supposedly – purified and filtered air; an unknown chemical generated oxygen using bellows to force air through a concoction which included slaked lime. It was the first submarine to use compressed air to supply the boat. Originally she had been powered by oars, but later the system was replaced by propeller drive, with the former oarsmen working at a hand crank. Some argue that *Alligator* was the world's first submarine; a large claim, though its ingenuity is beyond doubt. She was among the first from which a diver could be released while the boat was submerged. It took the form of a diver lock and allowed him to exit and re-enter the boat, surreptitiously, to affix explosives on the hulls of enemy ships which could then, theoretically, be subsequently detonated by an electric timer.

---

* In 1862 the Confederates suffered a serious blow when they lost their major city, New Orleans, sited 100 miles up river from the mouth of the Mississippi River; the annexation of New Orleans, and the seizure of other towns and settlements in the vicinity, meant the Unionists could block the South's access to the river. New Orleans had been seized by Union commander Captain (later Admiral) David Glasgow Farragut (1801–70). Two years later, in 1864, Farragut used his fleet to capture the town of Mobile; it was masterful sailing. He navigated a dangerous passage through a minefield to win the key battle of Mobile Bay, the last major port held by the South.

Confederate forces centred their submarine development on the northern Gulf coast, with four submersibles operating in the Red River in Louisiana. The submarines would become known by a generic name, the *Davids*. It was a *David* which attacked the USS *New Ironsides* in October 1863, but its Confederate commander, Lieutenant William Glassel, pulled the explosive's lanyard too quickly and triggered a premature detonation of the charge attached to the end of a spar. Consequently, the attack failed and Glassel and his comrades were imprisoned. The name *David* covered a diversity of submersibles: they were, in the main, cigar-shaped, steam-driven and some 40ft in length. The derivation of the name is unknown, though it might have come from an engineer, David Chenowith Ebaugh, who was active in the area as a submarine constructor. Or perhaps it is biblical: valiant Confederate *Davids* pitted against Union Goliaths.

A difficulty faced Confederate commanders in the armouring of enemy ships: Union vessels were fortified in iron; their architects began cladding their vessels lower and lower to the waterline, reducing the vulnerable wooden target areas sought by marauding submariners. The *Davids* evoked terror in those pitted against them, but they had many drawbacks. The steam engines on *Davids* could not be used beneath the water; they emitted noxious fumes and swiftly consumed all breathable air. A chimney and air pipe poked in a tell-tale way above the surface and betrayed a craft's presence. They were also vulnerable to gunfire from ships' crews, being forced to engage the enemy at close range to have a chance of deploying their spar explosives; if they succeeded in attaching an explosive charge, it was as likely to destroy the submarine as its target.

The southern states sanctioned privateers as well as official submarine builders and operators. At the Leeds Foundry, New Orleans, a privately funded submarine, the *Pioneer*, was designed in 1861 by two businessmen, Baxter Wilson and James McClintock. They had built their reputation as engineers and manufacturers of gauges with which to measure the effectiveness of steam engines. By the time the war began, they had established links with Confederate leaders and, shortly after its outbreak, had sold bullet-making machines to the Confederate government. They held letters of marque which sanctioned them as privateers and stated that they were authorised to attack enemy vessels. As well as naval glory, a further incentive encouraged inventors and engineers: big bounties were offered to those who sank Unionist warships whose blockading strategies were beginning to slowly choke the southern states.

Wilson and McClintock's *Pioneer*, with its commander and two-man crew, was 34ft long, propeller-driven and its crew worked at a crank handle It successfully sank two vessels using towed torpedoes. In 1862 the Unionists overran New Orleans and laid claim to the *Pioneer*. It was sold for scrap six years later. Not to be thwarted, Baxter and McClintock made a hasty retreat from

New Orleans, fleeing the invading Unionists and setting up camp in Mobile, Alabama, to begin building another craft, the *American Diver*.

Though the *American Diver* would come to a sudden demise, the idea for its propulsion was advanced. Baxter and McClintock envisaged it being powered by an electro-magnetic unit, an idea so far ahead of its time that, sadly, it came to nothing. They turned their attention to the more usual steam power; it, too, failed to materialise. In addition to the customary problems associated with building a submarine, their endeavours were being undertaken in the chaos of war, in trying circumstances of haste, secrecy and budgetary constraint: Unionist forces and spies were everywhere. When the Union navy invaded Charleston harbor in South Carolina, it seized ten *Davids* and annexed several other submersibles which had become stranded in the mud of the Cooper River on which Charleston sits. Finally, Baxter and McClintock had to resort to more prosaic propulsion: four men worked at a hand crank to drive a propeller. But the power they could generate was insufficient for the craft to attack fortified Union ships, which were generally anchored offshore beyond the calmer confines of a harbour.

Given the vicissitudes of tide and swell, wind and weather, the crew would have been exhausted before getting within range of their target. The *American Diver* was not an easy vessel to propel by muscle power: 36ft and shaped like a brick, its hull was built of heavy iron plating. As it transpired, the *American Diver* would not see action. It foundered off Fort Morgan at the mouth of Mobile Bay. Though it never had a chance of maritime glory, its technology and construction, in the chastened circumstances of war, are testimony to the assiduity that runs throughout the submarine story.

The Redoubtable Horace Hunley

At this juncture in the chronology another important name enters the saga: Horace Lawson Hunley (1823–63). A one-time lawyer and cotton entrepreneur turned nautical engineer, he hailed originally from Tennessee. In 1861, alongside James McClintock, he began building a new Confederate submersible. At 30ft long it had a crew of three working at a hand-cranked propeller. What happened to it is unknown: some claim it was never built; others maintain it was scuttled in 1862 when Union forces invaded New Orleans. A second Hunley-McClintock boat was to have been propelled by battery, an idea of acuity but so far ahead of its time as to be impractical; no appropriate engine could be found. So, once more, it had to be driven in the usual way, by muscle power: a crew of four grinding at a crankshaft to turn a propeller. Given the confinement, heat and overall discomfiture, such crews needed steel nerves with physiques to match. The vessel, however, suffered calamity. It sank after being swamped by turbulent seas while operating off Mobile Bay, Alabama. Hunley, McClintock and their Confederate backers were not the sort to be easily dispirited: they built a third submarine, the *H.L. Hunley*, a robust, if inelegant, craft comprising a modified steam-boiler tank. The tank was of sufficient muscularity, if lacking in aesthetics: its line best described as brick-like. At 40ft long and just 4ft wide, it accommodated a crew of between eight and ten, crammed in and working furiously at a crankshaft to turn its propeller. Given its bulk and squareness, if it is true, as claimed, that it had a top speed of 4 miles an hour then its occupants must have been supermen. In its wake it towed a deadly weapon; if it would prove lethal to predator or prey, or both, rested with the Fates. At the end of a 200ft line was attached an explosive. The method of attack had a fiendish simplicity: the *Hunley* would dive beneath a Union ship, its plunge abetted by hefty weights affixed to its frame, dragging behind it the line which pulled a detonator and 90lb of gunpowder; when the line was yanked up the charge would explode against the hull of the enemy. The plot was tested on a barge which was duly blown to smithereens.

Buoyed by the success of the assault on the barge, the *Hunley* was taken by rail to Charleston, South Carolina, where she met with catastrophe: she sank on three occasions, drowning her crew and the redoubtable Horace Hunley. In total, her diverse calamities had cost the lives of twenty-three men. The Confederates were still undeterred, raising the craft from the seabed and altering its design and armaments. A so-called torpedo was hung from the bow, though in reality it was a type of gunpowder charge attached to the end of a spar. After the costly expenditure in lives and money on its predecessor boats, CSS *Hunley* would confound her many sceptics to achieve maritime immortality. On the night of 17 February 1864, she became the first submarine to sink an enemy ship, her victim being a new corvette of the Union navy, the USS *Housatonic*, a blockade craft anchored 3 miles off the Charleston bar. The commander of CSS *Hunley* at the time of the attack was Lieutenant George Dixon of the Alabama Light Infantry. While the *Hunley* was making her run at the target she was spotted by sentries and look-outs posted on the deck of the *Housatonic*.

She was approaching at just 2ft below the surface, off the ship's starboard bow, making some 3 knots. The *Housatonic* hastily tried to slip anchor to flee her midget tormentor, her crew deploying a hail of small arms fire. But it was too late. The *Hunley* went in for the kill. A vast explosion lifted the 1,240-ton *Housatonic* clear of the water and she sank swiftly by the stern in shallow water with the loss of five men. In the resulting maelstrom the *Hunley* sank too, drowning her crew of eight.[33]

In 1995 divers found the *Hunley* lying near her base 30ft down at Sullivan's Island, South Carolina. In her side was rent a large gash. There are diverse theories as to her demise: Charles Pickering, the *Housatonic* commander, fired a shotgun which holed her hatches; her hull had been peppered by the *Housatonic* crew using small arms; she might have been swamped by another ship going to the aid of the *Housatonic*; or that she was overwhelmed by the elements. The last explanation is prosaic but as likely as any other: the weather was worsening, a capricious sea suddenly boiled with violent waves from the explosion. Perhaps the vortex left by the stricken *Housatonic* swallowed her up. In truth, nobody will ever know how the little *Hunley* met her end.[34]

In 1863 a submarine project known as the *Intelligent Whale* ended in mayhem and murder. A group of American businessmen from the northern states hoped to cash in by building a private submarine for use in the American Civil War. But the submarine, which looked like a whale, was not completed until after the war. The alleged proprietor of the *Intelligent Whale* – his ownership was at one time hotly disputed – was Oliver Halstead of Newark, New Jersey, where the *Whale* had come to life. She had a crew of a four who worked at a hand crank to drive a propeller. Halstead and others are thought to have taken dives in the craft on the Passaic River, New Jersey. He was subsequently murdered, supposedly by a jealous former lover of his mistress.

The performance of submarines in the American Civil War had gone from patchy to calamitous. The conflict began, inconveniently, years in advance of the technology. The *Davids* and *Hunleys*, however, had triggered discomfiture, violence and alarm. The submarine was beginning to gain a reputation as *ominous*, a weapon of some seriousness, but it was still badly hampered by fundamental drawbacks. The lure of a machine in embryo and subject to primordial inadequacies, which offered potential and large rewards if such obstacles could be overcome, would attract inventors from around the world.

Garrett, Nordenfelt and Maxim

Among inventors of the submarine was the remarkable English clergyman George Garrett (1852–1902). The Reverend George William Littler Garrett came from Moss Side, Manchester, in Britain's northwest. Cottonopolis, as it became known, had been swept to prosperity by the hot winds of the Industrial Revolution.[35] With its chest-puffing brand of capitalism, Manchester had become efficient at exploiting a captive imperial market and fostering new ones: one of a handful of swaggering northern cities on which Britain's industrial prowess was built, it had emerged as the capital of the world textile industry.

Cheap coal, purpose-built waterways and the invention of the steam engine had galvanised its clothing industry. Powered by steam, its mills had transformed its spinning and weaving processes; in its wash it had brought both wealth and deprivation, spawning cotton barons and a teeming urban underclass. Garrett understood the transformative qualities of steam, its widespread utility in industry and the way it would revolutionise Britain's fighting and mercantile fleets.[36] Before following his father into the curacy, he had studied science and chemistry prior to attending Dublin's Trinity College and spent time teaching at the influential Manchester Mechanics' Institute (MMI).*

Founded by well-heeled, science-minded patrons, the MMI offered fertile ground for innovative thinkers such as Garrett, with his engineering persuasion and ideas for solving problems which bedevilled the submarine; one of the most engaging, yet baffling, technological developments of the day. Garrett's appearance in the progress of the submarine weaves in a colourful litany of inventive and industrial personalities.[37] In 1880 he had designed a submarine powered by a coal-fired steam boiler with a retractable chimney. It was crucial to extinguish the fire before the boat plunged if the crew were not to be overcome by poisonous fumes and the swift exhaustion of breathable air; the boiler was of a sufficiency to store steam for a four-hour submersion and to propel the craft at 2 knots. Ambient heat from the boiler, however, and accumulated coal fumes, made conditions virtually intolerable for her crew of three. The optimistic name for the vessel was *Resurgam* (*I shall rise again*). Great Britain had fallen behind continental competitors in constructing submarines; the British Admiralty still viewed with hauteur the spasmodic progress of the vessels, insisting they were merely gimcrack tin-fish. It did, though, deign to show an interest in the *Resurgam*. The apparent aloofness of the Admiralty was not entirely misplaced: the choppy progress of the submarine had failed to inspire, while each setback or calamity sent frissons of *schadenfreude* through those who ruled Britain's illustrious surface navy.

Garrett was not a submarine virgin. Two years before building *Resurgam* he had built a baby version of his craft: at 14ft with a hand-cranked propeller, it was prone to leaks and other scares. Out of its sides he poked his arms through greased leather sleeves to test the feasibility of pinning explosives by hand on to enemy hulls; he might have been a vicar but, like most submarine pioneers, he had, it appears, a distinct touch of madness. Before his baby *Resurgam* he had fashioned a diving suit, which he had tried to sell to the French. It was, though,

---

* The MMI spawned a number of radical bodies: the Trades Union Congress; Manchester University Institute of Science and Technology; and the Co-operative Movement.

Resurgam II, with steam engine and foldaway smokestack, which caught the public imagination and, too, the sceptical eye of the Admiralty.

Though *Resurgam II* held promise, it failed to answer unresolved issues. The fire and steam boiler were impractical and the vessel unstable. Nevertheless, after it had been tested in Liverpool harbour, the Admiralty requested its inspection at Gosport naval base on Britain's south coast. It would have been sensible to have transported it by rail. But a sensible submariner was an oxymoron and, in 1880, Garrett began the journey by sea. It was a costly decision. *Resurgam II* was lost while under tow off the coastal town of Rhyl, on the north Wales coast.

Thorsten Nordenfelt and Hiram Maxim

It took more than an occasional sinking to thwart early submariners. Garrett persisted with his experiments, his efforts sponsored by Thorsten Nordenfelt (1842–1920). Nordenfelt was a Swedish banker, steel maker, inventor and gunsmith who had based himself in Britain. He had made money as the energetic proprietor of the Nordenfelt Guns and Ammunition company, which had forged an alliance with Vickers. It would prove beneficial: Vickers would grow into an engineering and armaments empire.

Nordenfelt was well connected and determined. He became involved with Maxim, another successful enterprise run by the American-born British businessman, Sir Hiram Stevens Maxim (1840–1916), the inventor of the world's first automatic machine gun in 1884, of which the Catholic writer Hilaire Belloc (1870–1953) said in 1898: 'Whatever happens we have got the Maxim gun, and they have not.'

Hiram Maxim was another of the astute and inventive businessmen who enrich the submarine annals. Maxim always nurtured a desire to build aeroplanes, but he seems to have had little luck. He raised the money to finance his aeroplane designs by creating an unusual product: in Europe, travelling fairs had for centuries been popular with troupes of performers, alchemists and animal acts; crossing frontiers they were the earliest personifications of international trade. Recognising the commercial possibilities offered by the international travelling fair, Maxim invented the nearest he could get to an aeroplane: a whirling fairground ride, a tethered 'flying' machine. It was so successful it became, literally, a money-spinner. His best-known invention was even more successful: the ubiquitous mousetrap. In the 1890s, Herbert Austin – later to become a car industry mogul – worked with Maxim on developing a giant steam aeroplane. Such was the creative coterie which progressed the submarine.

Vickers and the Importance of
Barrow-in-Furness

Submarine constructors, like all ship builders – though those who strove to raise money for conventional craft were backed by centuries of tradition – would, in the course of their business, attempt to assemble a consortium of engineers and financiers willing to wager their skills and capital in return for a share of a growing and, with a large slice of good fortune, prosperous company. Some were driven by ego, while others were drawn by a misplaced imaginary glamour or by the lure of untested technology. The submarine held undoubted promise, but commercially, at this stage, it was only for the brave. Some investors, however, found the combination of risk and the slim possibility of reward irresistible. Maritime compacts for the construction and operation of fleets were commonplace: labyrinthine, discreet and protectionist, members bought shareholdings, garnered funds, exploited networks of financial and political contacts. While axial to the world's shipping corporations in amassing their fortunes, such cartels were detrimental to those who were devoid of patronage and trying to exist outside this privileged circle.

Submarine building was maturing: from a scattering of oddball inventors chasing madcap obsessions, a serious construction industry was beginning to slowly crystallise. It would eventually become commercially incestuous, however, with building dominated by a handful of companies. Though submarines were usually the wayward offspring of those who, by nature, were robustly independent – brave, eccentric, brilliantly gifted or alarmingly deranged – they would all, sooner or later, succumb to the comforting and apparently secure embrace of private or state capitalism, the latter being in the form of naval support. The foremost player in armaments and shipbuilding was Vickers. It would increase its influence by extending its activities into submarine construction.

The industrial megalith of Vickers had its roots in Barrow-in-Furness, on Britain's north-west coast, 40 miles north of the marine citadel of Liverpool. It had begun there in 1871 as The Iron Shipbuilding Company, founded by James Ramsden, the general manager of the Furness Railway Company. Until the middle of the nineteenth century, Barrow had been a sleepy farming community. The arrival of the railway saw its awakening. With Britain caught in a ferment of industrialisation, Barrow grew as a centre of iron production and, by 1870, had the world's biggest iron smelting works. James Ramsden had to swiftly change the name of his infant business to the Barrow Shipbuilding Company (BSC) on discovering that another company in nearby Birkenhead also built iron ships. Given that Great Britain was caught in a maelstrom of industry and invention, such oversights were commonplace. The reputation of BSC flourished. It built a succession of ships for naval and mercantile fleets across the globe. In 1888 it bought the gun side of the Maxim Nordenfelt Guns and Ammunition Company, run by George Garrett's Swedish sponsor, Thorsten Nordenfelt, and changed its name to The Naval Construction and Armaments Company (NCAC). In 1897 the NCAC was bought for £425,000 by the Vickers family, which ran a steel business in the bustling south Yorkshire hub of Sheffield, the City of Steel, whose products would conquer the world.[38] Vickers bought out the rest of Maxim Nordenfelt for £1,353,000 and renamed itself Vickers, Sons & Maxim Ltd. It grew into the world's foremost shipbuilding, armaments and heavy engineering company. Barrow became the Royal Navy yard, as proud as Vickers itself, with an unrivalled heritage as the submarine capital of Britain and the world.

Though Thorsten Nordenfelt understood the inadequacies of George Garrett's *Resurgam*, and that it had failed to live up to its Micawberish name, he and Garrett would build another submarine, a modified *Resurgam* with some essential differences, one being that it would be armed with a torpedo (see Chapter 3)

Nordenfelt I was launched in 1885. She was 64ft long and 9ft in diameter, with a surface range of 160 miles and 15 miles underwater. A cigar-shaped profile was a precursor of contemporary craft and incorporated horizontal propellers to push her down to a maximum depth of 50ft. Made of iron plate, with a conning tower, she had an external torpedo tube and was fitted with a 25mm machine gun. Built by the Bolinders yard in Stockholm, her trials were difficult; there were problems with stability and the morbid presence of carbon monoxide. Nevertheless, she was seen as sufficiently workable for Greece to buy her, being delivered to the Salamis naval base in 1886. She failed to meet expectations and was scrapped by the Greek Navy in 1901.

After the Greeks, the Turkish

National pride being an intoxicant, and the readiness of submariners to sell without compunction to whoever wished to buy, following the Greek acquisition it was inevitable that their ancient adversary, Turkey, would feel compelled to enhance their own fleet. They ordered not one but two submarines to be built by Vickers at Barrow-in-Furness; the principal criteria for the Turkish purchase being that they were in every way superior to the submarine purchased by the Greeks. *Nordenfelt II* (*Abdulhamid*) was built in 1886. At 100ft long, with two internal torpedo tubes and two guns, it also had a bigger engine than *Nordenfelt I*. But stability was poor; on the surface it could be swamped by heavy seas or the wash of passing ships. To cap it all, Turkey were unable to muster a crew willing to man it; though given its perilous tendencies this is hardly surprising. Dismantled at Barrow and then transported by ship to Turkey, the craft was re-assembled at the Taskizak Tersanesi yard in Istanbul. The next submarine, *Nordenfelt III* (*Abdulemecid*) failed to materialise.

Later, *Nordenfelt IV* was built in 1887 at Barrow for the Russian Navy. At 125ft it could supposedly cruise for 1,000 miles on the surface: if it could is debatable. Being keen to recoup the capital, and with luck to turn a profit, submariners were not averse to gilding the lily: in their struggle to break through, they had to be salesmen as well as technicians. The Russian sale ended ignominiously. On its delivery voyage, *Nordenfelt IV* became grounded at Jutland, Denmark. The Russians lost heart and refused to pay for it.

Isaac Peral and Spanish Endeavour

Across the world the submarine and its development triggered flurries of activity. In 1884 in Spain, a young naval officer watched advances being made in other countries. Today his memory is revered, a replica of his invention in dry dock; a wondrous machine from another age, popular with the throng of tourists who pay homage at its resting place in Cartagena harbour, where it was built on Spain's Costa Blanca coast. The *Peral*, launched in 1888, was designed by Lieutenant Isaac Peral y Caballero (1851–95).[39] It is proof of Peral's resolute character that it took four years of determined effort, navigating financial and technical problems, naval scepticism and political bureaucracy, before he managed to bring his craft to fruition. His life was short, sad and unfulfilled. An engaging figure of originality and technical élan, for four years he suffered with a brain tumour, finally succumbing to meningitis at the age of 44.

It was claimed that his vessel, which was 70ft long, could dive to a depth of 100ft. Its overall design and advanced navigation system made it one of the most capable military submarines yet devised. The early research was undertaken in Cadiz, with a budget of 5,000 pesetas approved by Peral's naval superiors and later increased to 25,000 pesetas. There were advanced aspects to the machine. It was among the first to be driven by electricity. Some say it was *the* first, but others would claim the crown. The *Peral* also used chemicals in a process which recharged the air supply. In breathing experiments volunteers were used as guinea pigs in a locked and airtight chamber with oxygen being pumped through a tube. It was reported that, of the six candidates selected for the test, only one had to be brought out prematurely, after an hour or so. The remaining five stayed in the room for another five hours in conditions supposed to loosely replicate the restricted confines of a submarine. The tests involved buckets of water being used to maintain levels of moisture and an array of measuring devices. An auxiliary 4 kilowatt (kw) engine drove air through a sodium hydroxide air purifier.

In 1889 the *Peral* made successful trial firings of two of Robert Whitehead's torpedoes (see Chapter 3). In an early submarine it was no mean feat to even launch a torpedo; its sudden departure from the firing tube would rock and unbalance a boat, imperilling stability.

The *Peral* was powered by a pair of electric motors, each of 30hp, and range and speed varied according to the charge in the batteries. Given the limitations of human propulsion, and the heat, dangers and inadequacies of steam, electric drive seemed the way forward. The two motors drove twin screw propellers. The craft had a searchlight to examine the seabed. The engines employed a current from a 420-cell accumulator battery, but the technology was costly, unreliable and early accumulator batteries and generators were too heavy, with the batteries alone weighing 30 tons.

There were adverse reports that the 77-ton submarine was underpowered and that it could not retain its charge; the limitations of battery power meant it had insufficient range. It was claimed, however, that it had an impressive underwater top speed of 9–10 knots. If such performance figures were true, it put it in the same category as U-boats which were not seen until twenty-seven years later in the Great War. As well as the technical worries and inherent limitations, there was also confusion about how the *Peral* could be deployed. The concerns proved too much for risk-averse politicians and for entrenched sceptics whose opinion prevailed in the Spanish Navy.

To Peral's chagrin, the project was discreetly abandoned and he quit. His departure was a cause of regret: two years after its launch, his boat had executed successful torpedo firings and, in an important innovation, could claim to be one of the first to have attempted a type of properly functioning underwater navigation system. There had been plans to build a more advanced submarine, but relations between Peral and the layer of politicians, bureaucrats and naval chiefs had by then, however, become intolerable. For years he had contended with political drift, budgetary constraints, internecine rivalries and red tape. He had demanded more autonomy in building a second submarine and guarantees of freedom in the appointment and direction of its constructors. His early loss denuded the submarine of a significant talent.

The way the project had degenerated into a debacle was unfruitful. For a period the compact between Peral, the Spanish Navy and government agencies had been positive. Budgets had been increased and there was sympathy from the bureaucracy. On a personal level, Peral was rewarded with honours and financial recognition. The way the affair spiralled into acrimony personified the difficulties pioneers had in persuading backers of the veracity and practicability of their plans, and, also, in maintaining their confidence during the sometimes lengthy programmes of complex experiment. Inventors keen to articulate their unproven, and to lay persons generally unfathomable, visions would always face difficulties.

Peral had his detractors as well as admirers. One was Commander Murray Sueter (1872–1960), a foremost figure in Britain's new arsenal.[40] Sueter wrote that, although Peral had been harshly treated:

> ... progress should never be sacrificed on the altar of self-aggrandisement. Pioneers would do well to cultivate a loftier, higher and nobler aim ... [nor has] any individual the right to assume that he is indispensable in the development of a weapon that has been considerably advanced by the pioneers of earlier days.

There seems scant evidence for Sueter's admonishment or the suggestion that Peral had sought glory while ignoring the endeavours of his inventive predecessors.[41] Sueter also noted:

> Spain had been experimenting with subs as early as 1860. It is recorded an engineer Narcisso Monturiol constructed a boat named the '*El Ictineo*'. She was a copy of Bauer's boat. ... Experiments were conducted with *El Ictineo* at Barcelona and Alicante during which a depth of 18 metres was reached; the crew of 10 men stayed underwater for five hours ... the results appear to have been satisfactory but apparently led to no definite results.[42]

In recording the endeavours of early submariners, it is prudent to resist being too categorical; perhaps Peral had simply failed to chronicle his findings, as did others. Though this is irritating to historians trying to track their accomplishments, Peral and his ilk were firstly engineers, not scribblers whose primary aim was to keep an eye on posterity. Sueter was distinguished, courageous and unafraid to speak his mind in a profession in which candour could hamper career progress; he was not, however, devoid of ego. Sometimes his sense of certainty and entitlement came close to scuppering his own career when, as an example, he allegedly wrote to the king claiming credit for the invention of the tank.

French Immersion: Goubet, Zédé and Laubeuf

In Paris in 1885 French civil engineer Claude Goubet (1837–1903) built a little battery-driven submarine. Short and fat, 16ft long, it had an odd internal configuration: its two-man crew sat back to back in the middle of the boat. Cynics commented that the layout served as an example of the French making the simple complicated, with one operator steering forwards and the other backwards instead of a sole operator helming in the ordinary way. In reality, both operators had different duties, but it was true the vessel carried all manner of curious devices, one involving a pendulum and a type of pumping mechanism to aid stability, which it did not. Another novelty comprised a pair of outsize scissors with which to snip through protective nets at harbour entrances and other entanglements which could impede submarine progress; the scissors met with mixed success, though the extensive if, on occasion, not famously adept Brazilian Navy, keen to keep abreast of European developments, took an interest in submarine and scissors.

The boat proved disappointing in trials in the Seine River and, later, off Cherbourg, being underpowered, incapable of holding a charge, unstable and clumsy to manoeuvre. Wits insisted this was a design flaw with the two helmsmen steering in opposite directions. At one time it was felt pedalling would be more efficient; it was tried, though it is unclear if pedal-power supplanted or merely supplemented Goubet's first choice of battery drive. In 1899 he built a larger model that underwent tests off Toulon. It must have been an improvement as it was adopted by the Russians, who had considered buying fifty of Goubet's original, tiny submarines. The acquisition failed to materialise; given its limitations a bulk buy would have been unwise. Some of Goubet's more esoteric creations were stripped of their innards and inelegantly redeployed as floating pontoons. His second submarine, which Russia bought, proved difficult to control and was alarmingly unstable. There were accounts that it once dived to 30ft and remained submerged for eight hours. Its occupants kept in touch by primitive telegraph with observers on the surface, who, as the hours ticked by, became rather worried.

The French naval architect Gustave Zédé (1825–91) was influenced by a template which had been laid down by one of his distinguished peers, another naval architect, Henri Dupuy de Lome (1816–85). Dupuy de Lome undoubtedly knew his boats. But one of his more fanciful ideas, though he died before it could be enacted, was for a fleet of submarines to ferry platoons of soldiers. It was part of another grand plan to invade Britain, though the technology of the time was too primitive. Britain had many foes and naively continued to nurture them within her borders. In drawing up his plans to invade Britain, Dupuy de Lome had learned what he knew about iron ships and steam engines while spending time in Britain in the 1840s. As a young man he had spent a fruitful period happily ingesting knowledge in the maritime centre of Bristol in Britain's south-west. His interval there could be construed as a successful espionage mission. France, through Dupuy de Lome, would have found the wisdoms he acquired in Bristol useful in its exertions against her old enemy. While in Bristol Dupuy de Lome had made a minute study of the construction of Isambard Kingdom Brunel's (1806–59) SS *Great Britain*. He had chosen his inspiration well: Brunel's stellar abilities would give Britain roads, bridges, the template for a superlative railway system and three awesome vessels including the iron-built SS *Great Britain* (1843), the biggest ship afloat and the first propeller-driven transatlantic vessel.

Dupuy de Lome was accomplished and designed a range of fighting ships, including *La Gloire* (1859) *Normandie* (1860) and *Invincible* (1861). *La Gloire* (5,630 tons), an armoured frigate with massive steel plates stretched across a wooden hull, was the earliest sea-going Ironclad. She was rendered obsolete a year later by Britain's HMS *Warrior* (1860), the world's first iron-hulled warship. Dupuy de Lome's talents were not limited to marine craft, however. He invented a hot air balloon, one of the few that could be steered (most went where the wind decided). He was also among the first to understand that electrical propulsion offered an important pointer to the submarine's future. In 1888, in the significant naval stronghold of Toulon in the Mediterranean on France's Cote d'Azur, Gustave Zédé, a friend and admirer of Dupuy de Lome, launched a remarkable little submarine, the 31-ton *Gymnote* (Electric Eel).[43] It was one of the first to use compressed air to expel water from its ballast tanks. She made many dives, but suffered from an up-down see-saw motion and, alarmingly, even for those doughty crews who had grown blasé about such incidents, ploughed into the bottom on several occasions. She suffered another impediment: being battery powered her range was limited and her duties had to be close to home. She could be used as a coastal or harbour-patrol craft where she might easily return to base to recharge her batteries. The French Navy acquired her and made modifications to enhance both her usefulness and manoeuvrability: a variable pitch propeller, two sets of hydroplanes and manual diving rudders fitted at her stern were an attempt to improve stability.

In 1893 a bigger version, the *Gustave Zédé*, almost 150ft long and weighing 266 tons, was launched in Toulon. But it took almost a decade before it was finished. The ten years were lost because of three major problems: technical difficulties, as every new submarine presented fresh conundrums; protracted and troublesome sea trials; and a frustrating degree of indecision and uncertainty which stemmed, in the main, from the alarming degree of political, bureaucratic and naval mayhem which ran unabated in France throughout the construction period. When *Gymnote* and her successor were laid down, the French government had seemed favourable towards the navy. The influence of the Young School, *La Jeune Ecole*, had grown and the approach of the naval chief, Vice Admiral Hyacinthe Theophile Aube (1826–90), was enlightened. An advocate of fresh thinking he was a fierce critic of obsolete naval traditions which had hampered the French fighting fleet. As in other navies his promotion of the submarine and willingness to accept new ideas would prove fatally unpopular with more conservative peers. Nor did his views curry favour with politicians hindered by a lamentable grasp of the submarines' potential and the enormity of its implications. They remained sceptical about committing monies from defence budgets which were already tight. There also prevailed a jealousy that the *Gustave Zédé* was imitative of Peral's submarine and that France, in its pomp, should be able to do anything better than that produced by the Spanish. If national pride is at stake, political peevishness knows few boundaries.

France was ensnared in political turmoil, so defence chiefs came and went with astonishing swiftness, including diverse Ministers of Marine. Some politicians and defence leaders praised while others castigated the submarine and its technology. The stark differences of opinion helped further stall its advance. The volatility in the French administration, the way politicians were shifted with a rapidity that destabilised the navy and the rest of her military, can be gleaned from the length of Lockroy's tenure as Minister of War. Lockroy was appointed on 25 October 1898 and dismissed from office eight days later. His predecessor, Charles Chanoine, lasted only a month. Lockroy's successor, Charles de Freycinet, showed glue-like tenacity, clinging on for seven months. French submariners watched in despair as ministers came and went, jettisoning policies in their wake. In the chaos, the exotically named Hyacinthe Aube was kicked out and the progressive notions of *La Jeune Ecole* shelved.

The *Gustave Zédé* made promising tests and, in 1897, a smaller version called the *Morse* (Walrus), incorporating various improvements, was laid down. When used as a harbour or inshore boat a battery-driven submarine had usefulness. But what of its principal role as a roaming predator? How could her potential be unleashed while her range was limited by an urgency to recharge her batteries?

Another who would play a crucial part in submarine affairs was the talented French marine engineer Maxime Laubeuf (1864–1939). France had not been alone in pondering the notion of having a boat with dual propulsion: a submarine equipped with a steam reciprocating engine on the surface and an electric engine for when the craft ran submerged. It was an attractive idea and, like most major breakthroughs, so extraordinarily simple it seemed glaringly obvious; in reality it was only obvious once somebody had said and done it. Laubeuf's thinking was cleverer still: his boat would carry fuel oil stored between its two hulls – the internal 'pressure' hull and the boat's external hull. Accumulator batteries could be recharged by a small generator powered by the vessel's steam engine. Laubeuf incorporated the innovations in 1899 into a 200-ton submarine called the *Narval*, famous as the first boat to have a double hull. Its underwater range was 10 miles with a claimed 100-mile range on the surface. The craft won a submarine design competition organised by Edouard Lockroy, the transient French Minister of War. Lockroy had known several previous incarnations. He had been a campaigning journalist – part of Victor Hugo's milieu – a left-wing politician and, at one time, had been the Minister of Marine.

Twenty-nine submarine designs from around the world had competed in Lockroy's contest. In winning the competition Laubeuf had made a spectacular entry into the global submarine business. The French, greatly emboldened by Laubeuf's success, immediately ordered four more submarines of a similar, slightly larger design.*

France saw the *Narval*, and the later boats that were built to a modified template, as potent additions to its armoury in its ceaseless quest to challenge Britain and its naval supremacy. In submarine annals the *Narval* left an indisputably important mark, but formidable problems still had to be resolved if submarines were to achieve their potential. Within the cramped parameters of *Narval* the ambient heat from the boiler was unbearably intense and, before it dived, the crew had to close the boiler, an operation that could take several minutes and leave both the craft and crew vulnerable to attack.

America Moves Ahead

In America in 1885, Professor Josiah Horace Tuck (1825–1900) at Annapolis, Maryland, produced a new twist on the steam engine which many of his peers

---

* France had a pressing incentive for investing its money in improving its submarine fleet: when the colonial powers were carving up Africa, France became enmeshed in the Fashoda incident in 1898, in which General Herbert Kitchener (1850–1916) later Lord Kitchener, elevated as a national hero after leading Britain's successful campaign to regain the Sudan, had claimed the entire Nile Valley for Britain. The affair blew up into a significant territorial dispute with France, settled only by a simmering diplomatic truce, but which, once again, had brought France and Britain to the cusp of war.

had chosen to propel their inventions. His power-plant for his submarine *Peacemaker* comprised a fireless steam engine, steam being generated by 1,500lb of caustic soda which drove a 14hp Westinghouse steam engine, albeit not very successfully. Though a more suitable name might have been *Warmonger*, some inventors took the view that their contraption would be so forbidding that nobody would dare challenge it, thus ensuring an uncertain peace; given the name of his boat it seems the professor subscribed to this explanation. (Tuck's craft resembled a porpoise but *Peacemaking Porpoise* would have been a mouthful.) Its captain stood in the craft with his head in a goldfish bowl-type viewer to see where he was going. However, maintaining a constant depth was difficult, as it was for other submarines, and instruments were basic to non-existent, making it impossible for the captain to gauge the angle of dive or when he might hit the bottom.

Peacemaker made brief trips in New York harbour with one underwater excursion lasting five hours, the caustic soda generating a surprising sufficiency of steam. She had been built at the DeLameter Iron Works, New York, which was run by Cornelius Henry DeLameter (1821–89).*

With a slice of maritime history to DeLameter's credit, Tuck could not have had a better authenticated builder. Despite originality and promise, *Peacemaker* had a brief history and showed itself largely impractical. Professor Tuck's experiments were brutally truncated in 1903 when relatives discovered he had spent most of the family fortune on his submarine peregrinations and, consequently, had him committed to a lunatic asylum.

Simon Lake and *Argonaut*

In America the naval architect Simon Lake (1866–1945) was a pioneer whose gifts and influence would be far-reaching.[44] Born in Pleasantville, New Jersey, he came from a distinguished engineering background. His grandfather, the Honourable Simon Lake, was a founder of Ocean City, Maryland, and Atlantic City, New Jersey, who with his brothers was responsible for the construction of a significant number of bridges, roads and railroads in the locality. His father, Christopher, ran a foundry and machine shop. With such lineage there was

---

* Cornelius DeLameter's company had distinguished itself in the Civil War building steam boilers and mechanics for the USS *Monitor*, the first Ironclad commissioned by the US Navy whose innovations included one of the first rotating gun turrets; *Monitor* was lost in 1862 off the dreaded Cape Hatteras, North Carolina, the disaster due in part to the weight of the turret and her perilously low freeboard.

an inevitability that Simon Lake would follow his forebears into engineering, though the branch of technology in which he chose to build his own reputation was still judged unusual. After his formal education at High School in Toms River, New Jersey, followed by the Clinton Liberal Institute at Fort Plain, New York, and the Franklin Institute, Philadelphia, where he studied mechanical engineering, Lake joined his father's company in 1883, of which he would later become a partner.

Gifted from an early age he began to make his mark as an inventor of nautical mechanisms, one of them being an ingenious steering device, with some of his appliances being adapted and utilised by fishing craft. He launched his first *Argonaut* submarine in 1894. A later *Argonaut* he designed had retractable wheels; the notion in some ways reminiscent, though very considerably advanced, of that conceived by the adventurous French priests Fournier and Mersenne in the seventeenth century. It was driven by a 30hp gasoline engine with air fed into it from two pipes on the surface. The *Argonaut*, named after the heroes in Greek mythology who sailed with Jason in the ship *Argo* in search of the Golden Fleece, made several successful voyages. In an especially ambitious passage of 2,000 miles, it survived a violent storm which caused widespread maritime havoc; an epic voyage in terms of durability and navigation. Jules Verne, the author of *Twenty Thousand Leagues under the Sea*, which Lake said had been his initial inspiration when he had first read it as a 12-year-old, sent a telegram from Amiens, France, in 1898 congratulating Lake. Some saw Simon Lake as the real-life Captain Nemo.

In New Jersey in 1901, the Lake Torpedo Boat Company was formed; it flourished and subsequently produced numerous boats for the United States and overseas, among them the impressive *Protector*, built in 1901 and sold to Russia in 1904. Lake came second in a US Navy competition to find the most advanced submarine design. But his abilities and designs caught the eye of the Imperial Russian Navy and, for a while, production was based in St Petersburg (the Russo-Japanese War of 1904–5 gave further impetus to submarine design). Lake was a designer with stellar gifts and his boats, more than others, began to look like contemporary submarines. They had a periscope, which he termed an 'omniscope', and his craft had little squat conning towers, a distinct pointer to the future and of designs to come. Diving planes were fitted on hulls to the fore of the conning tower and his creations had free-flooding ballast tanks, the judicious control of their filling and emptying enabling the vessel to dive and to rise.

Lake later designed numerous classes of boats for the US Navy, beginning in 1908 with the streamlined USS *Seal*, which was the first in the G-class range of vessels and which set a depth record of 256ft in November 1912 (see

Appendix K). Among many admirers of his craft and their advanced designs was his principal rival, the formidably talented John Holland.[45] Some see Lake as the father of the modern submarine; the assertion has undoubted credibility, but there are other contenders. Though his company closed in the 1920s his extraordinary influence can be traced down the decades in submarine design right through to the nuclear age leviathans. His supporters are unshakeable in their belief that it was Lake, rather than Holland (see Chapter 2), who was the more significant of the two in submarine technology. Lake's biographer Herbert Coley wrote:

> Perhaps no man in the past century has had as much to do with the shape of history as Simon Lake. That statement is intended as a query rather than as a statement of fact. It may be debatable but it is also defendable. He is responsible for the modern submarine.

The modest Lake had an attractive line in self-deprecation:

> I think it is nonsensical for me to write my autobiography at this time. I am only 71 years old and I have not accomplished one half the things I wish to do.[46]

Through the centuries the submarine had inched ahead incrementally. With resourceful thinking and the use of unorthodox apparatus the cardinal dilemmas of stability, contaminated air and propulsion were being properly addressed. Though submariners were still demimonde, their progress uncertain and picaresque, there was a sense that submersion beneath the seas in a curious transport, while unlikely to be everybody's first choice, was perhaps not quite as far-fetched as had been first believed.

Notes

1   *Oxford Dictionary of National Biography: William Bourne* (Oxford University Press, 2004)
2   Da Vinci, Leonardo, *The Da Vinci Notebooks* (Profile, 2005); Laurenza, Domenico, *Leonardo's Machines* (David & Charles, 2006); *Leonardo on Flight* (Johns Hopkins University Press, 2007)
3   Williamson, James, *The Age of Drake* (A&C Black, 1938)
4   Bourne, William, 'A Regiment for the Sea Conteyning Most Profitable Rules, Mathematical Experiences and Perfect Knowledge of Nauigation, for all Coastes and Countreys: Most Needful and Necessary for Al Seafaryng Men and Trauellers' (1577)

(EEBO editions, Proquest, 2012); Taylor, E.G.R. (ed.), edited version: 'A Regiment for the Sea and other Writings on Navigation (Hakluyt Society, Cambridge University Press, 1963)

5   Trevor-Roper, Hugh, *Princes and Artists, Patronage and Ideology at Four Habsburg Courts 1517–1633* (Thames & Hudson, 1976); Evans, R.J.W., *Rudolf II and His World: A Study in Intellectual History, 1576–1612* (Clarendon Press, 2nd edn, 1984)

6   Swinfield, John, *Airship: Design, Development and Disaster* (Conway Maritime, 2012)

7   Gray, Edwyn, *Disasters of the Deep* (US Naval Institute Press, 2003)

8   Arnold-Forster, Rear Admiral D., *The Ways of the Navy* (Ward, Lock & Co., 1931) p.260

9   Author in conversation with anonymous submariner (National Maritime Museum, Greenwich, London, 17 February, 2012)

10 *Oxford Dictionary of National Biography* Smith: Wilkins: John Wilkins (Elder & Co., 1885–1900); Wilkins, John, *Mathematicall Magick, Or, the Wonders That May Be Performed By Mechanical Geometry in Two Books: Concerning Mechanical [Brace] Powers, Motions* (Eebo Editions, Proquest, 2011)

11 Ragan, Mark, *Submarine Warfare in the Civil* War (Da Capo Press, 2003); Parker, John, *The World Encyclopedia of Submarines: An Illustrated Reference to Underwater Vessels of the World Through History, from the Nautilus and Hunley to Modern Nuclear-powered Submarines* (Lorenz Books, 2007)

12 Blashka, Ivor, *The Great Engineers* (Hart, Methuen & Co.1928) chapters 6 and 7; Milton, Perry, *Infernal Machines: The Story of the Confederate Submarine and Mine Warfare* (Louisiana State University Press, 1985); Crowley, R.O, 'Confederate Torpedo Service', *The Century*, vol. 56, Issue 2 (The Century Company, 1898)

13 Matschoss, Conrad, *Great Engineers* (Ayer Publishing, 1939) pp.87–92

14 Black, Jeremy, *Naval Power* (Palgrave Macmillan, 2009) pp.112–115

15 Diamant, Lincoln, *Chaining the Hudson* (Fordham University Press, 2004) chapter 11

16 Parker, John, *The World Encyclopedia of Submarines: An Illustrated Reference to Underwater Vessels of the World Through History, from the Nautilus and Hunley to Modern Nuclear-powered Submarines* (Lorenz Books, 2007)

17 Black, Jeremy, *Naval Power* (Palgrave Macmillan, 2009) pp.112–115

18 Isles, George, *Leading American Inventors* (Henry Holt & Co., 1912) pp.73–74

19 Isles, George, *Leading American Inventors*, pp.40–73; Parsons, William Barclay, *Robert Fulton and his Submarine* (Colombia University Press, 1922)

20 Hague, William, *William Pitt the Younger: A Biography* (Harper Perennial, 2005)

21 Lavery, Brian, *The Ship of the Line*, vol. 1 (Conway Maritime Press, 1983)

22 Howarth, David, *British Sea Power* (Robinson, 2003) p.394

23 Quoted in Isles, George, *Leading American Inventors* (Henry Holt & Co., 1912) pp.68–69

24 Isles, George, *Leading American Inventors* (Henry Holt & Co., 1912) chapter 2

25 Quoted in Isles, George, *Leading American Inventors* (Henry Holt & Co., 1912) pp.72–73

26 Sweetman, John, *The Crimean War, 1854–1856* (Osprey, 2001)

27 Stuart, Matthew, *Monturiol's Dream: The Extraordinary Story of the Submarine Inventor Who Wanted to Save the World* (Profile Books, 2003) p.186

28 Stuart, Matthew, *Monturiol's Dream*, p.187

29 McNab, Chris and Keeter, Hunter, *Tools of Violence* (Osprey, 2008) p.234

30 Parrish, Thomas, *The Submarine: A History* (Viking Adult, 2004); Friedman, Norman and Friedman, Andrew, *U.S. Submarines Through 1945: An Illustrated Design History* (US Naval Institute Press, 1995)

31 Jenkins, E.H., *Histoire de la Marine Francaise* (Albin Michel, 1977)

32 Ragan, Mark, *Submarine Warfare in the Civil War* (Da Capo Press, 2003)

33 Chaffin, Tom, *The H.L. Hunley: The Secret Hope of the* Confederacy (Hill & Wang, 2010)

34 Hicks, B. and Kropf, S., *Raising the Hunley: The Remarkable History and Recovery of the Lost Confederate Submarine* (Ballantine Publishing, 2002)

35 *Making Sense of the Industrial Revolution: English Economy and Society, 1700–1850* (Manchester University Press, 2001)

36 Murphy, William Scanlan, *The Father of the Submarine: The Life of the Reverend George Garrett Pasha* (William Kimber & Co., 1987)

37 Bower, Paul, *The Garrett Enigma and the Early Submarine Pioneers* (Airflife, 1999)

38 Scott, J.D., *Vickers: A History* (Weidenfeld & Nicolson, 1963)

39 Humble, Richard, *Undersea Warfare* (Hodder & Stoughton, 1981)

40 Shores, Christopher, *100 Years of British Naval Aviation* (Haynes Publishing in association with the Royal Navy, 2009) pp.12–18

41 Sueter, Commander Murray F., *The Evolution of the Submarine, Boat, Mine and Torpedo, from the Sixteenth Century to the Present Time* (J. Griffith & Co, 1907) pp.62–65, 90

42 Sueter, *Evolution*, p.62

43 Harris, Brayton and Boyne, Walter J., *The Navy Times Book of Submarines* (Berkley Trade, 2001)

44 Poluhowich, John H., *Argonaut: The Submarine Legacy of Simon Lake* (Texas A&M University Press, 1999)

45 Harris, Brayton and Boyne, Walter J., *The Navy Times Book of Submarines* (Berkley Trade, 2001)

46 Coley, Herbert D., *Submarine, The Autobiography of Simon Lake* (Appleton-Century Company, 1938)

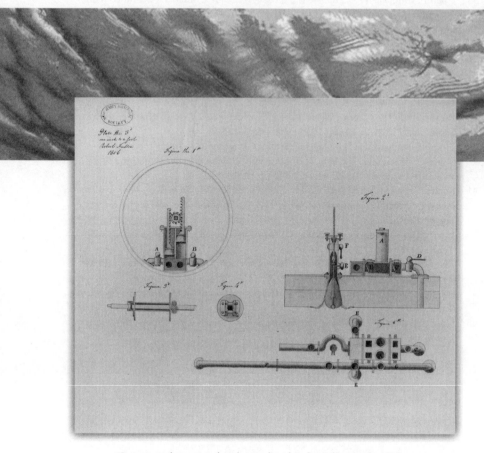

'Pumps, cocks, water chamber and anchor for "plunging boat".'
Robert Fulton, 1806. (LOC USZC4-6809).

2

Ducks and Devotions

As nearly as the human mind can discern now, the submarine is indeed a 'sea-devil' against which no means that we possess at present can prevail.

John Holland (c. 1900)

For inexplicable reasons satanic instruments of carnage seem irresistible to those of a medical or religious bent. The Irish American John Philip Holland (1841–1914), whose influence on the submarine was cardinal, was a monk with the Order of Christian Brothers for six years. Thoughts of death and destruction rudely interrupted his devotions, though his aficionado maintain he saw the submarine as a peaceful device; how, is difficult to see, though he did write about alternative uses. With his father a coastguard and his brother a Republican, the spirit of the sea and the seeds of revolution were in his genes. Michael, his brother, was a member of the Fenian Brotherhood, an Irish independence movement which financed the first *Holland* submarine; Michael's immersion in liberationist activities forced him to flee to America to escape the British. John grew up in the whitewashed coastguard's cottage in the small fishing community of Liscannor, County Clare, facing the Atlantic. Later – Dublin's Easter Rising was in 1916 – the same seas would witness German U-boats seeking uncertain sanctuary off the Irish coast as they caused massive casualties to British and Allied shipping in the First and Second World War.

The Irish-speaking Holland – he would learn English later – was one of four brothers born to Maire Ni Scannlain. He was a child when his father died amid the squalor and disease of the Great Famine (1845–52), which ravaged Ireland and resulted in mass emigration, especially to America.[1] Holland was fortunate in his childhood that two enlightened influences would nurture his abilities. At the age of 12 he and his family moved to Limerick, where as a schoolboy he came under the aegis of the talented Bernard O'Brien, a teacher in the Christian Brothers. Brother O'Brien built ingenious mechanical devices, especially telescopes, and he encouraged Holland's early love of design and engineering. The second influence occurred when he was a teenager. In 1858, at the age of 17, he had taken the initial vows of the Order of Christian Brothers and started to train as a teacher at the North Monastery school, Cork, coming under the wing of the gifted James Dominic Burke. Brother Burke was steeped in engineering and science, and shared a love of the submarine with Holland. While critics of the monastic culture are today legion, its educative regime is indisputably demanding and few could deny its scions were not seriously educated.[2] Holland went on to teach at various schools in Ireland, but failed to take his full vows and became disenchanted with teaching. Fascinated by flight and the advance of the aeroplane he showed himself determined, well read, cultured, quietly humorous and an accomplished musician. His keenness to engage with the mysteries of flight and to design aeroplanes, with the high level of imaginative fluency that he brought to the subject, were such that he could have made it a career. Throughout these technical and cultural dalliances, however, he retained an unswerving passion for the submarine.

Ireland's plight had left its mark. In its wake the Great Famine brought cholera and cruelties such as 'levelling', in which landlords routed defaulting tenants and razed their homesteads. The indignities inflicted on the Irish by the British were extensive. How could the wretched and impoverished Ireland free itself of a nation with a mighty army and an unmatched fleet? The latter, John Holland convinced himself, could be challenged by the submarine. If the Confederate's little *Hunley* could sink the mighty *Housatonic* of the Federal Navy in 1864, then why couldn't an Irish submarine sink ships of the Royal Navy? At one time he created a toy duck. It waddled and paddled as all ducks do; an amusing contrivance which delighted teachers and pupils. In its ability to dive and swim underwater, and to surface, the plaything offered a clue to that which would become his lifelong enterprise.

In 1873 he rejected taking his perpetual vows with the Christian Brothers and followed his family to America, the Promised Land, to which they had emigrated the year before. He sailed to Boston, travelling steerage, finding employment in an engineering company and, although it was not his first love, as a teacher. During his period teaching at a school in the industrial township of Paterson, New Jersey, home of the Colt revolver and also known as Silk City, a foremost textile centre, he produced his first formal submarine design, though he had sketched many contraptions over the years. His first submarine would be financed by the Fenian Brotherhood.[3]

Established in 1858 in Ireland and America, the Fenian Brotherhood were avowed to ridding Ireland of the British and founding a republic. There were many sympathisers in the United States. The monies were arranged by his brother, Michael, a member of the Brotherhood, and further funding would emanate from stories about the submarine in *The Irish World* newspaper. Three years after his arrival in America Holland constructed a scale model, just under 3ft long, and presented it at Coney Island for approval by the Fenians. They found it convincing and sanctioned the construction of a full-size 'wrecking-boat'. Built at Paterson and completed in 1878 it was Holland's first real submarine. It cost in the region of $4,000 dollars and was called the *Number 1*. At 14.5ft long and 2.6ft high the boat had an inauspicious launch on 20 May 20 in the Passaic River; she immediately sank. It was Holland's mistake. He had calculated the buoyancy of the boat for salt water, but the upper reaches of the river comprised almost fresh water; a trimming error – an easy mistake for a pioneer to make, and one committed by later submariners in different circumstances. Undeterred, the boat was raised, Holland made the appropriate alterations to the trim, and *Number 1* gave a promising performance, diving and surfacing to the delight and amazement of all who had gathered. The Fenians thought it was a winner and agreed to budget another $20,000, sanctioning Holland to build a diving machine capable of inflicting terror on the British fleet; the sizeable amount indicative of the sympathy and funding in the US for Irish Republican causes.

Work began on the *Fenian Ram* at the DeLameter Iron Works, New York, on 3 May 1879, the same construction yard of the Ironclad *Monitor* and Professor Tuck's caustic soda-driven *Peacemaker*. Launched in 1881 it was 31ft long, 6ft wide and displaced 19 tons. Designed for a crew of three, her cigar shape, and the thinking which went in to her, owed something to the Whitehead torpedo, with cruciform control fins sited close to her tail. Horizontal planes on the hull could be tilted, enabling forward motion to drive her beneath the water line. Powered by a twin-cylinder 15hp Brayton petrol engine, she could dive to more than 45ft. Within limitations she was competent, but she lacked a battery and was devoid of a torpedo, as the art of firing torpedoes underwater was still being developed. To compensate, Holland produced an underwater gun which, though primitive, was curiously effective. Using high-pressure air it fired a 6ft projectile 12ft through the water to strike the underside of a target. It sounds fanciful but reports of its reliability were in the main favourable.

Given the power and immensity of Imperial Britain, the might of its navy and, also, the internecine rivalries and factionalism in the Fenians, their ambitions were naïve. Though spirited, the movement lacked discipline. The plot that it imagined would humble the Royal Navy entailed transporting the *Fenian Ram* by an innocent-looking merchant vessel to within striking distance of a British warship. The marauding submarine would slip into the sea to attack its target before returning to its mothership, secretly nosing back through an unseen underwater hatch from which it had been freed to execute its skullduggery. Though American Fenians claimed some 50,000 members, their track record had been dismal: two unsuccessful invasions of Canada in 1866 and 1870, and the fostering of somewhat feeble Irish discord in 1867. The Fenians generated as much ferment in their own ranks as they did beyond them.

The submarine's construction was paid for out of a 'skirmishing fund' administered by the Irish-American journalist John Devoy (1842–1928), a prime mover in the Brotherhood.[4] From the start of the project relations between Holland, who was sympathetic to the cause but primarily a technologist, and a cauldron of revolutionaries, promised to be fraught – and it was. Holland made dives in the boat, firing a dummy projectile. But the long construction process, the refinement of the engineering and the ceaseless testing and underwater trials required a continuance of both money and patience. Some of the Brothers demanded that the monies be used for more skirmishing and less innovation; with revolution in the air, patience had become a rare commodity.

In 1883 a band of renegade Fenians forged Holland's name and stole the boat, using a tug to tow it up Long Island Sound to New Haven, Connecticut. Clueless about how to operate it their inept handling of the craft obliged the harbourmaster to declare it a hazard to navigation. The botched submarine snatch had become comedic. In mounting frustration the Fenians had beached her and later tried, without success, to sell her to the Russians. The outraged Holland refused to help, declaring he would prefer to let the vessel rot in their hands. She was partially stripped of her mechanics and faced an ignoble demise, rusting and forsaken in a waterside shed. She was, however, saved from decay and later displayed in Madison Square Gardens in New York as part of a fundraising effort for the Easter Rising in Dublin in 1916. Today the *Fenian Ram* and the *Number 1* are on show in Paterson, New Jersey, where Holland conceived them.

A year after the debacle, with Holland severing ties with the Fenian Brotherhood, he found new employment with Edmund Zalinski's Pneumatic Gun Company, later starting a business with Zalinski called The Nautilus Submarine Boat Company. It was a promising new chapter for Holland, but it too would end in frustration.

Edmund Zalinski (1849–1909) was a talented Polish Jew with a distinguished military background, seeing action in the Civil War, and he proved his technical prowess by later becoming professor of military science at the celebrated MIT, the Massachusetts Institute of Technology. Entrepreneurial and inventive, he was determined to build a submarine which would be armed with his own creation, a dynamite gun, though his underwater ambitions would have fared better had he adhered more closely to Holland's counsel. He and Holland built the *Zalinski Boat*: 50ft long, 8ft wide, powered by a Brayon engine like that in the *Ram*, it was constructed on a little island off Fort Hamilton, Brooklyn, New York. From the outset the project was hampered by meagre funding and stymied by Zalinski's unwillingness to heed Holland's advice about submarine fundamentals. They were both driven and knowledgeable and had definite ideas: as such the relationship could only end in tatters.

Zalinski was a former artillery officer who wanted a vehicle for his gun; to him the success of the gun was as important – perhaps more so – than that of the submarine. Mounted on the bow, Zalinski reckoned the gun's projectile had a range of ½ mile. It carried an explosive charge which would detonate on impact (or before). In Zalinski's determination, to cut costs the boat's construction was largely of wood. It was damaged at its launch and, though repairs were followed by promising trials in New York harbour, it failed to live up to expectations. Holland and Zalinski parted company and closed their infant business. This was not unique: submarine enterprises surfaced and sank with an alarming suddenness, sometimes leaving creditors foundering.

Holland had been introduced to Zalinski by William Kimball, whose role in the submarine saga would become critical. Kimball (1848–1930) was a lieutenant in the US Navy and would enjoy a meritorious career, rising to the rank of rear admiral. A specialist in torpedo warfare he had graduated from the US Naval Academy and would become one of the most influential promoters of Holland and his endeavours. There was still indifference and cynicism in the world's navies towards the submarine and Kimball was instrumental in flagging up the importance of Holland's work to Congress and the Navy Department. He was unstinting, though not entirely successful, in trying to persuade commentators, politicians and naval chiefs that they should endorse Holland's work; that the US Navy should acquire his patents and back him with resources, permitting him to undertake a credible programme of trials instead of trying to maintain himself while eking out piecemeal funding.

Nevertheless the naval leaders declined to offer Holland their support. In his career it becomes apparent that once he had configured the blueprint of the modern submarine he was helped in bringing it to fruition by a determined nexus of lay supporters; it was they, rather than politicians or decision-makers in the military, who would be largely responsible for the eventual acceptance of his designs. Another key ally of Holland was the young Charles Morris (1853–1914), a gifted engineer and staunch advocate of submarines.[5] His father owned a dredging company and the dock in New Jersey where the ill-fated *Fenian Ram* had been moored. Holland worked as a draftsman for the Morris and Cummings Dredging Company, taking work where he could find it; the usual lot of the impecunious inventor in the interval of agonised uncertainty which commonly precedes recognition. Holland and Morris were innovative engineers, once collaborating on the design of an aeroplane.

There were others who had a major impact on the progress of the submarine. Elihu Frost (1860–1925), to whom Morris had introduced Holland, became central. A well-connected and influential lawyer, Frost was among those who helped to fund Holland and his experiments. Like Kimball, Frost too would assist in bringing the Holland designs to the attention of the US Navy. Though initially close, the relationship between Holland and Frost started to wane when business and politicking began to engulf the project; when the eagle-eyed, wishing to turn a buck, began to circle. Such unpleasantness, however, was still a distance off.

In 1888 a submarine competition by the US Navy offered an opportunity which Holland's supporters saw as a likely breakthrough. The rules included a stipulation that the winning craft could turn in less than four times its own length and that it had positive buoyancy other than when it dived. Holland won the competition. But the US Navy still refused him a contract. In 1893 came success: after calling for more design submissions the navy finally placed an order for *Holland V*, the *Plunger*. The five years between the first competition and the second request for designs by the US Navy indicate the patience which was needed by Holland in dealing with the military. While others might have quit in frustration, Holland had tenacity, retaining an unswerving belief in his creation.

The *Plunger* had to be built to naval specifications which were not to Holland's liking. The boat had to have electric propulsion while underwater, but the navy stipulated that it must use an oil-fired steam engine on the surface. The first had become the convention, but the latter was ludicrous: the steam engine was too big, heavy and hot. Its imposition showed that naval staffs still had little understanding of the strategic concept of boat engineering and architecture. Holland wanted gasoline as the use of steam power would impair his design. Consequently, his relationship with the navy and government bureaucrats would grow fraught. He would accept no meddling by naval constructors or clerks vested with chaperoning state monies. His supporters said only he, as its creator, properly understood the submarines' intimacies, while his detractors allege that he was curmudgeonly and stubborn. Doubtless the truth lay in the void between.

Holland asked the fiscally adroit Frost to help, and he did so by forming the Holland Torpedo Boat Company, expertly exploiting his range of contacts to raise funds. Another backer appeared. The industrialist Isaac Rice (1850–1915) had grown wealthy in railways, batteries and electricity. In this era of bustling capitalism, in which America's economic powerhouse rose like a colossus, Frost and Rice saw the potential and recognised a chance to make money. In 1899 they forged a takeover in which the Holland Torpedo Boat Company became a subsidiary of Rice's Electric Boat Company, controlled by Rice. With a quickening of the commercial momentum a third player emerged: the Washington lawyer and lobbyist Charles Creecy, who had connections in the naval and political milieu. Creecy became a lifelong friend of Holland, who he met through Frost's father Calvin, who was also a lawyer. Creecy and others later quit the Electric Boat Company, being at odds over policy and direction.

Holland modified his *Plunger* plans to produce the streamlined *Holland VI*, the acme of design. She bristled with Holland's invention and style, encapsulating centuries of innovation with all the silly bits sieved out. *Holland V1* had a 45hp petrol engine on the surface and an electric motor while submerged, with a dynamo to recharge her batteries. She could make 6 knots submerged using battery power and 7 knots on the surface while using her petrol unit. Fitted with an internal torpedo tube she carried three torpedoes fired by compressed air, the air also being used to expel water from her ballast tanks and which shifted water between her two small trim tanks positioned fore and aft.

She had two ballast tanks. The first was sizeable, full to the brim to ensure the craft would sink; filling to capacity stopped water slopping sideways and imperilling her equilibrium. A smaller tank was filled only to a level which gave marginal buoyancy, governed by such considerations as the weight and number of crew, usually between seven and nine. If stopped when submerged, her slight buoyancy would bring her slowly to the surface. Hydroplanes on control surfaces made her dive or rise. Launched in 1897 she began her trials the following year. Built at the Crescent Shipyard in Elizabethport, New Jersey, her construction was supervised by a Yorkshireman, Arthur Busch. Busch established his credentials at the famous Harland and Wolff shipbuilding yard in Belfast, Ireland, before emigrating to America in 1892.[6]

Creecy persuaded Holland to exhibit his submarine in Washington for inspection by naval chiefs. It was a smart move. Their number included the US Navy's chief engineer John Lowe, another Englishman. Born in Liverpool, Lowe had emigrated to America and joined the army, before being wounded in the Civil War and joining the US Navy. With Kimball, Lowe was one of the few who appreciated the scope of the submarine. While most adhered to a notion which persisted for years – that its main role would be as a surface craft operating close to home in a defensive posture – Lowe recognised its real potential as a lone, underwater, long-range predator. A crucial participant in the early testing programme, Lowe was aboard *Holland VI* for her acceptance trials. It was Lowe who advised the US Navy to buy her.

In surveying the operational personnel, rather than those of a business or political bias, the part played by the American engineer Frank Taylor Cable (1863–1945) should not pass unnoticed.[7] Cable was an instinctive engineer with a careful approach to solving problems. *Holland VI*'s batteries were made by a company called Electric-Dynamic, one of Rice's businesses, and by whom, in 1897, Cable was employed. Cable's introduction to the *Holland* project was in unpromising circumstances: *Holland VI* had sunk at her moorings and Cable had been summoned to help with her repairs. Having instituted them and suggested other technical changes, he found, as did other engineers if given a chance to scrutinise the technology, that to his delight he had become enthralled by it. To those so inclined, such was the magic of the submarine. Cable's conversion was not new: submarine history is rich with engineers who, having had first-hand experience of its mechanics and science, were then beguiled. Subsequently, in 1898, Cable joined the Holland Torpedo Boat Company. He captained the boat during testing in New York harbour and, with Holland, introduced modifications to enhance its performance and handling.

Frost had embarked on a worldwide drive to exploit Holland's patents and, with Rice, would build a company powerful enough to strike a deal with the US Navy. It had been difficult for Holland, a one-man band, to have the same degree of authority and clout that a properly funded company had in dealing with the US Navy. While Frost and Rice tightened their grip on the business, so Holland's influence declined. He felt his ideas were being hi-jacked and that he had been sidelined by businessmen. Supporters of the boat lobbied Congress and the naval hierarchy with a renewed vigour. On 11 April 1900, the US Navy finally bought *Holland VI*. She was commissioned on 12 October 1900 as USS *Holland VI* (SS-1).

After years of struggle it was a salutary time for John Holland, the resolute, frail inventor, plagued by poor health since infancy. He had crossed continents to fulfil a dream, his triumph marred by a growing discomfiture at his sense of alienation. The following description is of Holland on the day of the launch ceremony:

> A slender man of moderate stature, wearing a dark suit and a black bowler, with a large cravat bulging under his winged collar ... the tense expression on the little man's face was almost hidden behind thick spectacles and a walrus moustache.[8]

Holland's designs caught on and the business prospered. Rice and Frost swelled their coffers licensing versions of Holland boats to the Dutch, Japanese and British navies, the latter having dismissed with disdain those in their 'little tin fishes'. However, though a leap forward, *Holland VI* was still seriously bereft. Among her shortcomings she was devoid of a periscope; her commander had to glean his bearings through a minute observation window. In reality, if a boat dived, its commander and crew had only the sketchiest notion of where it might come up, if ever.

Rice cajoled the British Admiralty into buying five Holland variants, but their acquisition failed to meet with universal euphoria. In Britain, submarine warfare was not cricket. Navy controller Admiral Sir Arthur Knyvet Wilson (1842–1921) allegedly said in 1901 that 'submarines were underhand, unfair and damned un-English'. His view was that captured foreign submariners were pirates and should be hanged. Knyvet Wilson would not have approved of a tradition which later echoed his strictures as, on returning to port in the Great War, victorious submarines took to flying the Jolly Roger. Some historians claim that Wilson's oft-quoted remarks were taken out of context; contrarily, and sometimes overlooked, is that it was Wilson, as the Controller of the Navy, who first sanctioned commission of the submarine.

John Philip Holland's antipathy to the British and the sale of his invention to the Royal Navy caused him unease. His Republican instincts had mellowed over the years but misgivings lingered. For its part, the British Admiralty was not at ease over the matter either. Acquiring the designs of a truculent former monk, in a deal brokered by an American battery magnate, caused considerable chagrin in the Admiralty, in which most grandees shied away from commerce, eschewing it as an alien habitat of chicanery and wheeler-dealers; nor, it was felt, had Britain's imperial might been built, and its naval supremacy secured, by the costly purchase of Irish Republican contraptions.

The British Admiralty had its critics, but after centuries of dominating the oceans it was not totally bereft of guile. In being slow to adopt submarine technology it is difficult to determine if it was guilty of dilatoriness, or if it had been quite exceptionally wily, watching developments with a canny eye while letting foreign navies bear the cost of experimentation: certainly a diversity of expensive submarine flops had been paid for by other navies with which they were now saddled, and from which the Royal Navy had gained valuable knowledge at somebody else's expense. It is inarguable though, at this point, that Britain lagged behind indigenous developments taking place on the continent. France set the pace with her home-grown submarines and innovations; many were competent, others of flair, while some were plain dotty. Germany came late to the technology, shrewdly or otherwise, by failing to develop its own boats until 1906; when it did so, spurred by thoughts of conflict, it was able to avoid some of the hazards and pitfalls which had beset earlier designers.

Relations between Holland, Frost, Rice and a naval constructor new to the business, Lawrence Spear (1870–1950), grew gangrenous. They thought Holland clueless in business, drowning in a ceaseless stream of his own inventions. Holland reckoned they were crass and ignorant about submarines, had filched his life's work, duped him with bogus contracts and pursued profit at the expense of advancing the technology. Spear, from Warren, Ohio, had studied naval architecture at Glasgow University, Scotland. In 1902 he quit the US Navy to accept a lucrative offer to be the naval architect and vice-president of the Electric Boat Company. In the pecking order it effectively made him Holland's boss. Much of Spear's career had been on surface ships in the naval construction corps and his submarine experience compared to Holland's was negligible.

Years after *Holland VI* was launched, Richard Knowles Morris, the grandson of Charles Morris, an intimate of Holland and the superintending engineer of *Holland VI* during its construction, was given access to his grandfather's papers. He published an excellent and informed account of Holland's endeavours and tracked the infighting in the Electric Boat Company. He wrote:

> Spear was an able technician ... thorough, conservative, traditional ... not familiar with submarines, in theory or in practice. If a man with no experience in submarines were placed over Holland in the face of his objections, the inventor [Holland] knew that his days in the company would be numbered. He had watched the modification of the basic principles for which he had so long fought. To modify a design is not to invent. Invention involves the introduction of new principles, forms or methods – singly or in combination – by which a hitherto unrealized objective may be attained. At least from Holland's point of view, Spear was a modifier and not an inventor. Nor was the difference between the two men to be explained solely on the grounds of Holland's frustration. The variations in design which Lawrence Spear began to introduce made a virtue of convention and moved the boats farther away from the type which Holland conceived.[9]

Spear said he would incorporate bow superstructures on Holland's submarines, fitting a flying bridge, claiming it would help 'habitability and comfort' while the boats were cruising. It was the type of remark guaranteed to induce rage in Holland who took pride in stripping his designs to bare essentials, ensuring clean, uncluttered lines. Irritated by what he saw as Spear's meddling, Holland had an angry riposte:

The Navy does not like submarines because there is no deck to strut on ...
Sweep out all interesting but useless devices that encumber the present boats
... She cannot have a deck on which men can enjoy sunlight.[10]

There were differences in the company which ranged across the spectrum.
From engineering minutiae to the commercial ambitions of the business, to the
military purpose and long-term potential of the submarine. Relationships went
into free-fall with charge and counter-charge, accusations and rebuttals. Writs
flew, lawyers grew fat and Spear's career took off.*

Holland's career went in the opposite direction. In 1904, aged 63, he was
effectively forced to quit the Electric Boat Company, sending Rice a bitter
note of resignation. Dated 28 March it read:

Dear Mr. Rice,

As my contract with the company expires on the 31st inst., and as it is
proper that I should then withdraw from my directorship, I beg to offer my
resignation. The success of your company can never be as great as what I
ardently desired for it.[11]

The acrimony did not diminish with his departure. The following year the
company brought a legal suit against Holland which blocked any possibility
that he would ever be allowed to engage with submarines in the future. He
fought the injunction and lost. Holland had never been physically strong. His
path had been arduous; he was exhausted and unwell. A blanket ban denied the
world a stellar talent. One can only guess at different creations he may have
produced. He returned to an earlier passion, flight, another mystery of the day,
designing what experts said would have been an accomplished aeroplane. In
this he had been beaten to posterity by American brothers Orville and Wilbur
Wright, who in 1903 had made the world's first powered flight at Kitty Hawk,
North Carolina.

Holland died in reduced circumstances aged 73 at the start of the First World
War; forty days later the German submarine *U-9* torpedoed and sank three

---

* In 1911 Spear became the president of the New London Ship and Engine Company
(NLSEC) which included the exploitation of diesel technology. Diesel engines, patented
in 1894 by Rudolf Diesel (1855–1913), in which fuel could be ignited without a spark,
would, eventually, supplant less safe and uneconomic petrol engines in submarines. In 1930
the NLSEC merged with the Electric Boat Company, of which, in 1942, Spear became
president and, later, chairman, a post he held until his death.

old, armoured British cruisers, built in the 1890s, *Cressy*, *Hogue* and *Aboukir* while on patrol off the coast of Holland (see Chapter 7). In an hour a 'tin-fish' submarine of 450 tons with a crew of twenty-six had sunk 36,000 tons of shipping and cost the lives of more than 1,400 men. Fourteen years before the start of the First World War Holland wrote:

> As nearly as the human mind can discern now, the submarine is indeed a 'sea-devil' against which no means that we possess at present can prevail.[12]

John Holland was extraordinarily prescient, but his belief in the submarine as a passenger carrier seems – always with hindsight – uncharacteristically jejune. He wrote:

> The progress of the submarine in commerce will be rapid ... within the next ten years ... I expect to see the submarine boats engaged in regular traffic.

He did not see them being used commercially on long voyages such as Atlantic crossings, but envisaged their deployment on less taxing trips:

> On a short route such as across the English Channel it would be excellent. No other water journey causes an equal amount of suffering. The most hardened traveller becomes sea-sick there. The fogs and heavy traffic are constantly causing collisions ... and storms toss the stoutest boats about like cockleshells ... [whereas] the boat will lie as steadily as a water-soaked log.[13]

He imagines several advantages for passengers:

> There will be no seasickness, because in a submerged boat there is absolutely no perceptible motion. There will be no smells to create nausea, for the boats will be propelled by electric power.[14]

Visionaries have blind spots and Holland was no exception. The first submarines after his death were rank and dangerous. A century later most boats are in the hands of the military with a relatively small number used for exploration or as toys by billionaires. A further role has emerged: ferrying narcotics by submarine for Colombian drug traffickers. The devout bowler-hatted idealist, toy duck maker and educationalist would turn in his grave.[15]

Notes

1   Donnelly, James, *The Great Irish Potato Famine* (Sutton Publishing, 2002)

2   Wilson, R.F., *The Christian Brothers, their Origin and Work* (BiblioBazaar, 2009)

3   Jenkins, Brian, *Fenians and Anglo-American Relations during Reconstruction* (Cornell University Press, 1969); Jenkins, Brian, *The Fenian Problem: Insurgency and Terrorism in a Liberal State, 1858–1874* (McGill-Queen's University Press, 2008); O'Broin, Leon, *Revolutionary Underground: The Story of the Irish Republican Brotherhood, 1858–1924* (Gill and Macmillan, 1976)

4   Golway, Terry, *Irish Rebel: John Devoy and America's Fight for Ireland's Freedom* (St Martin's Griffin, 1999)

5   Parrish, Thomas, *The Submarine: A* History (Penguin, 2005)

6   Moss, M. and Hume, J.R., *Shipbuilders to the World: 125 Years of Harland and Wolff, Belfast, 1861–1986* (Blackstaff Press, 1986)

7   Cable, Frank, *The Birth and Development of the American Submarine* (Harper & Bros, 1924)

8   Morris, Richard Knowles, *John P. Holland, 1841–1914, Inventor of the Modern Submarine* (United States Naval Institute Press, 1966) p.3; Burcher, Roy and Rydill, Louis, *Concepts in Submarine Design* (Cambridge Ocean Technology Series, Cambridge University Press, 1995) pp.12–14, author's note: technical and primarily contemporary submarines with mentions of John Holland and early craft

9   Morris, Richard Knowles, *John P. Holland*, pp.117–118

10 Morris, Richard Knowles, *John P. Holland*, p.118

11 Morris, Richard Knowles, *John P. Holland*, p.121

12 Holland, John P., *The Submarine Boat and its Future*, reprinted from *The North American Review* (The North American Review Publishing Co., 1900) p.2

13 Holland, John P., *The Submarine Boat and its Future*, pp.4–5

14 Holland, John P., *The Submarine Boat and its Future*

15 McCue, Gary W., *John Philip Holland, 1841–1914, and his Submarines*, commemorative booklet on the 100th anniversary of the US Navy's first submarine, USS *Holland SS-1* (The Holland Committee, 2000); Stacy, Harold G., *The First Holland Submarine* educational pamphlet (Paterson Museum Publications, 1961); Morris, Frank, *Submarine Pioneer: John Philip Holland* (Bruce Publishing, 1961)

The devil's device: the Whitehead torpedo.

The United States, *Holland* Submarines and Torpedoes

Harry Caldwell

The first submarine captain in the US Navy was Lieutenant Harry H. Caldwell (1873–1938), the skipper of the USS *Holland*, later designated *SS-1*.*

Caldwell's appointment as commander brought the authority of an influential surface officer to the USS *Holland* and provided a valuable gravitas to the infant American submarine service. In August 1900 Caldwell skippered the *Holland* during exercises off Newport, Rhode Island, in which he performed an ominous feat which caused submarine sceptics in America, Britain and Europe to readdress their misgivings. He proved the awful stealth of the submarine by closing on the USS *Kearsarge*, the flagship of the North Atlantic Squadron, to within target distance and without detection. Had his attack been real, the result would have been calamitous. Unhappily for Caldwell, and as an indication of the reluctance by the US Navy to accept the inroads being made by the submarine, his imaginary 'hit' was not accepted: in an ill-spirited interpretation of the rules it was decided that the *Kearsarge* had already been 'hit' by other vessels and so that scored by Caldwell in his valiant *Holland* did not count. If one sought proof that military exercises were too often used to score political

---

* Caldwell had served aboard the cruiser USS *Olympia* at the Battle of Manila Bay (1898) in the Philippines in the Spanish-American War (1898–1901). He was the former flag secretary to Admiral George Dewey (1837–1917) in the Spanish-American conflict.[1] It was never a problem recruiting good men into the submarine service.

points than to demonstrate strategic possibilities then this incident would be a prize example. Ignoring pettifogging and mean gamesmanship, the implications of Caldwell's mock attack were irrefutable. The success of the *Holland* in the manoeuvres would also prove startling to clerks who pored over their ledgers fretting about budgetary considerations. Government monies were as tight as ever and, compared to surface vessels, the submarine looked a bargain: the USS *Holland* cost about $150,000; the price of the torpedo with which it could have sunk the *Kearsarge* was $3,000; the *Kearsarge* cost in the region of $5 million. Had Caldwell's attack been real she would have sunk in minutes.[*]

In France the *Jauréguiberry* battleship was subject to a successful mock attack from the submarine *Gustave Zédé* as the French fleet manoeuvred off Ajaccio, the Corsican capital. Laid down in 1891 and launched in 1897 the ship had been named after the so-called 'scientific' Admiral Bernard Jauréguiberry (1815–87), a foremost philosopher and astronomer as well as naval commander. She was one of the more handsome vessels of the time. Several French fighting ships laid down in the 1890s were often less becoming. As the pride of the *Marine Nationale Francaise*, the realisation that she could have been sunk by the *Zédé* sent shock waves through the French naval establishment and reverberated around the globe. The terrible dangers posed by the submarine had now been twice writ large. Only the foolish and complacent would ignore them.

Irrespective of their military potential, now becoming clear, and their competitive price – though there were accusations the navy was overpaying the Electric Boat Company and that the craft could have been produced for less if profit margins had been trimmed – there was still as much resentment in the US Navy towards submarines as that in the Royal Navy. The fact that submarines had been used in the Civil War and Revolutionary War, albeit with patchy success, and that John Holland had made remarkable strides in the US with the *Fenian Ram* and later craft, did nothing to assuage the hostility. Britain had an excuse for its recalcitrance: its experience with the contraptions had been limited to experimentation, some novel, much of it quirky, none under proper naval aegis. The US, however, had first-hand military experience. Some conventions in the US Navy were influenced by those which for turbulent centuries had stood the Royal Navy, and consequently Britain, in good stead; not all, the US Navy always had its own way of doing things. Pride,

---

[*] Caldwell retired from the US Navy in 1909, returning to active service during the Great War. He later became a writer and editor in cinema films. With his wife, Katherine Clark, they were involved in some seventy-five movies, including *Seventh Heaven* and *Ben Hur*.[2]

however, often rides with prejudice; as in the Royal Navy, that too had infected the US fleet. American commanders had played a noble part in a diversity of conflicts, building illustrious careers, and some were as convinced as their British counterparts of the invincibility of the surface marine. In their minds it would not be assailed by the submarine, a small, silly and seemingly eccentric contrivance: frail and scuffed, too big for its boots, an impertinence to be swatted as one would any other irritant.

The continuing opposition to submarines manifest in the US Navy served to steel its band of disciples. Determined not to be thwarted in their conviction that the device represented the future, they pressed on with its promotion and development. The little *Holland* was towed to Delaware City and on to the US Naval Academy via the Chesapeake and Delaware Canal. At the Academy the naval cadets pored over her, fascinated by the exotic new weaponry about which they had heard so much. It was a chance for Harry Caldwell and *Holland*'s crew to show off their innovative and deadly baby to a questioning and informed audience. The crème de la crème attended the Academy, the future stars of the mighty US fleet. This was a brilliant chance for its students to dissect a novel and potent machine destined to change forever the face of naval warfare; how many realised its potential at the time is impossible to gauge.

It is unsurprising naval grandees remained suspicious of the submarine: it looked eccentric, fragile, a down-at-heel underwater transport largely unproven in the heat of battle. Submarines appeared as odd as their creators. John Holland was the epitome of a lunatic inventor: head buried beneath bowler hat, face hidden by outsize walrus moustache, a wing-collar so stiff it looked as if it was holding his head on, and pebble-lensed spectacles. Senior naval officers were at home with colossal warships as buffed and spruced as themselves. While undue regard for the superficial is tiresome, the cosmetic would always retain a place in any navy worthy of the name. Holland's intellect was a match for most naval officers, but a drawback he had to face, as did other marine inventors, was an absence of naval pedigree. In the high navy echelons submarine inventors were seen as rather peculiar outsiders; the inventors themselves were entirely unfamiliar, and sometimes impatient, with naval nuances and customs – the navy way. The superintendent of the Academy was Commander Richard Wainwright (1849–1926) and, along with his peers, had come from proud military and maritime stock.*

---

* If having illustrious naval forebears and fighting traditions was true of the Royal Navy, it was also certainly so in the US Navy. Wainwright had been executive officer on the battleship *Maine* when she was blown up in Cuba in 1898, and he had commanded the gunboat *Gloucester* in a heroic action at the Battle of Santiago de Cuba in the same year.

Wainwright was as polished as one would expect in an officer of high rank, and warmly supportive of the visiting *Holland* and her technology. He was gracious in welcoming her crew, captained by the equally magnanimous Harry Caldwell, with whose reputation Wainwright was familiar in Caldwell's previous incarnation as a successful and seasoned surface commander. Winning acceptance for the submarine would have been even more difficult had the *Holland* skipper been an unknown officer bereft of a strong record in the US fleet. During its inspection at the Academy Wainwright took dives in the *Holland* in Chesapeake Bay, declaring himself enthusiastic about its abilities, albeit adding the commonly held rider that, while of immense usefulness, it could never entirely transform war at sea; nothing, of course, could ever do that.

Friends and Foes

By 1901, as builders grew more familiar with submarine technology, construction gathered pace. Boats such as *Porpoise*, *Adder*, *Moccasin* and *Fulton* were launched, each more refined than its forerunner. Holland and Spear were in supervisory roles during the building of the boats, but by then their relationship had begun to seriously sour.*

The *Fulton* was involved in a remarkable experiment set up by Holland. Its crew stayed submerged for fifteen hours in Peconic Bay, between the north and south forks of Long Island, New York, the boats being built at the nearby Crescent Shipyard, Elizabethport, New Jersey. John Holland had calculated that the air would last seventy hours, but stressed that it was only a theoretical reckoning and that the crew could have been imperilled had they been submerged for longer. It was an impressive test which confounded sceptics. Interestingly, given Holland's claim that submarines were steadier than surface ships which gave them an advantage as passenger carriers, when the *Fulton* surfaced its crew learned of a violent storm which had passed overhead; strong tides and currents had been running on the bay floor. They, however, had felt nothing.

As well as the mindful Holland, construction of the early American submarines was also invested with the pedigree of Lewis Nixon (1861–1940),

---

* In 1905 President Theodore Roosevelt (1858–1919) made dives on the *Plunger* during a two-hour stint. Describing the experience as enjoyable and diverting his endorsement gave the callow submarine service the White House imprimatur. Presidential backing enhanced the credibility of the submarine, its designers, commanders and crews.

a naval architect of repute who in 1895 had founded his own ship building company at the Crescent Shipyard.[4] Nixon, a high-flying graduate of the US Naval Academy, had later studied naval architecture at the elite Royal Naval College, Greenwich, London. Lewis Nixon's Crescent Shipyard built many of America's proudest fighting ships, as well as its first submarines. Though John Holland's oxygen experiment with the *Fulton* had been a success, submarines were still a dangerous calling in which crews and commanders endured calamities as well as triumphs. On their completion at the Crescent Shipyard, boats were dispatched to the Goldsmith and Tuthill yard, New Suffolk, New York, for trials. Today there is a shrine in New Suffolk in remembrance of the pioneers and the submariners who later served in two world wars. While in New Suffolk misfortune befell the *Fulton* when she sank at her moorings. She was retrieved and repaired but her travails were not over. On a trial run in the Atlantic from Sandy Hook, on the eastern seaboard of New Jersey, to Delaware Breakwater, east of the city of Lewes, her battery gas exploded. Three of her crew were injured and the craft badly damaged. Such unfortunate events gave ammunition to those who set their faces against the submarine.

Among the most authoritative of the Holland critics was Rear Admiral Charles O'Neil (1842–1927), the chief of the Bureau of Ordnance and a sailor with a formidable record. Born in Manchester, England, O'Neil's parents had emigrated to the US when he was 5, settling in Boston, Massachusetts. His career reads like an adventure story. He went to sea at 16 and on his second voyage his ship foundered in the Indian Ocean. He drifted for days before he and fellow survivors were rescued by a French slave ship. His rise from enlisted sailor to senior officer, significant in itself, was studded with feats of daring and heroism. O'Neil was an undisputed architect of the modern US Navy.[5] An authority on naval ordnance, he had extensive expertise in gunnery; he designed a variety of naval guns, becoming superintendent of the gun factory at the Washington yard of the US Navy and, also president of the US Navy Board of Construction.

To have an officer of O'Neil's gravitas as a *Holland* critic could not be dismissed lightly. He had jurisdiction over the *Holland* and, too, the ear of the Congressional Committee. In 1901 he complained that an old fault with the *Holland* had repeatedly recurred during the boat's testing. The main motor armature had shown, from its inception, a proclivity to burn itself out. It was a fundamental design fault which should have been rectified long before. Rice, Frost, Spear and the rest at the Electric Boat Company were too busy trying to make money selling their patterns when they ought to have fixed it: being lax in urgently rectifying it had unnecessarily debased their credibility and that of the craft. In this O'Neil's strictures were valid. However, he used the wretched fallibility of the armature – it broke down five times in nine months – to launch a more general broadside: submarines were eccentric and torpedoes capricious.

Robert Whitehead and Giovanni Luppis

Torpedo development had been quietly progressing.[6] The most promising advances were made by the English engineer Robert Whitehead (1823–1905) who, in 1891, had started the Whitehead Torpedo Factory at Ferry Bridge, Wyke Regis, south Dorset.[7] As with Garrett, steam and coal were in Whitehead's genes; his father was an industrialist and his grandfather had been important in cotton in Lancashire when steam began to galvanise the industry. Whitehead was well trained: apprenticed at 16 to an engineering company in Manchester, he had worked in France as a marine engineer and as a consultant on land drainage and silk weaving in Italy. In Trieste he refined and adapted – with others around the world – the marine steam engine. In 1856 he became chief engineer to a company building warships for the Austro-Hungarian Empire in the coastal town of Fiume. In 1864 Whitehead became associated with Giovanni Luppis (1813–75), a former officer in the Austrian Navy.[8] Luppis had worked for years developing waterborne weapons and had invented an unsuccessful embryo torpedo: long, floating, packed with explosives, and driven by a clockwork motor. It inspired Whitehead to try and perfect a driverless underwater device which would detonate on impact; it had to be practical, portable and safe for use by its handlers. In 1866 he produced the Luppis-Whitehead torpedo, propelled by compressed air and fired from a tube. But it would not run at a constant depth. He solved the problem with a hydrostatic pendulum, the secrets of which he guarded for years. With its delivery by submarine the torpedo would transform war at sea. The torpedo caught on with navies around the globe, including the British.

Whitehead became rich, having signed a contract with Luppis which gave Whitehead the rights on future sales. Luppis, from an aristocratic family which had made money in shipping, died in Milan, aged 62, bitter that he had forsaken the rights. He did not die entirely unrecognized, though: the bizarre title of Baron von Rammer ('the sinker') was conferred on him six years before his death. From the death and destruction represented by the torpedo emerged a surprising story of song and romance which would later enchant the world (see Appendix F).

Eliphalet Bliss

In addition to the efforts of Whitehead and Luppis, the performance of the torpedo would be advanced by patient endeavours in France, and from keen minds in Britain's torpedo and mine school at the Royal Navy's HMS *Vernon*. The US Naval Torpedo Station (USNTS) at Goat Island, Newport, Rhode Island, also made a hugely distinguished contribution to its progress.[9] The USNTS had been established in 1869, thirty-two years before Admiral Charles O'Neil made his scathing remarks, during which time the torpedo had achieved a degree of acceptance as evidenced in its sales: by 1880 over 1,400 Whitehead torpedoes had been sold to navies around the world. In 1891 the Whitehead torpedo business began negotiating with the Eliphalet Williams Bliss Company of Brooklyn, New York, to produce torpedoes for the US Navy. Eliphalet Williams Bliss (1836–1903) is another of those remarkable figures who pepper the submarine story and whose role in the boats and in the development of the torpedo tends to be forgotten. Born at Fly Creek, Otsego County, New York, Bliss grew up on a farm. Early on he showed a strong inclination towards engineering, finding work in the Parker Gun Factory, Meriden, New Haven, Connecticut, famed for exemplary craftsmanship and founded in 1865 by Charles Parker. Bliss did well at Parker, staying seven years and being promoted to foreman. He later set up his own business in Brooklyn, New York, incorporating it in 1885. Originally in Adams Street, Brooklyn, by 1890 it had bought property in Bay Ridge, Brooklyn. Bliss was involved in metal production and machining, exporting some products to Yorkshire, England, for use in the wool industry, and his metal was also used in the building of the iconic Brooklyn Bridge in New York.

Bliss became a thriving enterprise, at one time employing 1,800 people with factories covering two blocks in Brooklyn. In 1892 an agreement was signed in which the US Navy would buy 100 Whitehead torpedoes from Bliss. It was, in effect, the US Navy endorsing the Whitehead torpedo and admitting its superiority over several alternative designs which were on offer at the time and others which were still being developed. Bliss tested its torpedoes in Peconic Bay, New York. In one incident a rogue torpedo shot through the hull of a small and entirely innocent craft, though, thankfully, it was devoid of occupants at the time. E. W. Bliss and other companies were among several to benefit from torpedo and armament contracts for the Spanish-American War of 1898, the Great War and the Second World War.

Working on torpedoes would always be dangerous. In 1881 two naval officers attached to the Torpedo Station at Goat Island were killed in an explosion while conducting experiments in Narragansett Bay, Rhode Island. Multifarious and alarming experiments were undertaken at Goat Island, as they were at HMS *Vernon*, into different forms of torpedo propulsion, including a diversity of methods such as chemical, electrical and rocket firing.

Robert Whitehead – and later with his son John – is acknowledged as the inventor of the torpedo. But others were important in its advance. The main problem with the Whitehead torpedo was the uncertainty of its directional control, the point O'Brien had made. A Russian engineer, Petrovich, had produced a primitive gyroscope which Whitehead used in early trials.[10] The US naval officer John Adams Howell (1840–1918), an inventive New Yorker, had served in the Civil War and commanded a squadron which blockaded Cuba in the Spanish-America War. Howell – with others – is credited with the self-steering torpedo and the gyroscope by which it was guided. In 1895 the former Austrian naval officer Ludwig Obry devised a system which utilised the gyroscope in a torpedo. Obry's device was ingenious: any alteration from an intended path was picked up by the gyroscope, which informed the rudders in the torpedo's tail of the necessary changes.[11] Robert Whitehead used Obry's innovation in his torpedoes but later utilised one of Howell's designs. There would be chagrin if the French physicist Jean Bernard Leon Foucault (1819–1868) was overlooked as the inventor of the gyroscope in 1852. Though Foucault made the first modern gyroscope, others had a hand in bringing it to fruition, including Johann von Bohnenberger. A model of his creation, believed to date from 1817, is in the Smithsonian American History Museum. Its mechanics are in the *Illustrated Descriptive Catalogue of Optical, Mathematical and Philosophical Instruments*, listed as *Bohnenberger's Machine*, in the first volume of the catalogue, dated 1856, published by Benjamin Pike Jnr. If one were to pick out a single factor which gave the submarine its potency it would have to be the development of the torpedo.[12]

Notes

1   *Autobiography of George Dewey* (Naval Institute Press, 1987; originally published 1913, Charles Scribner's Sons)
2   McKenna, Patrick, www.spanamwar.com/caldwell.htm
3   Swinfield, John G., *Airship: Design, Disaster and Development* (Conway Maritime, 2012)
4   Morris, Richard Knowles, *John P. Holland, 1841–1914: Inventor of the Modern Submarine* (University of South Carolina Press, 1998). Author's note: As ever with John Holland and his circle, including Lewis Nixon, Morris's *tour de force* is indispensable
5   *US Navy Department Library: List of Historical Manuscripts*
6   Friedman, Norman, *Naval Weapons of World War One* (Seaforth Publishing, 2011)

7 Wilson, H.W., *Ironclads in Action* (Sampson, Low, Marston, 1896)

8 Gray, *The Devil's Device: Robert Whitehead and the History of the Torpedo* (Annapolis Naval Institute Press, 1991)

9 Barber, Francis Morgan, Lecture on the Whitehead Torpedo, U.S. Torpedo Station, Newport, Rhode Island, 20 November 1874, reproduction (unknown publisher, 2010)

10 Poland, Rear Admiral E.N., *The Torpedomen, HMS Vernon's Story, 1872–1986* (M, 1993) pp.42–43; Gray, Edwyn, *Nineteenth-Century Torpedoes and Their Inventors* (US Naval Institute Press, 2004)

11 Humble, Richard (ed.), *Naval Warfare* (Little, Brown, 2002) pp.151–152; Poland, *The Torpedomen*, p.42

12 Wildenberg, Thomas, *Ship Killer: A History of the American Torpedo* (Naval Institute Press, 2010); Gray, *The Devil's Device* (Naval Institute, Annapolis, 1991)

Trials in the Solent in 1904; The Prince of Wales (the future King George V) took a trip in *A-1* in March that year. A few days later she was rammed and sank.

4

Great Britain Finds Her Stride

At the end of the nineteenth century the Royal Navy was a microcosm of the larger community it strove to protect, and whose global influence it secured through its vigilance of the empire. In broad terms its officer class equated to the shore-based elite: often of wealth, born to rule, attitudes unquestioned, and imperious about the emergence of the new arsenal that included the submarine, which was patronisingly dismissed as being of limited potential and of real interest only to weaker powers. The Royal Navy would endure upheaval. Submariners were still seen as oddballs though the British Admiralty had inched its way towards a stance of begrudging interest with a quickening of progress in the US.

The Admiralty had observed the American building experience with a critical diligence, minutely studying both its catastrophes and successes. Captain Frank Cable had been sent to Britain to help in the instruction of the crews of the five *Holland*-type submarines, the plans of which the persuasive Isaac Rice had sold to the Admiralty, and which were being built at the Vickers, Sons and Maxim works in Barrow-in-Furness on Britain's north-west coast. By the end of the nineteenth century Barrow had grown into a premier shipbuilding hub, constructing an impressive range of craft for the Royal Navy and for export to continental navies.

The Importance of Barrow-in-Furness

Barrow's coastal location and proximity to steel gave it a march on its competitors. Over the years it had built up a reservoir of skilled shipbuilding workers. Another factor in its success was the intervention of the industrialist Henry Schneider (1817–87). In 1851 Schneider had discovered the richly endowed Burlington iron ore mine at nearby Askam. It made him a fortune and became, itself, a sizeable employer. With the coming of the Barrow railway, in which Schneider and James Ramsden (1822–96) were major investors, the fortunes of Barrow-in-Furness and those of its neighbouring towns and villages would be transformed. A concentration on submarine building would further enhance its world-class reputation as a centre of excellence in naval construction.

Britain's first submarine, *Holland I,* was built in Barrow and launched on 2 October 1901. Its flotation was not hailed by trumpets, but a silence so profound it might have induced deafness. The Admiralty had ruled that the *Hollands* were merely experimental craft and their birth should be treated with caution and discretion. The submarine was still an embarrassment.

Bacon at the Helm

Reginald Bacon, Britain's first Inspecting Captain of Submarines (ICS) and the possessor, in the opinion of Admiral Fisher, of one of the best minds in the Royal Navy, came swiftly to the conclusion that the *Hollands* were too small and underpowered. He determined that, following the *Holland*-class, a more accomplished type would be built:

> ...The Holland boats were too small for sea-going work ... if submarines were to become vessels of practical value, their size and speed above and below water, and also their sea-going qualities, would have to be increased. These could only be attained by an increase in tonnage.[1]

Bacon wanted to increase the power of the petrol engines to 500hp with an accumulator battery of twice the capacity of that being used in the existing boats. Another major improvement he insisted on was in raising the conning tower to some 6ft above the deck; it gave a fairly high position from which to navigate the boat and raised the officer in control above the seas which constantly washed over the craft when it was moving.

Destined to become Admiral Sir Hugh Spencer Reginald Bacon (1863–1947), he left a crucial imprint on Britain's fledgling service. His tenure with submarines got off to an amusing, if inauspicious start:

On taking up my appointment I called on Sir William White, the Director of Naval Construction, and Sir John Durston, the Engineer-in-Chief. Both washed their hands entirely of submarines and refused to have anything to do with them. Sir William advised me never to go below water, as he had once made a descent in a submarine in a London dock and had been stuck at the bottom for an hour or so. The Engineer-in-Chief refused to be associated with the problem of petrol engines when worked in confined spaces. So I took over constructional and engineering control with regard to both design and practical working. This suited me down to the ground.[2]

Bacon would subsequently discover, from another member of the party, that the incident which had induced White's shyness about submarines occurred in January 1887 in Tilbury Docks in London. He wrote:

It appeared that after the party had partaken of a good lunch the boat was submerged ... It went down with rather too much of a bump and stuck fast in the mud ... water was all the time leaking into the boat, so each one of the crew and passengers had, in turn, to work hard at the control-pump to keep the water reasonably under control. The captain of the boat was suffering from heart disease; and, what with work and anxiety, his heart began to palpitate. I know this was so, as when he asked my friend to feel the palpitations, he found they were those of a 40 horse-power pump. The anxiety of all on board was therefore increased by the fear of the death of the only man who knew anything about the mechanical arrangements of the submarine. Two other members of the party had had experience of surface boats being grounded. They suggested the idea of rolling the submarine to loosen it in its bed of mud. [In the early, small, light craft, personnel would gather as a group at one end or the other to make the craft tilt at bow or stern, or rock it from side to side, their combined body-weight being sufficient to induce movement.] Eventually after considerable rolling they got the water to creep between the hull of the boat and the mud and up she popped to the surface.[3]

As the leader of the British submarine service Bacon brought wit and acuity. Drawn to the technically challenging, his diverse knowledge encompassed nautical design, electricity, dirigibles, torpedoes and mines. He had at one time been a torpedo instructor at HMS *Vernon*. In the 1890s, a decade before being put in charge of submarines, he had helped in the design of surface torpedo-craft. By 1900, though still querulous about the utility of submarines, the British Admiralty had sanctioned the deployment of mines, having previously banned them, and instructed HMS *Vernon* to initiate a programme of anti-submarine weapons. As the idea of war took root, long before 1914, the anti-submarine measures become urgent and Bacon was put in charge.

Bacon was a progressive thinker: always drawn to the innovative, he was a man of his time. But he had flaws. He did not suffer fools gladly and this trait could at times be damaging, although sometimes it was crucial in dealing with the navy's top brass. Nor, on occasion, did he tolerate the wise. He had, though, many redeeming qualities. Candour was one, as he showed when writing about his appointment as Britain's first submarine chief:

> I knew nothing about submarines; no more did anyone else. So the first thing to do was to sit down and think out what were the difficulties that we were likely to come across, and arrive at methods by which they could be forestalled. The result was rather peculiar; for all the problems that I originally considered to be likely to be difficult to solve turned out to be simple, and several of those that appeared simple gave, in the end, an infinity of trouble.[4]

Malicious Gossip

Teething problems in the boats triggered gossip that John Holland had deliberately fed the British Admiralty duff and dangerous specifications, being embittered by his declining influence in his company, having reservations about selling to the British and still harbouring lingering Republican tendencies. The mongering was led by the rabid Fenian activist John Devoy and seized on by submarine sceptics. Fenians had their own motives: to spread consternation in the Royal Navy; to bloat their influence; to spite a former supporter who was now reaping rewards and whose first efforts had been funded by the Fenians. After the Fenian raiding party stole the *Ram*, deleterious relations between the Fenian Brotherhood and Holland had lain festering. The gossip was mendacious blether. If early boats encountered problems, which they did, it was because they were still dangerous, experimental contraptions.

It was intended that *Holland I*'s primary role would be in home waters and used for coastal defence. Later, as the *Hollands* became redundant, they were used for target practice by the surface fleet. Submarines were gaining in competence, but it would take time before they could be deployed as independent, long-range predators.

The British *Hollands*

Holland I displaced 120 tons and could cover 20 miles underwater driven by a 70hp electric motor. Beneath her deck she had sixty lead-acid battery cells, which weighed 25 tons. On the surface she was powered by a 160hp Otto 4-cylinder petrol engine, which gave her a speed of just over 7 knots.[*]

In her bows a fuel tank held 600 gallons of petrol. She could dive to approximately 100ft, but contemporary research suggests she would have had difficulty at depths in excess of 60ft. The way a submarine dives sounds simple – it is not. The boat increased its weight by flooding ballast tanks with water. *Holland I*, a midget by the scale of today's leviathans, had a main ballast tank and an auxiliary tank. Kingston valves – named after the English inventor John Kingston (1786–1847) – permitted seawater to flood the tanks. The torpedo compensating tank could be filled to make up for the loss of weight after a torpedo had been fired. Keeping a boat level or trimmed after the sudden exit of a torpedo was another conundrum with which designers and commanders would have to concern themselves. More valves helped ensure the stability of the craft by allowing the transference of water ballast to tanks situated fore and aft. When dived, water had to be let into the main and auxiliary tanks in a controlled way so she settled gently, leaving only her conning tower above the surface; in trade parlance this is known as being 'awash'. If the commander wanted to submerge his craft the electric motor was accelerated to 5 knots, sufficient with the use of her hydroplanes, which act like diving rudders and were attached to the stern, to drive the boat beneath the water. To bring her back to the surface, water had to be expelled from her ballast tanks; she carried fifty-three bottles of compressed air with which to 'blow' or empty the tanks.

Navigation

Navigation was a nightmare. The gyrocompass had not been invented, while magnetic compasses could be driven haywire inside a steel structure such as a submarine. Bacon commented:

---

[*] Nikolaus August Otto (1832–91) was the German inventor of the internal combustion engine. The first Otto engine had been developed in 1876. Diesel engines, invented in 1893 by the German Rudolph Diesel (1858–1913) were fitted to later submarines. They were more efficient and had a lower ignition point, making them safer, cheaper to run and easier to repair.

It therefore seemed that the right place for the compass was outside the boat with an optical tube leading to the steering position.[5]

She was among the earliest submarines to have a proper periscope; well, *almost* proper. It turned 180 degrees allowing the commander to see behind his craft, but with the technology still raw the image he saw was upside down. (The periscope was something the inventive Bacon would later improve.) On surfacing a commander and crew rarely had any precise idea of where they were. Life was alarming, hazardous and topsy-turvy. The entrance and exit were through the boat's conning tower, which had a diameter of 32in, so fat submariners were rare. As with canaries used to detect gas in coal mines, three white mice were aboard early British submarines and entered on the pay roll as part of the crew. At a trace of petrol vapour or carbon monoxide boats had to immediately surface.

Unsavoury Creations

Holland I was 63ft in length with a width of 12ft. With a crew of eight – sometimes nine – she was cramped, fetid and insanitary. In early boats hygiene always ran a poor second to hostility. If compared to ensuing boats she had a luxury fitment: 'heads', or a lavatory. On later vessels the 'heads' was scrapped and replaced by a bucket. On even later submarines the 'heads' had 'blow-backs,' the vileness of which needs no amplification.

Twelve years after the *Holland*, Britain built its successful *E*-class submarines. Though far more advanced than the *Hollands*, sanitary arrangements remained primitive:

> In *E-17* we did have heads right aft. One of the exhaust pipes ran through it and you got boiled if you went in there. But because you'd got so little food and drink you'd go days without wanting to go. In *C. 18* and *D4* [classes which preceded the *E*-class] we had no heads. Our Captain used to say: 'everybody below', and they'd carry it out on the bridge, then come down, dive to twenty feet, wash it away, and come up again. But the conning towers were hollow, only casings. You could go down there in a bucket, and empty it through the holes in the side. If you were going to dive there was no worry about the mess. If it was only passing water, you did it over the lee side [the one protected from the wind]. Down below doing extended diving, you used a bucket a quarter full of diesel oil. It wasn't offensive then.[6]

Richard Compton-Hall, the former director of Britain's Submarine Museum at Gosport, near Portsmouth, noted:

> Constipation was the principal health-hazard amongst British crews and, even when proper heads were installed, the crews were sometimes loathe to use them because of the dangers of the system going into reverse if sea pressure overcame blowing pressure – an occurrence descriptively known as 'getting your own back'.[7]

Compton-Hall recalled the commanding officer of a submarine in 1915 in the Great War who flatly refused to use existing arrangements:

> He insisted on coming to the surface daily where he perched on the bridge rail like an overgrown seagull. One day he was literally caught with his pants down by a German Zeppelin which bombed the submarine accurately and severely; but the Captain was unrepentant and refused to change his daily habits.[8]

In the submarines which immediately followed the *Holland*, such sleep as might be had entailed 'hot-cotting' in tiny berths or 'cots'; as a crewman woke for his watch another would take his vacated bunk. The *Holland* submarines had no cots; the crew curled up where they might, crammed in between torpedoes and assorted paraphernalia. In its space and personal convenience the submarine would always be incommodious. Even in today's nuclear-powered behemoths space is tight and personnel must still be prudent in their use of water, taking 'submariners' showers': showering, turning off the water to soap themselves, then turning it on again to rinse off. A world which values conservation and energy could learn a great deal from some of the essential tenets of submarine culture; as it could about people having to live harmoniously in close proximity to one another.

Squalling Infant

With commander and crew obliged to exist cheek by jowl, the *Hollands* were less comfortable than vessels of the surface navy – though sailors might baulk at 'comfort' used in any context in a warship – where a physical divide usually afforded a degree of privacy, albeit often meagre, and which also helped officers to maintain their authority which, when exercised, came with the backing of centuries of convention. The submarine service was quite different. It was a rebellious, squalling infant, virtually devoid of the customs, trappings and inherent authority of rank which pertained in the senior service. The severe constriction of boats demanded a greater level of informality; it also added to the notion, within reason, of a rank system which was more dependent on command by consent; though, as effective officers understood then, and now, respect is always better if won than imposed. Crews had to 'fit in'. To operate a submarine needed skill and intuition. There were sufficient pressures on and below the water without being cooped up in perilous and unsavoury circumstances with one whose habits or personality might grate. The crew of *Holland I* comprised in reverse order of rank: able seaman, leading seaman, leading stoker, chief engineering artificer, torpedo instructor (petty officer), diving coxswain (petty officer), second captain (sub lieutenant) and captain (lieutenant).

Delafield Frank Arnold-Forster

The captain of Britain's first submarine was a young naval officer, Lieutenant Delafield Frank Arnold-Forster, a nephew of the parliamentary and financial secretary to the Admiralty, H. Oakley Arnold-Forster MP. Having connections was not vital in the ascent of a young officer, though rarely a hindrance. Among candidates for the captaincy of the other *Hollands* was Murray Sueter, whose spirit would be felt later in airships; he was part of a coterie drawn to the new arsenal, their backgrounds embracing a mix of experience in dirigibles, torpedoes, mines and submarines, an attraction which baffled and bothered more senior naval figures. Arnold-Forster played the banjo, his efforts celebrated today with occasional banjo and ukulele concerts at Barrow and the Submarine Museum in Gosport. The scene is evocative: a brave young commander plucking at his banjo as the fragile *Holland* bobbed precariously at sea – if he did or not is questionable, but it is an attractive picture. Delafield Frank Arnold-Forster was lovingly raised, well connected and had the world at his feet. Submarines were harsh and unforgiving, but for daring young men full of vim they could also spell fun, excitement and camaraderie; eager pioneers at a new dawn. They were also innocent; still to come were the four years of carnage which would claim 8.5 million military lives. Arnold-Forster survived but the spirited young officer class which he personified would be decimated. He had a range of skills which were complementary to the needs of the new submarine service, and his previous specialisms included the use of torpedoes and mines, with which the surface navy had become increasingly familiar.*

Typical of young officers who would find their way into the fledgling submarine service, Arnold-Forster joined the navy in 1891, serving in Antigua, Grenada and Copenhagen. A taste for travel, seeing foreign countries, serving in exotic locations, was always an attraction for naval candidates. It seems he was unsure if submarines would provide travel opportunities which could match those he had enjoyed in the surface fleet. Before 'switching sides' he was sceptical about the submarines' future and its utility:

> I don't believe in them but I suppose somebody will be wanted to do preliminary experiments and it might be useful experience. Anyhow, no harm in asking.[9]

On visiting Barrow-in-Furness, Arnold-Forster was understandably keen to survey construction of his new command. But he could not find anybody who would show him its location or to even admit that a submarine was being built. It was an indication of the prevailing reluctance by the Admiralty, and Vickers, to acknowledge their involvement in something as sly and underhand as a submarine. Perhaps, also, they were concerned about security; or coy of association with a risky experiment which could go wrong, damaging reputations and blemishing careers. Whatever the motive the boat was built in a shed with a sign which announced that it was a yacht, not a submarine, under construction. To add extra credibility to the pretence the fabricated parts of the boat were labelled Pontoon One. Today such measures might seem feeble, even comical. But there were at the time a range of sensible reasons. The Great War was still fourteen years away, but a febrile atmosphere was already beginning to build. Britain's military was at full stretch with hefty commitments throughout the empire and a wider encompass. In 1900 British deaths in the Boer War exceeded 11,000. Troops of the Allied forces fought to quell China's Boxer Rebellion. On 9 November 1900 at Vickers' Barrow slipway the world's largest battleship was launched, the 15,150-ton *Mikasa*, flying the Rising Sun flag, the

---

* Arnold-Forster had studied at HMS *Vernon* in Portsmouth, which had opened in 1872 as the navy's torpedo and mine school, a year after the navy had adopted the Whitehead torpedo. How serious he was about submarines is uncertain, given that he only stayed in the service for some ten months. He left on 18 March 1902 to take up a post as Torpedo Lieutenant with HMS *Ariadne*, a flagship of the Royal Navy's North American squadron. He went on to a successful career in the Royal Navy, rising to the rank of rear admiral.

mightiest vessel in the Imperial Japanese Navy. Vickers was consolidating its position as the world's foremost armaments maker and shipbuilder. Barrow was becoming frenetic as the global powers set about enhancing their arsenals. There was more tension to come. Queen Victoria's death cast a pall across Great Britain, the imperial sovereign whose colonial family was growing increasingly fractious. Quite simply, Queen Victoria *was* the empire. Rioting shook tsarist Russia, a harbinger of the coming cataclysm. Kitchener led 240,000 men in South Africa. Britain's Premier, the 3rd Marquess of Salisbury, put an end to hopes of Home Rule for Ireland, declaring that a free Ireland would hamper his government's war in South Africa; his dictates would have rankled with John Holland in America. In Buffalo, New York, two weeks before the launch of *Holland I*, the American President William McKinley died from wounds inflicted by a Polish anarchist. Vickers was unquestionably shy about its involvement with submarines; but given the global volatility, if it chose to draw a veil of secrecy round the building of its submarines, opting for a policy of discretion over openness, it was understandable and with reason.

Small and Stumpy

When Arnold-Forster finally caught up with his little boat he was unimpressed:

> What surprised me most when I did find her was her small size. She was only sixty-three feet long and was shaped like a very fat and stumpy cigar.

A glance inside *Holland I*'s miniature conning tower bursting with gadgets had him scribbling:

> ... the ingenious designer in New York evidently did not realise that the average naval officer has only two eyes and two hands; the little conning tower was simply plastered with wheels, levers and gauges with which some superman was to fire the torpedoes, dive and steer, and do everything else at the same time, and the inside of the boat was stuffed with wonderful automatic devices.[10]

Arnold-Forster had moved from the surface fleet, at ease with the relative spaciousness of 'big' ships, against which submarines were incommodious midgets. There were other fundamental differences. In submarines, compared to the stiffer surface navy, almost anything went. Officers and crew devised appliances and made up working practices as they went along. The art of the submariner was utterly new; there were no templates to follow, no precedents to guide. Somebody had to make it up. Early submarines were demanding and perilous, but there was a freedom for the lower ranks – and commanders – which was on occasion absent or stifled in the conventional navy. Sometimes there was even fun. While the cramped *Holland* was being made:

> … shipshape and less like a box of conjuring tricks, those with artistic ideas tried their hands at painting periscopes in various ways to make them invisible. The early periscopes were long and bulky, not like the neater little fittings on modern submarines, and there was plenty of surface for paint. A barber's pole gave one enthusiast an idea. He painted a dummy periscope in spiral stripes of all the primary colours. When whizzed round by a small electric motor it ought to have been invisible – but it wasn't, and the periscope painting craze gradually died out.[11]

How to Breathe

It had been decided that a converted gunboat, HMS *Hazard*, aptly named as it later transpired, would serve temporarily as a makeshift mothership for the submarine service. Various examinations were conducted on the *Hazard*, including breathing tests. Known as 'fug' experiments, they involved submariners being locked in bread ovens:

> Another queer diversion whilst awaiting the completion of the boat [*Holland I*] was what we called 'fug trials'. Awful things had been prophesied about the danger of breathing the same air for several hours inside a submerged submarine. To see what would happen, half a dozen of us used to shut ourselves up with the doctor in the hermetically sealed bread room of the small gunboat *Hazard*, then lying in the basin at Barrow. We had cards and music and every hour the doctor took everyone's pulse and temperature, including his own. Though apparently something serious should have happened, nobody felt any worse. The séances in the bread room led later on to breathing trials on more scientific lines in the submarine itself.[12]

Reginald Bacon, the submarine chief, recalled air-purification experiments and the nightmare of being trapped with a flute player:

> In one we spent a memorable night hermetically sealed in one of the submarines [being built in a building] in Barrow … it was a night not to

be forgotten; not because of the foul air or purification details, but because the elderly representative of the Holland Boat Company had brought a flute wherewith to while away the time. At the best of times the flute is not an inspiring instrument, but the dirges to which we were treated that night, in the bowels of the submarine, I believe caused us all, ever after, to look on a flute with a large measure of personal enmity.[13]

To conduct more detailed 'fug trials' Bacon had built an airtight room just large enough to seat four men:

> This was occupied by four long-suffering officers until the amount of carbonic acid gas rose to what was then considered a dangerous amount. We found that human beings, at a pinch, could put up with considerably more 'stuffiness' than that for which they had previously been given credit. In fact, our experiment showed that under normal conditions of working, foulness of air need not be looked on as a danger; but for prolonged sojourns under water, such as lying on the bottom for considerable periods, both air purification and oxygen would have to be resorted to.[14]

Of noxious gases Bacon said:

> ... the nose is the main detector, but this organ is unable to differentiate between a considerable quantity and a small percentage of vapour. Its action is qualitative rather than quantitative.[15]

There was little information available about the effect on crews of stale or poisoned air, as Bacon described:

> Of course, the result of the exhaustion of oxygen and the effect of carbon-monoxide was well known; but, although we know better now, it was then by no means certain that human bodies in close confinement did not give off poisonous exhalations![16]

John Haldane

Bacon was helped in his experiments into foul air by the Scottish Professor John Scott Haldane FRS (1860–1936), a physiologist as intrepid as the submariners. Haldane became famous as a scientist who used himself as a guinea pig, conducting experiments in which he locked himself in sealed chambers to ingest poisoned air, gauging its effects on his physical and mental state. The inventor of the gas mask used in the First World War, and developer of the oxygen tent, Haldane became a world authority on respiratory, pulmonary and breathing illnesses, from silicosis, the dangers from toxic fumes which endangered coal miners, to the decompression hazards which faced divers and submariners.[17]

Fumes from petrol engines were one of the worst hazards. Bacon was blunt:

> Unless it is absolutely necessary, no wise person likes to work with petrol in a confined space. However careful everyone may be, there is still always the danger of a fortuitous leak, followed by a spark, then an explosion.

His opinion of steam-driven submarines was that they were even more dangerous than petrol-powered craft:

> Steam engines and boilers had been tried in some of the French boats; but in one case, when bad weather came on quickly, and the boat had to be closed up in a hurry, the crew arrived in harbour in a parboiled condition. This was quite sufficient to condemn the system. The dangers inherent in petrol had, therefore, to be cheerfully accepted.

If French submariners were literally parboiled is unknown. Bacon mentioned an explosion in a boat caused by an officer starting the main motor to ventilate the craft to get rid of the smell of petrol: 'A variation of the old lunacy of looking for a gas leak with a candle.'[18]

Of Mice and Men

Canaries were used in coal mines to signal the presence of gas; beneath the waves it was the squeak of mice. Sailors always like pets, and it was said the white mice on early submarines were so well fed that they could be comatose, their alertness impaired by corpulence, or too fat to bother about a whiff of petrol or toxic fumes from batteries. Bacon said:

> [An] advantage of a small animal was that it could be kept low down in the boat, well below the mouth of a man, and would thus give ample warning of low-lying poisonous gas. White mice were preferred to brown because they were tamer and more easily handled.[19]

Arnold-Forster would have no bad words said about his mice. Like the rest of the crew the mice had to endure the rigours of foul weather, the fragile boats being tossed around in stormy seas. He noted:

> When it was at all rough, the boat running on the surface was all awash and nothing could be seen from the little conning tower. Everything had to be battened down; those below had to stop there; those on deck, the captain and the coxswain, had to hang on as best they could. They could stop inside, of course, the captain using the periscope for looking out, but its lenses had an annoying habit of clouding over at critical moments; then he was done, and had to trust entirely to Providence and the compass. It was in these *Holland* boats that the famous white mice were kept in cages ... if certain defects occurred in the petrol engine, small quantities of carbon monoxide, a highly poisonous gas, found its way into the boat. White mice are far more sensitive than man to the ill-effects of this gas, and their behaviour in the submarine gave warning to the crew of its presence. If a mouse actually died, it was high time to come to the surface, open up everything, and blow the boat through with fans. The presence of petrol vapour or battery gases, which were also dangerous, could be detected in good time by smell.[20]

First Dive

As the *Hollands* were completed they were dispatched from Barrow to Portsmouth to form Britain's first submarine flotilla. Though aboard the boat for its initial trials, Arnold-Forster was not aboard for its first dive in the shallow waters of Barrow docks. This was undertaken by Bacon, in his capacity as Inspecting Captain of Submarines, accompanied by a navigation specialist and an engineer. Arnold-Forster and a team of divers had to stay in a safety tender on the surface in case of an emergency. Chains were placed around and under the boat, in a manner which had become the convention, to pull her to the surface if she encountered unforeseen difficulties.

Holland I first dived at sea on 6 April 1902 under the command of Arnold-Forster. She had been launched seven months earlier, in October 1901, but her completion had been delayed by a slipway accident which had occurred at the time of her launch. The duration of the repairs that were thought necessary as a consequence of the accident obliged the determined Bacon to try to speed up the trials to get the ambitious development schedule back on track. Consequently, *Holland I* was used to train crews for some of the other *Holland* submarines in advance of their completion.

Arnold-Forster wrote of trials in *Holland I* after he had helped tow her by steam launch to the deeper waters of Morecambe Bay, which lies due east of the Isle of Man, south of the Lake District, and on which sits the submarine capital of Barrow-in-Furness. An impressive expanse of water, notorious for its shifting sands and treacherous tides, it was ideal for testing the first boats and the competence of their learner commanders and navigators. Arnold-Forster described his experience:

> The first real dive and underwater run was made in Morecambe Bay, and an American crew that had done some trials in the United States were sent over by the Holland Boat Company to go out with us for our first effort. After the boat was carefully trimmed down everyone except the American working the diving-wheel, the 'boss-diver' as he called himself, was seated about the boat on canvas stools opposite their work, and warned that if they moved they might upset the balance, and perhaps cause a nose-dive into the mud.[21]

It is not difficult to imagine the excitement and apprehension of Arnold-Forster and the crew as they made their first dive in the small boat:

> Then the motor went ahead, the diving rudder was put down and green water was seen through the conning tower windows. Gradually the depth gauge showed we were running under water for the first time, and those who could see it watched anxiously whilst listening to the hum of the motor and the queer-sounding American orders given by our temporary captain. The boat ran, as these boats always did, with her nose well down and to those who could not see the depth gauge it seemed as though we were bound for the bottom. When a bucket got loose and clattered down the engine-room floor plates it sent hearts into mouths.

On the surface *Holland I* was a 'brute' to handle but Arnold-Forster found her 'very handy' underwater. The basin at Barrow, in which she had been tested, was sizeable but insufficiently capacious for safe manoeuvring:

> One day she alarmed the inmates of the *Hazard*, her parent ship, by poking her big nose right through the ship's side into their berths. Her plates were so stout it did not hurt her at all, but the ship had to go into dock.[22]

Within the decade submariners in the vulnerable little boats which followed Arnold-Forster into the unpredictable waters off Barrow-in-Furness would see airships sailing overhead. The skies above Morecambe Bay were a favoured test area. Airships were also being built by the increasingly omnipotent Vickers at Barrow and would play their own distinguished part in Britain's 'new' arsenal (see Appendix A). After first taking the controls of his submarine, Arnold-Forster wrote about the difficulty he had in trying to keep it on a level plane and how he had run the boat just beneath the surface: 'I worked the diving wheel for the first time and kept her at about ten feet for two miles.'[23] Lessons about stability learned in early submarines benefited airships in the years which followed; stability and balance could oblige airships to sail with bows slightly tilted up or down, using the belly of the airship as a wing (Appendix A).

Arnold-Forster wrote of the death of one of his crew:

> At breakfast I was told that a Leading Stoker was missing and his cap found floating near the torpedo boat. It looked as though he must have fallen overboard so I started dragging at once and found his body at 11.00 and sent it to the mortuary. The next three days were perfectly awful what with arranging the inquest and funeral and running trials with No.2 [the second Vickers-built *Holland*] between whiles. We buried him eventually on Wednesday with naval honours …[24]

During 1902 and 1903 *Holland I* and the other boats underwent trials in different seas and conditions, including the turbulent Irish Sea. Successful dummy attacks took place on anchored and moving 'enemy' ships, including the *Hazard* mothership. Crucial to the trials were the Americans who had come to England from the Electric Boat Company to help in the instruction of officers and crews, passing on knowledge they had gained through their trials of the *Holland* in the US. To the British submariners they were the 'Yankees', the most experienced being the technically deft Captain Frank Cable who, with John Philip Holland, had played a key role in the construction and operation of the first *Holland* submarine in America.

Frank Cable: Boss Diver

Frank Cable had an intimate understanding of the submarine and its foibles, having piloted it on its most important and risky trials. A consummate engineer, he furnished the British with invaluable insights into what made it tick and why sometimes it did not. Cable knew each nut and bolt. The concept of voyaging underwater, let alone attempting to blow other vessels out of it, was entirely new, a perilous and adventurous science: to have aboard someone as expert as Cable was beyond price. Bacon was fulsome:

We were most fortunate in being trained by Captain Cable, who was a thoroughly sound and careful captain. His favourite remark was that he 'did not go down in submarine boats for his health' and so he took no unnecessary risks and his crew left for America, carrying with them our cordial regard. Another thing that he took back with him was a firm belief in the periscope for submerged work.[25]

When Isaac Rice had achieved his significant coup in selling the *Holland* submarine design to the Admiralty, it was the promise of Cable and his colleagues coming to Britain from the US which had helped clinch the deal; a corollary that gave the Admiralty, always trepidatious about such commitments, confidence that in its acquiescence to Rice's blandishments it had not bought a pup but had made a wise purchase. Aboard the *Holland*, Cable would be called on to act in ways far beneath his status: he was the metal stress and dive expert, helmsman, navigator, prophetic reader of waves and weather, all-round good-egg, first-class engineer, general dogsbody and fixer. The call would go out: 'Get Frank. What does the Yank say?' Cable was an old salt, a sensible counsel, one of the few who had done things now being undertaken and lived to tell the tale. Cable would sit on his canvas stool watching the sea, lit by the sun, turn from pale green to a darker hue as the *Holland* plunged deeper, retailing his wisdoms to the 'Limey greenhorns'. To the Americans Cable was called the Boss Diver. Aside from the commander, the Boss Diver was the most important person aboard. In Britain the title became Diving Coxswain, an unwieldy mouthful which was quickly reduced to Coxswain; its etymology harked back to halcyon days when it was not steam, petrol, diesel or nuclear power, but the might of sail which ruled the oceans.

Periscopes and Problems

Bacon's assessment that the *Hollands* were too small, their capability limited and their overall design unseaworthy, largely owing to their low freeboards, caused him to try and halt production, a move which the Admiralty refused to sanction. He was, nevertheless, given consent to order a sixth and larger submarine from Vickers, in addition to the five *Hollands* which were already on order and in the process of being built. Its construction would incorporate his suggested modifications.

Bacon's previous innovations included the refinement of the periscope. Once, while steering a boat, something which he especially enjoyed, he had an accident which snapped off the periscope. The periscope had been invented by the eminent Dublin scientist Sir Howard Grubb (1844–1931), and Bacon had helped modify it for the *Holland* submarines, enhancing its strategic use. Bacon never lacked gall and was so delighted by the device that, on occasion, he claimed it as his own creation: 'I hit on the idea of a tube long enough to reach from the boat to above the surface of the sea.' He described various refinements, how he copied a pair of binoculars, inserting a double concave lens in front of a prism and having to lie on his back to use it. He declared boldly:

> This immature 'optical tube' as I called it was slung on the poop of the *Vernon* and lo and behold! I found an excellent view of the dockyard and the surrounding mud flats. This was the first attempt at a periscope in England, and I believe the first made in any country. I found that it could not be patented, as there was a surgical instrument of a similar nature for examining a patient's bladder. This original tube was fitted to the first *Holland* boat, and it enabled all her trials, as well as those of the second boat, to be carried out in safety.[26]

During testing in the notorious Irish Sea the *Holland* would prove disappointing. It lacked power and a worrying design fault had begun to emerge. The freeboard was so low that even in moderately calm waters the conning tower had to be kept shut if the boat was not to be inundated. It meant boats suffered the disadvantages of being submerged while still on the surface. It restricted the amount of fresh air that commanders could drive through a boat, important for safety and health, for cleansing and refreshing the craft. Even the commanders' habit of standing – though squeezed – in the conning tower, head and upper body outside the boat, entailed the risk of flooding the craft in unkind seas. Something had to be done. Bacon and Admiralty architects would oversee revisions.

The *Holland* boats had a mechanical spark plug which Bacon said was the cause of incessant problems:

> The petrol engines which had been sent over from America behaved worse than anything else, chiefly owing to the fact that the sparking-plugs were mechanical, giving a 'break' in the high-tension circuit inside the cylinder. But there were many other failures; in fact, so many were the minor troubles and breakdowns, that I came to the conclusion that we would never make real headway until I had taken the boat away from the fathering care of Messrs Vickers' works, and made the crew themselves do as much of the repair work as was possible and thus learn to keep the boats efficient by their own labours. As soon, therefore, as the second crew was sufficiently practised, I took the first two boats to Portsmouth.[27]

While the other *Hollands* were being completed, *Holland I* was assigned to HMS *Vernon* to be used as a target boat in the anti-submarine programme. She had to return to Barrow to be rebuilt after several attempts had been made to blow her up. On one occasion she survived a 200lb charge detonated only 70 yards (yd) from her. Her impregnability emboldened supporters; her easy destruction would have seen the anti-submarine lobby bathed in *schadenfreude*.

Bacon's Admiralty reports on the trials of the boats in his little flotilla were perspicacious. In a letter to Admiral Sir Charles Frederick Hotham (1843–1925), he included an assessment of the boats and how they and their personnel had performed. Hotham was of influence: commander the Pacific Station (1890–93); commander-in-chief the Nore (1897); commander-in-chief Portsmouth (1903). In his detailed analyses Bacon pondered on the deployment of submarines and warned of the dangers posed by foreign submarines:

> We must conclude that near approach of an enemy's port known to contain, or suspected of containing submarine boats, is extremely hazardous. The strain of incessant look-out is great and it is always an absolute certainty that a good boat may come within torpedo range at any moment without being seen. I am quite positive that the risk is one that should not be run. I venture to think that our present experience, even with these little boats [the first *Hollands*] warrants our saying that a ship should not approach within 20 miles of an enemy's port with a view to remaining there for a moderate time unless it is blowing a gale of wind: even then care should be taken not to come close. That our new boats [to be known as the *A*-class] will put further limitations on the free action of ships in moderately narrow waters I am convinced, but it is not my business to speculate.

Bacon advised Royal Navy ships' captains on the ways in which they might counter submarines:

> If a submarine is sighted at a dangerous distance go straight at her. It is bound to upset the captain of the boat. You will expose the least target and he will have to dive or alter course. The chances are he will altogether be put off his stroke.[28]

The Admiralty considered using the convoy system in which vulnerable merchant vessels were chaperoned by fighting ships. Bacon had misgivings:

> As regards the use of destroyers accompanying I am sceptical, but an inferior scout is better than none at all. They should not be able to track a well-

handled boat and injure her but they will form an additional obstacle to be avoided. In looking out for boats ... search the horizon thoroughly with as powerful a glass as possible. In this way boats on the surface may be detected before they have thoroughly made out the ship. Search the water about a mile to a mile and a half off for optical tubes. Note carefully disturbances among sea birds.[29]

His reports warn of the perils surface commanders would face from enemy submarines, but he remained critical of the *Hollands*:

The small horizon on the surface is their curse; the difficulty of trimming in a sea way except after considerable experience is another defect. Both these objections should be largely got over in the *A-type*. Optical tube has to be long and can only be got down by taking off internal portion owing to the limited height of the boats. This will be got over in *A*-class who [*sic*] will have a shorter and larger tube which will considerably increase their efficiency. Submerged speed is too low in *Holland* boats making the number required for defence or offence much larger than with higher speed boats. These defects are all I hope overcome in our new *A-type* boat. They should be infinitely more invisible yet more seaworthy than the *Holland* type. On the surface of the water at natural load–line rolling is practically unknown. But while submerging when in diving condition, under certain conditions of sea, rolling becomes most marked, even as much as 20 degrees each way. At present I have ordered the boats to keep head to sea if rolling occurs while trimming. The cause is undoubtedly the small water line area when in this condition and the resultant loss in wave formation which tends to check rolling. These boats also have no bilge keels. There is nothing therefore alarming in this sudden tendency to roll provided care is taken to keep the boat head to sea in the act of trimming. Fitting bilge keels will I hope get over this considerably.[30]

Bacon was indefatigable in analysing the difficulties faced by his captains. While such reports can lack minutiae, his demonstrate intimacy and an appreciation of the nuances of submarining and boat characteristics. He was a commander who steeped himself in this entirely new art. His reports do not suggest a leader remote from his men, as his critics alleged, or one blind to their concerns, rather he shared their problems and offered solutions:

He [the captain] has to keep his boat compensated for immediate diving, all consumptions being made up for in water ballast. He has to navigate by rough methods. See without being seen, which means alertness and common sense. He has to recognise friend from enemy (this is not very difficult with a good tube). He has to estimate course of enemy and distance to cut her off and dive at requisite time to show his optical tube as little as possible. At close range he has to estimate her speed by time of approach and vision, adjust his director and fire. Meanwhile he has had to keep a casual all-round observation to see that other ships and boats are clear. He has to study light and shade. So he has plenty to do without hurry or mistake and it requires much practice even with a naturally good man. And it is in the man rather than the machine that the success of an attack depends.[31]

He advises his Admiralty superiors about attacking harbours:

Experience with these boats has more than ever convinced me that the most elementary defences are sufficient to keep out boats. I do not believe any narrow entrance can be forced by a boat especially if light nets are used in front. In daytime she must use her optical tube and betray her presence. At night time she must navigate the surface and become a 2nd class torpedo boat. But to any fleet not in a well-defended harbour merely anchored in a roadstead they should be, if within striking distance, a veritable terror. The boats would know the bearing and distance of the ships and diving and running for a known time could rise within striking distance having shown no sign on the surface. This is the class of attack the French are so fond of.[32]

His observations confirm a technical panache. More surprisingly, given the causticity of remarks about his aloofness, they show he was protective, almost, at times, headmasterly towards his commanders and crews. Whatever doubts persisted in others, it was his conviction that the principle of submarines had been established and he would brook no intervention from those who still questioned their validity.

It is patent that he was determined to maintain the integrity of his charges, men and craft, sometimes seeming to make light of grave incidents. In their clipped tone his missives are 'naval': of sharpness and brevity; brisk to tart. They would be mulled over by seasoned salts in the Admiralty who in battle-scarred careers had suffered worse than trifling explosions or fumes from a leaking battery.

In his bulletins a certain officer insouciance can be gleaned: it was both customary and expected. Bacon's apparent airiness in describing hair-raising events was part of the habit of command. It was *de rigeur* that a senior naval officer did not dwell on such affairs:

The condition of the boats has been satisfactory on the whole. No.2 has had a run of particularly bad luck. Her top joint on the cylinder cover had to be remade. This is a heavy job necessitating lifting the stern of the boat. This again gave out. She then had a small explosion which laid up her crew. The first day she was out again she broke her optical tube and rammed the 'Hazard' and now she will want a thorough overall on account of the condition of her tail shaft, intermediate shaft and bearings. No.4 had a leakage of some of her battery containers, this however was put right in a month. No.3 was laid up a month refitting her cylinder joints and previously for a month refitting battery containers. No.1 was only laid up 4 days. No.5 also only 4 days. [33]

Impervious to Admiralty pressure for quick results, Bacon was determined to conduct the trials at his own pace and in his own way. His missives show a confidence which could irritate older hands. To some Admiralty buffs he was still a stripling. Of an unswerving self-belief the tenor of his observations could border on arrogance; he was, though, Britain's *only* senior submarine chief and one of a handful in the world who knew *anything* about them. So if his reports had at times an irksome precocity, their uniqueness made them deserving of attention:

In this period ... the absolutely initial period ... the main underlying feature has been to instil care of handling in the officers of the boats. No hurry and caution have been the watchwords. To have in any way hurried ... to have attempted to run before they could thoroughly walk, would merely have resulted in carelessness. If the results obtained are neither dramatic or great ... [then] the teaching has been sound [and] the riper the fruit will be when gathered later. To have hurried would have been to court disaster. To have lost a boat through 10 seconds flurry would have been a blow to an experimental service which it would have been criminal to have incurred. [34]

Despite captious remarks about Bacon's deliberation, his caution and circumspection, he remained unapologetic in choosing prudence over haste, describing various restrictions he placed on his captains and making a virtue of carefulness over rashness:

I am in no way ashamed to say the captains of boats have themselves protested at times at the limitations I have imposed on them, but I have always endeavoured to instil into them that risks that are legitimate in war, or rapidity of action that is warranted by large experience, are at present out of place, and that knowledge and confidence are more useful equipment on active service

than premature quickness even in manoeuvres. We have had to test the boats
in varying weather and sea, as well as the reliability of the methods and fittings
under more or less prolonged conditions of use, and in looking back I do not
regret a day of the quiet practice or more or less infantile manoeuvres that
we have carried out. The improvement in reliability of the boats and their
handling has been most marked ... I am quite satisfied with all the captains
... some naturally have proved themselves more qualified than others for the
particular work ... it is extremely satisfactory to note they have all done well
and that in no sense has anyone proved to be a failure. The only fear as regards
the safety of the boats is that familiarity may breed overconfidence and that
some day an officer in taking an off chance may come to grief. Provided
certain general rules are adhered to the boats are safer than surface boats but
if overconfidence breeds carelessness accidents will follow. But I hope and
believe that the conditions are so simple, that care is so ingrained, that the
boats will be safely worked and accidents forestalled.[35]

Bacon had learned the quixotic nature of his trade, spending hours in the
boats, and his insights were the first lessons from Britain's new submarine
service. The technology has changed today but essential truths still apply.
Bacon's analyses covered engineering, wave formation, the need for caution
but decisiveness, and the necessity of a commander to perform instant mental
arithmetic. Contemporary commanders must assimilate a welter of conflicting
information, sieving the relevant from the trivial, calculating dive time, depth,
distance, range and more: the menace of information overload is profound.
They have to be good managers, like any captain, but they also need scientific
and mathematical disciplines: algebra, geometry, trigonometry and physics.
Their predecessors needed similar abilities but had no electronic aids, though
a mistake by a commander today could be globally catastrophic. Learning to
'read' the sea; honing their instincts, getting a 'feel' for the diverse uncertainties
of wind and weather; the learning curve was always steep for those who aspired
to the command of a submarine:

The boats can work, roughly speaking, in any weather up to a sea usually
raised by a wind of 6 in open water. Wind below force 2–3 makes them
visible some distance off, but as soon as the weather breaks the optical tube
becomes very invisible. [Bacon could navigate a submarine but failed to avoid
tautological collisions.] Dull heavy weather makes it difficult for them to see
their enemy especially if painted lead colour. The optical tubes do not mist in
thick weather provided the boats dive and wash them.[36]

Bacon's commanders would become deft in handling torpedoes (see Chapter 3; Appendix F):

> The torpedo practice from the boats tube is excellent, but of course estimation of the enemy's speed is quite as difficult as in a torpedo boat, and therefore the chances of getting in a shot are about the same.[37]

For sceptics Bacon's message was direct:

> Even these little boats would be a terror to any ship attempting to remain, or pass, near a harbour holding them.[38]

This, then, is how submarines were seen: a dog in its kennel, one eye open, fangs bared, ready to spring out and nip the unwary; the idea of a submarine lurking far out to sea, independent, unleashed, quietly waiting for a passing ship, was unexplored. At the time it was beyond the technical capability of boats and even the imaginings of its most strident advocates. Bacon looked forward to having command of a more effective flotilla. With Fisher he had determined that war was coming and understood the importance of keeping his unit in a state of preparedness:

> The larger boats that we are building [the *A*-class] should be very much more formidable and at the same time more invisible. Practice in attacks is being continued three days a week.[39]

In his reports to the Admiralty, Bacon returns frequently to the health risks being run by his submariners. Little was known about the effects on those constrained beneath the sea in cramped and dangerous circumstances. In October 1901 there were tests to allay fears about breathing and people being cooped up under the waves. Seventeen people, including Bacon, were locked in a submarine overnight, with a doctor conducting tests to gauge the ill-effects, of which there were none. Supporters were pleased and the sceptics, once again, confounded. Unsurprisingly, claustrophobia was commonplace. Boats were chilled, damp or suffocatingly hot. They stank of sweat, oil, petrol and bodies. For those prone to headaches there was no respite from the closeness of others, the throb of the engine or the hum of the electric motor if the boat was submerged. There was constant tension with nerves stretched to the limit. Closeted underwater in a sunless, malodorous, glorified tin-can, devoid of fresh air, was entirely unnatural and always certain to trigger migraines, raise blood pressure and set pulses racing.

On his initial trip in a submarine, a young officer by the name of Cecil Talbot wrote of his first five-and-a-half unpleasant hours in a *Holland*. Talbot wrote that he had endured 'about as bad a day as it is possible to have'. He continued:

> We went over to Sandown Bay & attacked TB [torpedo boat] 26; there was a nasty lop in the Solent, so we had the hatch shut down all the time and in consequence the atmosphere got a trifle thick; I was very nearly sick from the stink and kicking about. We dived several times; we once struck the bottom with a bump, through trying to rise by blowing the auxiliary ballast in 7 fathoms.[40]

The person who scribbled those hasty first impressions of life in a submarine overcame his queasiness and went on to have an illustrious naval career, being decorated for a diversity of courageous deeds: Vice Admiral Sir Cecil Ponsonby Talbot (1884–1970).*

When war began on 28 July 1914, the young Talbot was already at sea in command of the submarine *E-6* patrolling the Heligoland Bight off the north coast of Germany. He was fortunate to survive a number of incidents as a submariner, including, in 1913, an explosion on *E-5* during trials in which three sailors were killed; *E*-class boats were a later category of submarine which bore the brunt of operations in the First World War. By the time of the Armistice, Talbot had been appointed captain of the submarine depot ship HMS *Ambrose* and its flotilla of ten submarines.[41]

---

* From a leading military family, Talbot had joined the Royal Navy as an officer cadet at the age of 13. He had been trained on HMS *Britannia*, an elderly wooden ship of the line based on the River Dart, Devon, England, where cadets lived and learned their trade. The life of a child sailor was led permanently 'at the double'. Talbot won top marks and subsequently saw lengthy and varied service in the surface fleet, as well as in submarines. He had begun his surface career on the warship HMS *Glory* at the China Station during the Boxer Rebellion (1898–1900). Married in Barrow on 12 August 1912, his best man was the eminent submariner Lieutenant Martin Dunbar-Nasmith (later Admiral Sir Martin Eric Dunbar-Nasmith; see Chapter 7). Talbot was the first naval officer to attend an army balloon course in 1908. In 1911 he was made the first lieutenant of HM Airship No.1, the Mayfly. Catastrophically its keel was removed and, consequently, the craft snapped in two while being hauled from its shed at Barrow; in 1926 Talbot was made head of the Admiralty's Naval Air Section.

Sickly Business

In the years which preceded the First World War, Bacon had tried to ensure that his young charges would be among the best-trained submariners in the world. It was not an easy task. Being a new science he was as much 'at sea' as the officers he led, which he had discussed with frankness on taking up his appointment. His tuition was all-embracing; it covered more than seamanship and the dexterity of his trainee commanders in handling a boat in extreme circumstances. He also looked carefully at their health and well-being, reporting on the 'Affections due to the Effects of Noxious Gases', he comments on the student submariners being treated for 'an affection due to some unknown cause'. Its symptoms included vomiting, dizziness, severe headaches which were, he continued

> ... either frontal or occipital, and in some cases the pain was described as going around the head. A feeling of languor was also complained of. On enquiry it was found that many others had been similarly affected, although to a lesser degree ... and the symptoms ... quickly disappeared ... [with exposure to] fresh air. The symptoms as a rule appeared only after a considerable amount of time had been spent in the boats and the severity of the cases was in direct ratio to the amount of time spent there.[42]

Bacon's analysis showed engine room staff were worst affected:

> I incline to the belief that they are in large measure due to the effects of noxious gases escaping from the gasoline engine by leakage. Gasoline being a hydro-carbon, the chief products formed as the result of its combustion are carbon dioxide and carbon monoxide, the latter occurring as the result of incomplete combustion. The greater part of these products are discharged externally but there can be little doubt that small quantities escape into the boats by leakage. The symptoms of those affected could be explained by the presence of these gases, but the former gas would require to be present in large amounts and it appears more probable that the principal factor is the presence of carbon monoxide in small quantities. Investigations are being made into this subject in order to arrive at a definite conclusion and at the same time every precaution is being taken to ensure as efficient ventilation as possible in order to remove or dilute those impurities.

He compiled a list of eight crew who had suffered various maladies: headaches, vomiting, dizziness and palpitations. Of the eight men, four were Engineer Rating Artificers and two chief ERAs, who worked with engines. They were off work from one to five days. Five of the six men Bacon felt were 'cured', while the sixth was sent to hospital with headaches and palpitations:

On examination he [the crew member] was found to be suffering also from weak action of the heart and it was considered inadvisable for him to continue in submarine boats.

Of the two who remained, one was a leading stoker and the other an able seaman; both would frequently lend a hand in the engine room or were often at work in its vicinity.[43]

In a section entitled 'Accidents Peculiar to Submarines' Bacon makes another reference to gases:

Carbon monoxide is an extremely poisonous gas and if inhaled, even in minute quantities ... must seriously impair health. With reference to the ERA who was found to be suffering from weak cardiac action and is at present undergoing treatment in hospital it is impossible to state whether this affection can be traced to the action of this gas. It would ... materially aggravate this complaint. Carbon monoxide doubtless causes in the living tissues profound pathological changes, but the nature of these changes is unknown apart from their functional manifestations. It is anticipated that in the future, owing to certain improvements in the ventilation arrangements, that this gas along with all other noxious impurities will be completely removed and the atmosphere of the boats be rendered purer than hitherto.[44]

From his annals it appears life outside the boats was as unhealthy as that inside. Under 'Catarrhal and Rheumatic Affections' he records that the greatest number of cases were among those frequently on deck:

... and are therefore more exposed to damp and wet. This probably explains why most cases were met with in the Seamen class ... all were mild in character ... probably the most important factor in causing these affections is the sudden changes of temperature from the interior of the boat to the outside.[45]

Admiralty-Speak

Toxic gas and petrol vapours were a constant concern. The later installation of diesel engines helped make boats safer, but not entirely safe; nothing could achieve that. A boat under Bacon's jurisdiction was involved in an accident in which gases had built up and in which an explosion had injured members of its crew:

> It was caused by an explosion due to an accumulation of gasoline in the crank pit of the engine ... and resulted in four of the crew receiving severe burns about the face, forearms and hands. All the burns were however of a superficial character and no permanent injury resulted [author's note: this is another example of officer insouciance; severe burns *superficial*]. One Chief ERA, however, suffered from a certain amount of shock after convalescence from the burns and appeared to have lost his nerve. Consequently it was necessary to relieve him from further service in submarines.[46]

This is likely to be Admiralty-speak: it means that the seaman was kicked out – it is possible, though unlikely, that the sailor in question might have been found a new role in the surface navy; such transfers occurred but were rare if the seaman suffered a continuing ailment. Bacon was cerebral but could slip into euphemistic navy guff as easily as any other naval grandee. The chances are that the sailor he refers to would face a haphazard future, as did generations of redundant mariners; theirs was a markedly different culture to that of a landsman – from a distinctive rolling gait to a language which was incomprehensible to those onshore – with such specialist skills as they had being misunderstood, misused or simply unwanted. It seems from Bacon's reports that the engine room submarine personnel had a particularly bad time. He writes of two cases of conjunctivitis:

> Both occurred amongst the engine room staff and were probably due to irritation attributable to charred oil. However both cases promptly recovered on removal from the boat for a short time.[47]

He draws a comparison between the well-being of the officers and the men; the first being – unsurprisingly – rather healthier than the second. He attributes this not to their different submarine duties but to officers enjoying a better lifestyle:

The general health of the officers ... has been uniformly good without exception. They have all worked under exactly the same conditions as the crews, and neglecting the few instances in which slight headaches occurred ... none have shown any signs of anaemia, nor are there any indications of their health having in any way suffered. This may be in large measure due to their contact with more hygienic surroundings when out of the boats [manifestly not *in* the boats where all aboard had to share a single bucket] to open air exercise being taken at every opportunity, to better food, to sleeping in well-ventilated rooms or cabins, in fact to their living a healthier life generally. Contrasted with the officers it must be admitted that the health of the crews ... has not been quite so robust. There is no doubt that when out of the boats their time is spent as a general rule amidst more or less unsanitary [*sic*] surroundings. They take less open-air exercise, spend less time in the open-air and altogether do not live so healthy a life. The effects of working in confined spaces has been at times evident in producing signs of anaemia to a more or less degree in some instances. Want of open-air exercise, deprivation of sunlight and prolonged working in an atmosphere which it is evident contains gaseous impurities of an undesirable nature, all these tend to the production of anaemia and the deterioration of health.[48]

There is nothing startling in this: sailors often joined the navy from poor backgrounds where they had suffered from inferior diets and all the rest; officers were drawn generally from the better-off classes with the attendant advantages this conferred.

The remarkable *Holland I* has a special place in maritime affection. She served with the Royal Navy for twelve years before being declared redundant. Purchased at the scrap value of £410 by the company of T. W. Ward Ltd. she foundered off Plymouth while under tow to the breaker's yard in November 1913.*

---

* Almost seventy years would elapse before her discovery. Late on the evening of 14 April 1981, she was found at a depth of 206ft by the mine-hunter HMS *Bossington*, which had searched an area off the Eddystone Light on behalf of the Royal Navy Submarine Museum at Gosport. By midnight the diving vessel *Seaforth Clansman* had lowered an underwater television camera and a diving bell. At noon the museum received a signal from the ship: 'Submarine in reasonably good condition. Hull is heavily encrusted but easily identifiable and sits with keel approximately two feet into the seabed with slight list ...' She was salvaged and an ambitious programme of restoration and conservation began immediately. One of the battery cells was returned to its maker, Chloride Ltd., and still delivered, after sixty-eight years on the seabed, an amazing 35 amps.[49] *Holland I*, with the Second World War submarine HMS *Alliance*, are among exhibits at Gosport. A visitor entrance has been cut in the Holland's hull, a door to an atmospheric past where the ghosts of Holland, Bacon, Cable and Arnold-Forster still seem to linger.

Bacon was moved by Fisher from the submarine service to become the first captain of HMS *Dreadnought*, Fisher's prestigious warship; in the First World War he commanded the Dover Patrol (1915–17) trying to halt the incursion of German U-boats in which, through no fault of his own, he achieved only limited success. His career suffered by his involvement in an unpleasant naval saga: the Beresford Affair (see Appendix G).

Notes

1   Bacon, Admiral Sir Reginald, *From 1900 Onward* (Hutchinson and Co., 1940), p.61; Bacon wrote two volumes of memoirs: *A Naval Scrapbook 1877–1900* and *From 1900 Onward*; his other best-known work, apart from his biography of Admiral John Rushworth Jellicoe, is *The Dover Patrol 1915–1917* in two volumes

2   Bacon, *From 1900 Onward*, p.53

3   Bacon, *1900 Onward*, p.54

4   Bacon, *1900 Onward*, p.54

5   Bacon, *From 1900 Onward*, p.58

6   Thompson, Julian, *War at Sea 1914–1918* (Sidgwick & Jackson with the Imperial War Museum, 2005) p.39–40, quoting submariner cited as Telegraphist Halter. Thompson's excellent book has verbatim quotations from written material and taped interviews in the IWM archives

7   Compton-Hall, Richard, *Submarine Boats* (Conway Maritime Press, 1983) p.146

8   Compton-Hall, *Submarine Boats*, p.146.

9   Arnold-Forster, D., Letter to his uncle, Oakley Arnold-Forster MP., 24 March 1901, from HMS *Hazard*; Royal Navy Museum

10 Arnold-Forster, Rear Admiral D., *The Ways of the Navy* (Ward, Lock & Co, 1931), p.241

11 Arnold-Forster, *The Ways of the Navy*, p.241; Williams, David, *Naval Camouflage 1914–1945* (Chatham, 2001), p.57–61

12 Arnold-Forster, *The Ways of the Navy*, pp.241–242

13 Bacon, *From 1900 Onward*, p.56–57

14 Bacon, *1900 Onward*, p.57

15 Bacon, *1900 Onward*, p.59

16 Bacon, *1900 Onward*, p.56

17 Haldane, J.S., *The Philosophy of a Biologist*, 2nd Edition (Oxford University Press, 1936); Goodman, Martin, *Suffer and Survive: The Extreme Life of J.S. Haldane* (Simon & Schuster, 2007); Lang, M.A. and Brubann, A.O. (eds), *The Future of Diving: 100 Years of Haldane and Beyond* (Smithsonian Institute Scholarly Press, 2009)

18 Bacon, *1900 Onward*, p.60

19 Bacon, *1900 Onward*, p.58

20 Arnold-Forster, *The Ways of the Navy*, p.244

21 Arnold-Forster, *The Ways of the Navy*, p.242

22 Arnold-Forster, *The Ways of the Navy*, p.243

23 Arnold-Forster, Letter to his father, 6 April 1902, from HMS *Hazard*, RN Museum

24 Arnold-Forster, Letter to his father, 14 May 1902, from HMS *Hazard*, RN Museum

25 Bacon, *1900 Onward*, p.64

26 Bacon, *From 1900 Onward*, pp.54–55
27 Bacon, *1900 Onward*, p.64
28–39 Letter/reports, No.1422/45, dated 31-5-03, sent by Sir Reginald Bacon,
    postmarked HMS *Latona*, Portsmouth, to Admiral Sir Charles Hotham,
    Commander-in-Chief, Portsmouth, held RN Submarine Museum, Gosport, UK
40 Thompson, *War at Sea*, p.39, quoting from diary of Sub Lieutenant Cecil Talbot,
    p.20, 13 April 1905, re: voyage of *Holland 4*
41 www.maritimequest.com is an excellent website of biographies and photographs
42 Bacon–Hotham, Letter/reports No.1422/45, 31-5-03
43 Bacon–Hotham, Letter/reports No.1422/45
44 Bacon–Hotham, Letter/reports No.1422/45
45 Bacon–Hotham, Letter/reports No.1422/45
46 Bacon–Hotham, Letter/reports No.1422/45
47 Bacon–Hotham, Letter/reports No.1422/45
48 Bacon–Hotham, Letter/reports No.1422/45
49 *Holland I*, Royal Naval Submarine Museum guide

Spit and polish aboard *A-1*, 1903. These men in all probability died in her on 18 March the following year.

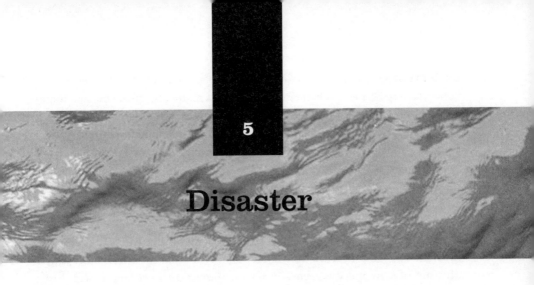

Disaster

The new *A*-class submarines were bigger, faster, of a superior range and more deadly. But they had a calamitous record. The first one out of Vickers at Barrow was HMS *A-1*, sometimes confusingly called *Holland VI*, being of quite different architecture but the sixth to be ordered by the Admiralty after the five American-designed *Hollands*.

The *A*-class had traces of the *Holland* but were the Royal Navy's first all-British submarines. *A-1* was laid down on 19 February 1902 and launched five months later on 9 July 1902; tacticians and accountants were pleased that submarines could be built more quickly and cheaply than conventional ships.

At 103ft in length – 40ft longer than *Holland I* – with a beam of just under 12ft she displaced 190 tons on the surface and 207 tons submerged. Her claimed surface speed was 11.5 knots, and 7 knots when dived. She had only one torpedo tube, which was later thought an aberration given that an imperative for the new class was the need to increase the fire power; later models in the class had two. On the surface the *A-1* was powered by a British 16-cylinder 450hp Wolseley petrol engine – the voracious Vickers had acquired the Wolseley Tool and Motor Car Company – and an 87hp electric motor when submerged. With a complement of eleven, again greater than the *Holland*, her surface range was 500 miles at 11.5 knots and 20 miles at 5 knots.

In its appearance the class looked more purposeful and was distinguished by its higher freeboard – 2ft higher than the *Holland* – which made it less susceptible to unkind seas, and, also, by its squat 7ft conning tower with an improved hatch system incorporated as a further safeguard against inundation. *A-1* was towed from Barrow to Portsmouth, but she suffered an explosion even before she left the yard; after repairs were expedited there was another near-miss en route to Portsmouth, where she would take her place as part of the submarine flotilla. The crew had to abandon her when seawater managed to reach the batteries; she had twice the battery capacity of the *Holland*. Such a concoction spells inevitable disaster and, within moments, lethal chlorine fumes had consumed the boat. Her travails would continue. Two years after her launch she was lost with all eleven hands in an accident so shocking it resulted in long-overdue tightening up of nautical procedures and regulations.

The Loss of *A-1*

A-1 was on exercises in the waters of the Solent, off the Isle of Wight, close to her Portsmouth base on 18 March 1904. It is today an area frantic with a diversity of craft and was a busy waterway more than a century ago. *A-1* was readying herself for a dummy torpedo attack on HMS *Juno*, a Royal Navy cruiser. Suddenly, while submerged, she was struck on the port side near her conning tower by a passing mail steamer, the newly built 5,883-ton SS *Berwick Castle*, built by Beardmore at the Govan yard, Glasgow, Scotland, on passage from Southampton to Hamburg, Germany. She was of the Union Castle Line (1900–77), its extensive fleet made distinctive by its livery of lavender hulls and red black-banded funnels.

A-1 sank instantly in shallow water of 37ft. Her loss, however, was not realised until the evening when she failed to return to harbour. The pilot of the *Berwick Castle* said later that he had not been notified a submarine was exercising in the vicinity, but thought his ship had been hit by a fake torpedo before continuing on its passage to Germany. There was severe criticism that the Admiralty had 'hushed-up' the incident, while others argued that its reportage had been exaggerated.[1]

The *A-1* catastrophe was amplified by occurring in what were – and still are – designated naval waters; both shore and water swarmed with naval personnel. Communications had been a shambles, and shipping procedures were unknown, ignored or misinterpreted.

Nobody had appreciated that the boat and its crew were missing until hours after the incident, by which time it was too late for a realistic rescue operation. It is likely a speedier attempt, in any event, would have been hopeless given the severity of the collision and the rapidity with which the submarine was inundated and sank. The disaster led to procedural changes and the customary inquiry. It was little more than a glorified ceremony of regret to the dead and bereaved; a genteel whitewash of inadequate probing with nobody being held to proper account. Nobody knew anything about submarines, certainly not lawyers and most of the military people involved in the proceedings. They were unsure how to conduct an inquiry into the disaster, this being the first of its kind. As a result of the calamity, a second hatch was fitted in later submarines at the foot of the conning tower in a thin attempt to prevent a recurrence of the cataclysm. *A-1* had become Britain's first naval submarine casualty, the first in what would become a long line. The event signified that the submarine service was maturing and in the agony of its growing pains it had shed a little of its boyish charm.

The coffin of *A-1* was raised a month after her sinking. She was repaired and returned to service and '... in the cramped confines of her primitive control-room the submarine's new captain, a dark-haired twenty-year-old lieutenant, Max Kennedy Horton, learned to master the arts of undersea warfare'.[2] Horton, who features later in this story, had a daring career.

Six years later, in 1910, *A-1* was reconfigured as an experimental craft for use by the Anti-Submarine Committee, set up secretly by the Admiralty under the presidency of Admiral Sir Cecil Burney (1858–1929).*

The *A-1* submarine ended as she had existed for much of her life: in unhappy circumstances. She went down, running as an experimental craft unmanned and submerged while on automatic pilot. Decades later, in 1989, her rusting corpse was found by fishermen in Bracklesham Bay, to the west of the Manhood Peninsula on the Sussex coast, looking out to the English Channel and the Isle of Wight, not far from where she first sank and eleven men died. She is guarded today by the Protection of Wrecks Act.

Thirteen *A*-class submarines were built at Barrow between 1902 and 1908. The fundamentals such as displacement and length were similar to those of *A-1*, but armaments were increased to two tubes and four torpedoes. There were also numerous technical changes which varied from boat to boat, so many that the *A*-class appeared to embrace several different types of boat. The *A*-class boats which survived the years up to the Great War were used for training, target practice and harbour defence at Portsmouth, Devonport Naval Base, Plymouth, and Ardrossan on the Ayrshire coast of south-west Scotland. In the years between their commissioning and the start of the Great War the *A*-class had a calamitous record. *A-2* was commissioned a few days after *A-1* and served on harbour patrol at Portsmouth during the war. In January 1920 she foundered in Bomb Ketch Lake, Portsmouth, and was inundated. In 1925 she was sold for scrap to H.J. Pounds of Portsmouth, a graveyard of military wrecks: in its heyday Pounds' scrap heaps comprised tanks, aircraft, ships and submarines. Money in armaments is well known; that made by scrap men tends to be overlooked.

---

* Burney was the number two to Jellicoe at the Battle of Jutland in 1916. From early in his career he had taken a keen interest in and become an expert on underwater warfare, a fascination with which his son, the naval officer Charles Dennistoun Burney, was also imbued (see Appendix B).

A-3 Goes Down

The submarine *A-3* was launched on 9 March 1903 and commissioned on 13 July 1904. On 2 February 1912 she was sunk in an accident so tragic it exceeded that of *A-1*. Of particular poignancy was that the collision which finished the boat occurred with the gunboat HMS *Hazard*, her mothership, the submarines' protector. It happened during exercises in the Solent, near the East Princess Buoy, and her entire crew of fourteen was killed. She was raised, the bodies of her crew extracted and buried with full military honours in Haslar Royal Naval Cemetery, by the quiet waters of Alver Lake in Gosport. The funeral cortege stretched for 2 miles. Today the cemetery, one corner of it devoted to Turkish sailors who died in another tragedy, is still deeply moving. A small chapel with whitewashed walls, dignified by its simplicity; weathered memorials on well-trimmed greensward record the loss of early submariners, interminable lists of unknown names notable for their youth and now largely forgotten.[3]

Submarine commanders were always youthful. *A-3* had been under the temporary command of Lieutenant Frank Thomas Ormand, aged 23. Three other officers on the boat, all lieutenants, were aged 21, 22 and 23; one was the second-in-command and the two others were aboard for instructional purposes. Ormand's own command was *A-4*. The commander of *A-3* was Lieutenant Charles Worthington Craven, aged 28, who later became Sir Charles Craven (1884–1944), the managing director of Vickers Shipyard at Barrow-in-Furness. Craven said at the subsequent inquiry that Ormand had had two years' experience and was a skilled submariner. At the inquest it was said the deaths would have been instantaneous, though nobody could possibly tell. When the boat was raised, a piece of wood was found jammed in its propeller which would have made steering difficult to impossible. A gash 6–8ft long and 1ft wide had been torn in her upper hull, a few feet in front of the conning tower. HMS *Hazard*, built in 1894 as a *Dryad*-class torpedo gunboat, also had a sad demise: she sank in 1918 after a collision in the English Channel with the hospital ship SS *Western Australia* off Portland Bill on the Dorset coast.

Ill-fortune continued to dog the *A*-class. On 16 October 1905 *A-4* was involved in sound and signalling tests. The wash from a steamer that had passed too close entered her through an open ventilator and found its way to the batteries, which gave of clouds of toxic chlorine gas. The boat had been instantly inundated and had plunged at the bow, sending her to the bottom, 90ft below. The gas made the crew choke and cough:

> … but there was no panic. While some of the men held back the water by
> wedging clothing into the base of the open tube Lieutenant Herbert, the First

Lieutenant, groped his way through the poisonous blackness, located the controls, and blew [emptied by compressed-air] the tanks. After minutes which seemed an eternity the little submarine rose slowly to the surface and Nasmith, Herbert, and the rest of the crew staggered out of the hatchway into the fresh air.[4]

The commander of *A-4*, Lieutenant Martin Nasmith, and his first lieutenant, Godfrey Herbert, went on to noteworthy careers in the Great War (see Chapters 6, 7 and Appendix O). As the *A-4* was being towed back to dock an explosion rent the submarine. She sank again, though without casualties, and was subsequently raised and put back into service. Sailors are as superstitious as any other group and the *A*-class was garnering an unwelcome reputation. In addition to the dangers, it was apparent that, though an improvement on the *Hollands*, they had other serious limitations: range, speed and endurance were insufficient and conditions for the crew severely inadequate and cramped. The craft also had too little ballast, from which the *Hollands* also suffered. Modifications were introduced as each submarine was completed. Surface speed improved as changes came through, but their performance while submerged remained disappointing.

The *A-5* Calamity

A-5 added to sailors' fears. Launched in March 1904 and commissioned in February 1905 she had made a much-heralded goodwill visit to the important maritime centre of Cobh – which has a significant seafaring history – on the south coast of County Cork, Ireland, later renamed Queenstown in honour of a visit by Queen Victoria.[*]

A-5 was visiting HMS *Haulbowline* Naval Base situated on the western side of Cork harbour, the first submarine to call there. The naval base was significant and virtually self-contained: a sizeable dockyard, dry-dock facilities capable of taking cruiser-size vessels, extensive accommodation for naval personnel and its own clinic and hospital. The visit of the little *A-5* had prompted great excitement and crowds of people, many of them naval officers, had congregated to see her. Most

---

[*]   When the *Sirius* sailed from nearby Port West to New York in 1838 she became the first steam vessel to cross the Atlantic; convicts deported to penal colonies left from Cobh; Irish fleeing the famine departed there for America, the land of immigrants; in 1912 Cobh was the last stop for the *Titanic* on its fateful voyage; in 1915 traumatised survivors from the *Lusitania* were brought to Cobh after its sinking by a German U-boat; it was from Cobh in the Great War that British and US Navy ships would conduct their Atlantic anti-U-boat campaign which, at its height, could have cost Britain and her allies victory.

had never seen a submarine. Accompanied by HMS *Hazard*, she was due to start exercises on 16 February 1905.

Some seventy naval officers had gathered to see her being put through her paces; instead, they witnessed her ignominy. Two hours after being filled with petrol on the 15th in readiness for her big day she blew up, the initial explosion being followed by a second blast some thirty minutes later. The blast was so intense members of the crew were blown out of the main hatch in the conning tower. Six were killed with more seriously injured. A spark from an electrical switch used to fire up her engine is thought to have ignited accumulated petrol vapour. The disaster was followed by a full military funeral; it was becoming a habit. Cobh closed down for the day as a sign of respect.

The forlorn hulk of the *A-5* was taken back to Barrow-in-Furness and rebuilt. She rejoined the fleet in October of the same year and was finally broken up, fifteen years later, at Portsmouth dockyard in 1920. With an audience assembled for its influence, one which it was intended would spread the word about the potential and potency of the submarine, it could not have been more catastrophic: had the explosion happened at sea, though equally tragic, at least *A-5*'s torment would have been discreet. Instead of returning to their ships and bases extolling the astonishing virtues of the submarine, navy personnel left *Haulbowline* shocked and alarmed.

Controversy and the Sinking of A-7

On 16 January 1914, ten years after she had been commissioned, the submarine *A-7* was carrying out dummy torpedo attacks in Whitsand Bay, Cornwall, in a flotilla of other submarines. When she failed to surface, with thirteen aboard, HMS *Pygmy*, one of her faux target ships, raced to the point at which she was thought to have disappeared and initiated a rescue. Reports said a large quantity of bubbles and a tell-tale oil slick had been seen on the surface and that the spot had been marked with buoys. There were contrary suggestions that the location had been inadequately registered and, consequently, the rescue attempt was badly delayed by drawn-out attempts to locate her. Her loss led to scathing criticism from defence chiefs, navy officers and controversialists in newspapers and journals. Politicians, generally ill-informed about the navy but always eager to scramble aboard a passing bandwagon, wanted to know why the Admiralty was stubbornly persisting with what they called its perilous 'coffin-ships'. They shouted in the Commons about the squandered lives of brave men and waved their order papers, condemning the wanton waste of valuable defence monies.

The Royal Navy tried for a month to raise *A-7*, but the sea refused to relinquish her. She had bedded herself too deeply in the glutinous ooze of the ocean floor. Hawsers were attached to wrest her from the mud and lift her to daylight: each one of them snapped. She had been fitted at her departure with extra hydroplanes on her conning tower; experimental components intended to enhance her diving and surfacing capability, all part of a continuing development programme. They would serve no purpose, though, in helping to liberate her.

Newspapers were in their element: it was a long-running and tragic story, rich with human emotion, and one which made the navy look more foolish and incompetent by the hour. Once again the perfidious submarine had heaped savage opprobrium on the Royal Navy. It would never be properly established what had befallen the stricken craft and, after much anguished breast-beating, it was decided to leave her where she lay.*

A-8 Adds to the Toll

A-7 had been close to tragedy before her own loss. While on exercises nine years earlier, she had set sail with her sister craft *A-8* on 8 June 1905. Both were running on the surface in Plymouth Sound. The *A-8* had the hatch in her conning tower open, as was often the convention. It had just been observed that the bows of *A-8* appeared to be tilting at a slight angle into the water when suddenly, quite without warning, she dipped violently and went under, her stern raised almost vertically into the air like an accusatory finger, tons of water flooding in through her open hatch. Some said she exploded as she slid beneath the surface; if so, it would have been seawater penetrating her batteries and filling the boat with chlorine. She was raised four days later on 12 June. The bodies were cut out and removed for the customary military funeral with all the standard pomp and ceremony. A rogue rivet was found to have worked loose on the bow plates, allowing water to penetrate her. If it was instrumental in her end nobody could tell, thought it seems likely. Fifteen of her crew perished. *A-8* was repaired and recommissioned, and went on to have a long career, being sold for scrap in October 1920.

---

* The *A-7* is today a protected wreck, mercifully safe from the ghoulish, free of souvenir hunters and prying divers. Before it was proscribed to dive upon her photographs had been taken: she had settled peacefully on the seabed, as if merely resting between manoeuvres. Barnacles encrusted her conning tower; her ghostly hull brown with rust, shrouded by weeds. Her men still locked inside.

Two months after he had joined the submarine service, Sub Lieutenant Cecil Talbot – the young man who had written in his diary about feeling sick on his first underwater trip in a submarine, and who subsequently achieved high rank in the navy – wrote of the *A-8* sinking:

> Candy [captain] & Murdoch [sub lieutenant], her coxswain and one AB were saved, the only people who were on deck, but the remainder went down ... Candy, noticing the boat was a bit down by the bows, ordered the diving rudder to be put up hard, instead of which it was put hard down, and she immediately dipped ... it appears that the people inside were alive for one and three quarter hours after they went down, when they were killed by the explosion from the chlorine gas; they must have become unconscious in about 20 minutes after dipping, from the chlorine.[5]

The Suicide Squad

Submariner Fred Parsons came close to being caught in the calamity of the *A-8*. He had joined the wooden three-decker training ship HMS *Impregnable* as a boy seaman at the age of 15 at Devonport in 1893. Later he volunteered for the submarine service. Married with two children he needed the extra money.*

On joining the submarine service Parsons and another seaman had to undergo a standard medical:

> When we saw the doctor, the first thing he said was: 'Hello, two more for the suicide squad?' He could have been right. Submarines were still very new, there had been several accidents; and little did we know that one of us was doomed to die in one within a month or so ... I was detailed to train in *A-7*, which along with *A-8* had been in Plymouth awaiting *Forth's* arrival [author's note: HMS *Forth* was a vessel fitted out *c.* 1905 as a submarine depot ship]. Then we moved to the *Defiance*, the torpedo training school.

Fred and the sailor with whom he had joined the submarine service held the ranks of leading torpedo men:

---

* Submariners could earn more than in the surface navy. Submarine pay was 2s per day, a reasonable amount at the time. Submariners received an extra allowance for the dangers and hardships inherent in their task. Colloquially the money was called 'hard lying' or 'hard liers'; officially it was called submarine pay. It nearly doubled a rating's wages. 'Command pay' was also given to commanding officers.[6]

We often did duty aboard the submarine and one evening while I was sitting by the fore-hatch, keeping an eye on the battery, which was on charge, Lieutenant Little went below in his boat, *A-7*. He saw me sitting there, and he knew me, as I was training in his boat. 'Hello Parsons,' he said. 'My Chief Petty Officer is leaving. Would you like to take his place?' I was delighted. 'If you like, sir,' I said. 'Not if I like – if *you* like,' he told me, giving me an old-fashioned look. I knew I'd put my foot in it, and years later when I met him as a retired Admiral, I said something and he gave me the same old look. Then I reminded him of this episode. I was detailed for *A-7* but my pal was detailed for *A-8*. And there our ways parted forever. One day we were out together doing exercises, and after surfacing and going ahead some way, *A-8* suddenly dived with her hatch open. The disaster occurred just off Plymouth Breakwater. The boat went straight to the bottom and all on board were lost. My pal among them. I thought then of the doctor's words '… the suicide squad'.*

Fred Parsons recalled that several of those in the submarine training classes which he attended changed their minds after the accident and asked to be returned to General Service:

I lived to have one or two near things, but I always reckon my lucky star must have been shining about then. There were only two of us of the same rating in training, and no objection was made to anyone who wanted leave. So, by a fifty-fifty chance it could have been me. My wife was very frightened by this, but as I pointed out to her, you won't go before your number is up, so it was just as well for me to carry on.[7]*

Lieutenant Little, the submarine commander to whom Fred Parsons referred, became the distinguished Admiral Sir Charles James Colebrook Little (1882–

---

* Batteries were expensive, dangerous and vital to a submarines' effectiveness; it was beholden upon those crewmen detailed to look after them to be hawk-eyed.

* Fred Parsons later joined the ill-fated British Terra Nova expedition of 1910–12 with Captain Robert Falcon Scott (1868–1912) to Antarctica, in which they were beaten to the Pole by thirty-three days by the Norwegian Roald Amundsen's team. One of the survivors, Mr Parsons, was awarded the prestigious Albert Polar Medal. He rejoined the navy and saw service in the Great War, leaving the navy in 1920 with the rank of petty officer. His trade was that of a boot and shoemaker and he set up shop in Plymouth where he had spent much of his naval career. He retired in 1962 at the age of 83. He died at his home, named '*Terra Nova*' after the ship on which he had sailed to Antarctica, in Churchill Way, Plymouth, in January 1970 at the age of 91, the last surviving member of Scott's tragic expedition.[8]

1973), known as 'Tiny', monikers being customary in the RN and guaranteed to cut recipients down to size. Little commanded HMS *Fearless* and the Grand Fleet Submarine Flotilla from 1916 to 1918.

The *A-13* Diesel and Ackroyd-Stewart

The last of the British *A*-class submarines was *A-13*, laid down on 19 February 1903 and commissioned on 22 June 1908. Because of the uncertainties of petrol engines, often unreliable and always dangerous, *A-13* was fitted with a diesel engine, becoming the first British submarine to be so equipped. A fallacy is that the Admiralty stood imperiously detached from technical developments of the day; it did not. Britain had not built, operated and administered the most successful navy in the world by having a dolt as its master. It maintained a beady eye over European and American advances, applying the same degree of scrutiny as that with which it monitored developments in Britain, carefully selecting those progressions which it could modify and turn to naval advantage. The Admiralty was profoundly disturbed by the death toll in submarines, some tragedies being rooted in the instability of the petrol engine and its noxious fumes. Sir John Durston (1846–1917), the Royal Navy Engineer-in-Chief from 1889 to 1907, retained major reservations about petrol engines being used in cramped and airless spaces with the possible build-up of toxic and explosive fumes. The Admiralty surveyed diesel engines and toyed with their fitment in submarines. In 1903 it ordered a British six-cylinder Hornsby-Ackroyd heavy oil engine producing 550hp. The engineering company of Richard Hornsby & Sons in Grantham, Lincolnshire, manufactured the Ackroyd-Stewart engines, one of which was bought by the Admiralty.*

Richard Hornsby (1790–1864) had founded his company, Richard Hornsby & Sons, in 1828. The Ackroyd-Stewart engine built here was brilliantly innovative, but for a small submarine it had drawbacks: it was too big and heavy, and to start it from cold required a hot poultice be applied to the

---

* Though the diesel engine took its name from the German Rudolph Diesel, who is almost universally credited with its creation, there were engineers across the world important to its progress. There is dispute as to who, if other than Diesel, invented the first heavy oil compression-ignition engine. A substantive claim is that it was created in 1890 by the Englishman Herbert Ackroyd-Stewart (1864–1927). Supporters argue it is not a claim, but a fact. Born in Halifax, Yorkshire, Ackroyd-Stewart is another resourceful engineer largely and undeservedly forgotten in the swirl of history. The competition was such that he and Diesel were involved in an acrimonious patents dispute.[9]

cylinder head and dispensed with once the engine had fired. Steam enthusiasts today extol the virtues of the machine, its inventor and manufacturer. In the writing of Britain's industrial, social and military history it is of regret that too often pioneers such as Ackroyd-Stewart and Hornsby are overlooked. Preliminary Admiralty tests on the contraption were promising: it was cheaper to run, more reliable and less volatile than a petrol engine, but owing to its increased weight and size, fuel capacity in the vessels had to be reduced. As the years passed, Vickers effectively became the engineering arm of the Admiralty – indeed, the military in general. Vickers agreed a deal permitting it to build, under licence from MAN Diesel in Germany, diesel engines which utilised its own fuel injection system.*

In 1904 France built the *Z* submarine with two diesel engines and, in 1905, the *Algrette*, powered by a single four-stroke diesel engine. It was clear to submarine lobbyists that the diesel engine personified the future: their cumbersome size, weight and an irritating reluctance to fire were problems which would have to be conquered.

Notes

1   Sueter, Commander M.F., *Submarines, Boats, Mines and Torpedoes* (J. Griffin & Co., 1907), p.151–53

2   Gray, Edwyn, *A Damned Un-English Weapon* (Seeley, Service & Co. Ltd, 1971), p.20

3   Author's visit to cemetery, 27 April 2012

4   Gray, *A Damned Un-English Weapon*, p.20

5   Thompson, *War at Sea*, quotes from Sub Lieutenant Cecil Talbot's diary, (8, 11, 20 June 1905), p.40–41; abbreviated by author

6   Thompson, *War at Sea*, p.39

7   Parson, Petty Officer Fred, 'Service in A-7', *Terra Nova* (The Naval Review, No.3, vol. 59, July 1971) quoted in Winton, John, *The Submariners: Life in British Submarines, 1901–1999: An Anthology of Personal Experience* (Constable, 1999), p.17–19

8   www.plymouthdata.info/PP-ParsonsFA.htm; Scott, Robert and Jones, Max (eds), *Journals: Captain Scott's Last Expedition* (OUP, new edn, 2008)

9   Klooster, John W., *Icons of Invention: Makers of the Modern World from Gutenberg to Gates* (Greenwood Press, 2009); Purday, H.F.P., *Diesel Engine Design* (reproduction *c.* 1920; original, BiblioLife, 2009)

---

*   MAN had extensive experience in heavy oil engines. Rudolf Diesel died in mysterious circumstances after boarding a ship from Antwerp to London. His decomposing corpse was found in the English Channel ten days later. He spent 1893–97 developing his engine at the MAN factory in the Bavarian city of Augsburg. Today MAN is a leading maritime and static diesel engine maker.

Lieutenant Boyle's *E-14* and crew.

6

Before the Tumult

In the decade prior to the start of the Great War in 1914, a diversity of occurrences encouraged the maintenance of a robust navy and submarine service. In 1905 the British Admiralty saw Admiral Togo's Imperial Japanese Navy obliterate the entire Russian Baltic Fleet, its ships outdated and crews ill-trained, in a day. Mutineers in Odessa, Russia, then seized the battleship *Potemkin*, the pride of the Black Sea Fleet; its officers were thrown overboard and the red flag raised. In 1911 India was Britain's shiniest imperial jewel when George V, King emperor, and Mary, the Queen empress, made their royal progress; two years prior, however, in 1909, Sir Curzon Wyllie (1848–1909), a high-ranking official of the British government, was shot dead by Madan Lal Dhingra (1883–1909) of the Indian independence movement. The empire had grown fractious and unrest was seeping through sovereign Britain. In the River Mersey, off Liverpool on Britain's north-west coast, warships protected merchant vessels which were waiting to unload: industrial disputes, striking stevedores, dockers and railway workers had threatened a nationwide famine. An estimated 50,000 troops had been deployed on Britain's streets and the situation had spiralled into one of desperation. Some strikers had been shot dead. Across continents Marxism became an opiate, purveyed by Lenin, Stalin, Trotsky and such cultural icons as Maxim Gorky. China, Japan, Russia, the Ottoman Empire would each would be shaken by tumult. The world was beginning to spin off its axis, stumbling to war. Britain's new arsenal had taken on a terrible urgency and, as a consequence, the once despised submarine was being more widely accepted, though its potential was not fully realised.

In 1909 there was near panic in the House of Commons when the First Lord of the Admiralty, Reginald McKenna (1863–1943) told MPs the government had underestimated German naval growth and that, if its expansion continued, it would have a mightier fleet than the Royal Navy. In reality it lagged behind, but to make a case nothing was more persuasive than to suggest Germany's naval strength could excel that of Britain. New estimates, McKenna claimed, showed that thirteen new *dreadnoughts* would be completed in Germany by 1911, in addition to those in service; two more than Britain's total. The Tory leader Arthur Balfour felt '… the position was so dangerous that it is difficult to realise all its import'.[1] Important civil breakthroughs of military potential had emerged, with army and navy chiefs giving the same grudging consent to swift strides in aviation as that which they had initially bestowed on submarines.*

Any suggestion that the battleship would become largely obsolete, and that at some not too distant point conflicts would be settled primarily from the sky or below the water, would have met with contempt. The majesty of the battleship embodied empire. It personified Britain's imperial greatness and for centuries it had reigned supreme. The navy and its battleships were held in affection by a grateful nation. If the navy was in urgent need of renewal, its battle fleet tired and whiskery, it would have been curmudgeonly not to sanction funding; no matter the pressure on the national purse, or how convincing the arguments for financing new weapons of sky and deep.

In 1912 the First Lord of the Admiralty in Asquith's Liberal government, Winston Churchill, announced to a divided House of Commons that he wanted to spend a record £45 million galvanising the navy with the construction of four new *dreadnoughts*, twenty destroyers, eight cruisers and an unknown number of submarines. Even as he presented his proposals British battleships were being withdrawn from the Mediterranean in a radical redeployment designed to safeguard the North Sea. It was a fundamental change in strategy after talks had collapsed between Britain and Germany about limiting the numbers of big ships being built by each; the mere convening of the talks had demonstrated the financial strains the navy race had put on both economies. The switch of warships from the Mediterranean to the North Sea indicated the certainty of war in the minds of Churchill and the Admiralty. It also showed the seriousness with which the threat of invasion was considered.

---

* In 1909, three months after McKenna had caused Parliamentary alarm about the challenge to Britain's naval supremacy, in Germany the ebullient Count Ferdinand Adolf Heinrich August Graf von Zeppelin (1838–1917) had failed to keep an appointment with his Kaiser in Berlin having crashed his airship into a pear tree on a mountainside near Stuttgart. Shortly afterwards the Frenchman Louis Blériot won a £1,000 *Daily Mail* prize by becoming the first aviator to fly the Channel.

Radio and Other Advances

Civilian breakthroughs held major ramifications for Britain's increasingly confident submarine service. Shipbuilding techniques and submarine construction were being refined and submariners had undergone intensive training.[2] Strides had been made in the engineering and operation of craft. Crews and commanders had become more skilful; masters of the machine rather than its servant, learning its abilities and growing sensitive to its fragilities. The years of familiarisation had paid off. In Germany the Kaiser's belligerence had focused the role of the British submarine service, giving it direction and purpose. Civilian breakthroughs could be adapted for navy benefit. In America in 1913 Henry Ford (1863–1947) altered the face of industry with an assembly line for the *Model T*, the 'motor-car for the multitude'.[*]

Ford's methods seeped slowly into shipbuilding – rarely quick in changing its ways – and helped demonstrate the importance of simplifying submarine design and construction, training engineers and using 'fit-all' components: in the coming war standardisation from drawing board to slipway was key to British and German submarine success.

In 1901 Guglielmo Marconi (1874–1937) had set up his Wireless Telegraph and Signal Company. For the submarine service wireless represented a primary advance. In 1910 the world had been spellbound by its use in the capture of the American acid bath murderer, Dr Harvey Crippen, and his mistress Ethel Le Neve, escaping on the liner SS *Montrose*.[3] Marconi took the glory, but it was Admiral Sir Henry Bradwardine Jackson (1855–1929), a technically gifted officer who played a central role in naval radiotelegraphy and navigation.[4]

A Mixed Bunch

Officers in the Royal Navy during this period of great change comprised a range of talents. Some were of an intellectual bent, such as Reginald Bacon, while some were administrators or valiant leaders. Others were duffers. The eminent naval historian Arthur Marder waspishly summed up Admiral Jackson:

---

[*] 'Marine Fordism' would be seen decades later in the standardised British-designed, US-built *Liberty* ships, produced for the Second World War at breakneck speed: 2,751 were built in just four years by the father of modern American shipbuilding, Henry John Kaiser (1882–1967).

Modest, fearless, and very able, more particularly in the technical sphere. A pioneer of wireless telegraphy, he stood for the application of science to the practical work of the Navy. He never served as a C.-in-C. afloat, which is perhaps just as well, as his personality was hardly of the inspirational type.[5]

Marder quotes the naval commander, writer and submariner Stephen Hall-King (1893–1966):

> There were a number of shockingly bad admirals afloat in 1914. They were pleasant, bluff old sea-dogs, with no scientific training; endowed with a certain amount of common sense, they had no conception of the practice and theory of strategy or tactics.[6]

As war neared, the navy needed flexibility and new thinking to embrace the sweeping changes which the First Sea Lord, Admiral Jacky Fisher, had unleashed. The repercussions from the string of calamities which had befallen the luckless A-class had wounded morale in an infant service still trying to establish itself. The disasters bolstered the submarines' adversaries and added to widespread superstition and irrational fears. The prejudiced blamed the hand of John Philip Holland, despite there being only driblets of his alchemy which still lingered in the A-class genealogy. From more consequential opponents pressure mounted on Fisher to revise or even forsake his support for submarines and torpedoes. Such exigencies merely served to hone his steel, making him more determined that his little toys, as the critics sneered, should prevail; it was a reaction which personified Fisher. The more puissant the opposition, the more uncompromising he would become. Arthur Marder described him:

> Fisher was among the first to foresee the offensive possibilities of the submarine. He had written in 1904: 'I don't think it is even faintly realised – the immense impending revolution which the submarines will affect as offensive weapons of war.' It was, he kept repeating, 'the battleship of the future'. That submarines could destroy dreadnoughts and were therefore a formidable danger to the battle fleet, especially when at sea, was a not uncommon belief by 1914, inside and outside the service.[7]

Fisher's career was pocked by controversy. On becoming the First Sea Lord in 1904 he scrapped 150 ships. It drew plaudits from some and outrage from many. He described redundant vessels as a miser's hoard of old junk: too old to fight, too slow to run. His reforms were overdue, but interpreted by traditionalists as a declaration of war on the navy in which they had spent their lives and built formidable reputations and careers.

Fisher was pugnacious, finger-wagging, short, stocky, round-faced and opinionated. He would become, eventually, a submarine champion; his enthusiasm fired and nurtured by Reginald Bacon who, above others, had kept him informed about the development of the submarine – its weaknesses, successes and potential. While Fisher was at Portsmouth, where he had been the commander-in-chief, he had been able to keep a close eye on the progress of the embryonic submarine flotilla, controlled by Bacon, whose intellect he admired and who had long been one of his favourite officers.

Fisher recognised that the submarine could cause mayhem. At this premature stage of its development, however, he was not shy about embellishing its worth, which both he and Bacon knew to be severely limited. Fisher was also attracted to submarines because of the prevailing animosity towards them in the navy. He could never resist a fight, or starting one. Befriending the submarine tickled his combative streak. It gave him a rationale with which to taunt what he saw as a reactionary cadre whose resistance to change undermined the navy and diluted its credibility. In the military, as in politics, perception counts: if the navy looked archaic, its commanders relics from another age, then its authority would doubtless be diminished.

Britain was at a dangerous point where, yet again, it had to look to its navy to tender the security which it had lent in the past. But its navy had become mothy and hidebound. It needed fresh blood, new thinking and wholesale reform. Fisher supplied it with relish. His methods and manner could infuriate, but the rightness of his objectives was indisputable. A mercurial tangle of strengths and weaknesses, he could embroider his arguments to a point of absurdity. He had a scalding temper, a big ego and an implacable stubbornness, bursting with impudence and vitality. His approach to training and gunnery was revolutionary. His *dreadnought* warships marked a transformation in naval architecture. His backing for the turbine engine and oil in preference to coal would be vital to the navy's future, though diehards branded him an 'oil-maniac'. His endorsement of 'the new arsenal' of submarines – mines, torpedoes (see Appendix N) and a plethora of other changes – that he instituted cannot be overestimated. A dizzying catalyst of unquenchable spirit he did not usher in reform, as detonate it on a grand scale. For all his fizzing energy, however, Fisher was no deity. No individual could guarantee the seismic shift in *attitude* which had become critical. The world's mightiest navy was ossifying: impregnable to criticism, bloated in conceit, content in its certainties which were underwritten by centuries of success.

Naval decay could not have taken root at a more critical juncture. Britain was fully stretched at a time of imperial expansion. A diversity of conflicts flecked the world map. There was a growing European militarism and, in Britain itself, political uncertainty and economic instability. The demands on the British government for more soldiers, sailors and hardware were as pressing as ever. This episode in Fisher's career ended badly with his resignation as First Sea Lord, his downfall ensured by a public and protracted feud with Charles William de la Poer Beresford (1846–1919, the first Baron Beresford, the popular but embittered admiral. Beresford resented Fisher and waged a virulent campaign against him. The affair was of such acrimony it led to a Cabinet inquiry; Beresford's woolly allegations about Fisher's competence and other accusations were dismissed, but the poisonous nature of the dispute brought both careers to an ignoble end and, too, blemished that of Bacon (see Appendix G).

Fisher's ascendancy saw a chasm grow between the Admiralty and the War Office, in part due to Fisher's carping and belligerence. There would always be rivalry between the two services, but Fisher's belittling of the army, his suggestion that the War Office be reorganised along Admiralty lines, and his supposedly jocular remarks which implied that he saw the army as mere shells to be fired by naval cannon, turned competition to feud. At a time when co-operation between army and navy was essential, it was an inappropriate juncture for the chiefs of land and sea to be at loggerheads.[8]

Bacon wrote:

His [Fisher's] advent at the Admiralty was rather like a gust of wind sweeping into and disturbing the calm atmosphere … Mr Churchill having monopolised the red pencils and ink for his minutes, Fisher seized the green and used that colour exclusively. He summoned the heads of the shipbuilding yards, and personally gave them directions; he burned the long drawn-out correspondence which, for years, had niggled about patents, and objections to more than one or two firms building submarine boats; he threw the building of those vessels open to all, and at the same time launched a big shipbuilding programme. Everything began to move. Inertia disappeared. The huge machine creaked and groaned; but it began to work at an increased rate. He was known, feared, loved and obeyed.[9]

The Spirited Roger Keyes

On his appointment, Fisher took Bacon out of submarines and gave him a new role (see Appendix G). It denuded the infant submarine service of its gifted first chief, but beckoned in another talented leader, Roger Brownlow Keyes (1872–1945). Keyes would bring his own style to submarines, one in marked contrast to that of Bacon.[10] As submarine chief, Bacon and Keyes were like chalk and cheese.

Keyes had joined the Royal Navy as a 13-year-old in 1885. In charge of submarines from 1910 to 1914 Keyes was encouraging, approachable, a charmer of dash, though a legion of admirers might concede his enthusiasm could blur into a wild impetuosity. Where Keyes was approachable, Bacon could seem remote and chary. Bacon had climbed the ladder, waving a banner for innovation, thrashing around in Fisher's pond: a clever, precocious blade who threatened an entrenched naval caucus, drawing flak from an old guard reared on conventions once judged immutable and now subsumed by a new code and an altered arsenal which demanded fresh thinking. Bacon sailed through naval exams; Keyes struggled but brought other qualities, those of the hero. Likeable, fiery, buccaneering, there was always a nagging sense he might do something concerning if not entirely barking mad. His surface career had been a series of astonishing adventures. If a situation was seriously dangerous, perhaps with hand-to-hand fighting, cutlasses and boarding parties, the chances of survival slim, he was in his element (see Appendix H).

In 1910 Admiral Sir Arthur Wilson, the First Sea Lord credited with his delicious utterance that foreign submariners should be hanged as pirates, asked Keyes to become the Inspecting Captain of Submarines. Initially Keyes was unsure. Being the chief of submarines needed more than boldness; a technical appreciation was vital. The historian Paul Halpern, in his masterful editing of the *Keyes Papers*, notes:

> Keyes had never considered himself expert in technical matters and he protested to the Naval Secretary that he had no real preparation for this employment. He was told that Wilson wanted an officer with good prospects of eventually making the Admiral's list to bring the Submarine Service into closer touch with the rest of the Fleet. Keyes, whatever his sterling qualities of leadership, had never been considered an intellectual, and his actual academic record in the past was mediocre.[11]

Fisher's reforms had bred him a squadron of enemies. Those officers seen to have benefited from his patronage were tainted, as were navy branches, such as the submarine service, which he had been seen to favour:

While the Submarine Service owed a great deal to Fisher, as well as its first
I.C.S. [Inspecting Captain of Submarines] Captain Reginald H. Bacon, it was
also hurt in subsequent years from its early association with them.[12]

As Halpern points out:

> It is easy to see then why Keyes, despite his lack of technical background,
> had been chosen for the post in an effort to integrate the Submarine Service
> more closely into the remainder of the Fleet.[13]

Keyes had warmth and openness, qualities that Wilson recognised. He was the
right sort to heal wounds inflicted by Fisher's reforms. The submarine service
would always be *different* to the rest of the navy, but, to fulfil its potential it would
have to be seen as independent, not just an addendum to the surface fleet. But
at this early stage it was still fragile. Without fleet embrace it would have been
as nought. Fisher's reforms were necessary but divisive; he had kept submariners
in an exclusive state, separate from the main body of the navy, what Sydney
Hall – Keyes's predecessor and successor as head of the submarine service–
called a 'hugger-mugger' state of isolation. Such tactics kept Fisher's critics in
the dark, making it more difficult for them to dilute his reforms. But they
encouraged a detrimental rivalry and suspicion between so-called progressives
and a more wary and – arguably – conservative navy core. Keyes could bring
submarines in from the cold. What he lacked as a technically minded officer
he compensated for with a ladling of valour and persuasiveness. He was not an
easy touch. He had spine, definite ideas and, on occasion, a hot temper. Nor was
he easily dissuaded. Some thought him downright stubborn. He was what he
was: bold, spirited and sometimes impetuous. Arthur Marder recalls Churchill's
comments in unveiling the tablet to Keyes's memory in St Paul's Cathedral: 'In
many ways his spirit and example seemed to revive in our stern and tragic age
the vivid personality and unconquerable dauntless soul of Nelson himself.'[14]

Acknowledging his technical shortcomings as the submarine chief, Keyes
assembled a committee to help him. It included commanders who had cut
their teeth on the unfortunate *A*-class vessels and who were destined for
distinction in the Great War: Charles 'Tiny' Little, Noel Laurence and Martin
Nasmith. There is a belief that nothing good comes from committees, but
Keyes chose its composition well. He made his headquarters as Inspecting
Captain of Submarines in HMS *Dolphin*, a hulk moored at Fort Blockhouse,
the submarine depot at Gosport, Portsmouth. An office in the Admiralty went
with the job, a handy corner from which to spread the word about submarines
and to keep abreast of the politics and gossip which forever festooned the

early days of the submarine service. In 1910, when he began in his new role, there were seven submarine sections, which, with their depot ships, were established at different ports around Britain.[15] The Home Fleet was reorganised in 1912. Keyes had control of submarine sections in the Home Waters and was responsible to the respective commanders-in-chief of the Home Ports for those submarines assigned to port defence duties. He was also responsible to a newly created command, the 'Admiral of Patrols', for the activities of the others. The first Admiral of Patrols was the gifted Rear Admiral John M. de Robeck (1862–1928) under whom Keyes would serve in the Dardanelles during the Great War. De Robeck's staff officer, Captain William Cowan, had been a friend of Keyes from their days spent together while serving in destroyers. It was a harmonious trio and Keyes' position was enhanced in 1912 when he was awarded the title of commodore second class; the head of submarines would from then on be called Commodore (S).[16]

Continental Acquisition

The period in which Keyes led submarines from 1910 to 1915 was not without altercation. Policy decisions enacted during his tenure – his purchase of foreign-designed submarines and his involvement with steam-driven failures – brought rebuke from inside the navy. His adversaries included the technically adroit Hall, his predecessor and successor as submarine chief. Scotts Shipbuilding in Greenock, Scotland, built the 231ft, steam-driven, Italian-designed *Swordfish* submarine. The Admiralty always wanted big, fast submarines to keep up with the surface vessels of the fleet. The first British-built submarine to have a funnel, *Swordish* proved hopeless and was finally converted into a surface patrol boat. Vickers built another large boat, the 1,270-ton *Nautilus*. At 258ft with a crew of forty-two, she was laid down in 1913 but not completed until 1917. Powered by twin diesels of 3,700hp, she had a surface speed of 17 knots with 1,000hp electric motors which gave 10 knots when the craft was dived. Gargantuan and elephantine she did not see operational use, but was used as a test bed before her ignominious end as a battery charging craft. The two vessels were not the proudest legacies of Keyes' reign as the leader of submarines.

The submarine historian Edwyn Gray wrote:

His [Keyes'] enthusiasm often over-rode his better judgement and some responsibility for the introduction of inadequate submarine designs must be laid at Keyes' door.[17]

Keyes' opinion that steam-driven submarines were 'a simple and well-tried means of propulsion' brought a stinging rebuke from Fisher: 'Like damned fools … we are hankering after steam engines in submarines.'[18] Admiral Sir Geoffrey Layton's verdict on Keyes's handling of the submarine service was equally blunt: 'Keyes made a b— [*sic*] of the submarine programme.'[19] Layton was a former submarine commander whose craft and half his crew were lost in an atrocity in 1915 during the Great War (see Chapter 7).

In buying foreign submarines, Keyes had addressed that which had long caused consternation in military and political circles: the near monopoly of Vickers. Other defence contractors were as minnows. Coventry Ordnance Works, where the first submarine chief Bacon would wash up as the managing director, was nurtured by the government which had encouraged shipbuilders to form a consortium to give Vickers a run for its money. Keyes, abetted by his submarine committee, had decreed that future submarines should be built by new builders. In his search for constructors he had shopped overseas and become naively entangled with the benighted steam-driven submarines. His continental explorations led to a mishmash of inappropriate designs, wasting time and money when the nation could least afford it. Britain's over-arching need was invincibility; the priority should not have been the thwarting of the omnipotent Vickers. Keyes and his committee had decided in 1911 to break the Vickers monopoly, a move which inevitably put noses out of joint – not least that of Vickers – and which in accordance with the contract needed two years' notice.

Sydney Hall had a low opinion of continental boats, including those built in Italy where Keyes and his committee had made enquiries. European boats featured a bewildering array of novel contrivances, whereas Hall favoured simplicity and standardisation. He argued that, during hostilities, it would not be easy to get spares from foreign suppliers in countries with which Britain might be at war. Questions of morale also took on an extra significance at a time of growing international tension. Buying foreign would be a tacit admission of Admiralty dissatisfaction with British designs. Hall's views had an irrefutable logic. He wrote to Keyes:

> I think you have now advertised to Europe that we are not satisfied with our own designs and have lowered the whole of our prestige in submarine work for which we had taken a strong line and kept it.[20]

Hall conceded that, 'it is good news that you [Keyes] have succeeded in breaking the Vickers monopoly agreement or at any rate this is in sight …' but he chided Keyes about the need to maintain technical straightforwardness in the submarine fleet: '… training, interchangeability, stores etc etc. I always advised the Admiralty that simplicity and a homogenous lot was in my opinion worth more than any possible gain in material.'[21]

Keyes despatched a robust rebuttal, describing Hall's remarks as deeply unfair and 'scornful'. Midway through his lengthy riposte he wrote to Hall: 'Now I think I have been almost as rude as you were!'[22] Most historians side with Hall. Paul Akerman wrote:

> The difference between Keyes and Hall could not have been greater. Hall was a technical genius par excellence – Keyes was aggressive to the point of absurdity.[23]

In this aspect of his rumbustious career, history has treated Keyes harshly. He never claimed a technical panache. When approached about the job he demurred because of his technical limitations. He was not without flaws. But his other gifts were so bounteous they compensated for his shortcomings. In times of national emergency bold spirits are beyond price. His daring, or even absurdity, was all part of the package.

Keyes' inspection of foreign submarines caused relations between the government and Vickers to become fractious. This was not new. In making its submarines, ships, tanks, mines, airships and aeroplanes there are other examples of Vickers feeling slighted by government, sometimes with justification. Vickers, however, could also be high-handed if anybody dared remind it that, important though it was, it was only a supplier and not the government. While politicians were suspicious of Vickers' power and profits – there was a continuing resentment about its margins – they did not have money or mandate to assume its role. No politician with an eye on the ballot box would dare risk the ire of the electorate were things to go wrong: submarines were a new science with few templates to guide and no guarantee of success. Though perennially ill at ease about the relationship, *all* governments depended on Vickers to bear the cost of research and to carry the brunt of the risks. Eventually a thaw would set in and the usual state of stressed normality would resume between whichever transient politicians held centre stage and the less impermanent stronghold of fortress Vickers.

In sending his emissaries overseas, Keyes was doing the bidding of his masters and was made to subsequently carry the can. His critics assume a sterner line, as Akerman commented:

> He [Keyes] went abroad to obtain what he wanted … the results were catastrophic, unfortunately, as these efforts produced nothing else but a motley

collection of what at best could be called experimental submarine types, which added practically nothing to the strength of the British submarine service ... [this] caused the Royal Navy in 1914 to lay behind the Imperial German Navy with respect to submarines of the overseas type.[24]

Keyes' inspectors, however, had reported back that Britain had much to learn from foreign yards. In the *Keyes Papers* it was noted:

> To avoid a time consuming period of experimentation an order was placed for a FIAT-type submarine. This was based on the design of Engineer Major Cesar Laurenti and the submarine – designated *S.1* – was to be built by the Scotts yard in Greenock, Fiat's licensee in Great Britain.[25]

Keyes' submarine committee also inspected French Maxime Laubeuf submarines, which were being built at the Schneider yards in Toulon. Laubeuf was a designer of élan. His craft, though, were rejected. While appropriate for the Mediterranean they were seen as being too delicate for the North Sea. Nevertheless, in a moment of inexplicable abandon, the negative reports were ignored and two boats, dubbed *W.1* and *W.2*, were ordered. They would be built by Schneider's licensee in Britain, Armstrong Whitworth and Co. Another Italian boat, designed by Laurenti and to be built by Scotts, was the *Swordfish*, mentioned earlier. Not to be outdone, Vickers submitted designs for a large 'oversea' submarine; the government bought one, the *Nautilus*. When the war began, orders had been placed for several other designs: the Vickers–designed coastal submarine, the *V*-class and Admiralty designed *F*- and *G*-class boats. Keyes' experimental building programme was only beginning at the advent of the war in 1914:

> The service record of the continental boats was unsatisfactory. By the summer of 1914 the Germans were ahead in the number of overseas submarines. The Royal Navy had a plethora of different types in service or in production but few were effective as overseas vessels.[26]

Some of the building of the experimental boats was farmed out to private yards. Akerman:

> Scotts Shipbuilding of Greenock built three: *S1*, *S2* and *S3* submarines which originated from designs by Engineer Major Cesare Laurenti, Italy's leading designer ... unreliable and unseaworthy they were inappropriate for the demands of the North Sea, having been designed for the usually kinder

waters of the Mediterranean. After Italy's entry into the war on 24 May 1915 the British got rid of them by their transfer to the Royal Italian Navy in September 1915.[27]

Arthur Marder:

> In the pre-war decade ... the Admiralty saw the new craft mainly as a potent defensive weapon, a final insurance against invasion. Until the war, therefore, the principal duty of submarines in British war plans was to co-operate with the older destroyer flotillas for coastal defence. Tirpitz, it should be mentioned, showed no signs before the war of a belief in the submarine. He saw in it only a defensive weapon for German harbours and their approaches. The early war successes of the U-boats surprised him, and it was not until January 1915, or nearly six months after the war began, that he conceived the plan of a submarine blockade of Great Britain.[28]

As Paul Halpern maintains, one can apportion individual blame, but it was the Admiralty which had failed to register the potential of the submarine. It emphasised the notion that surface warfare would play the major role in hostilities. It was a wrong assessment and it was fortunate for Britain that Germany and Tirpitz initially shared that view. The one real example of 'big ship' conflict would be the costly and inconclusive Battle of Jutland in 1916.

When war came Fisher was brought back to his old job as First Sea Lord by Churchill, his admirer and friend, who was by then the First Lord of the Admiralty. Their closeness proved explosive. Fisher had replaced Louis Mountbatten (see Appendix E).

Enter the Kaiser

In the years preceding the Great War, a new reason had emerged for keeping the Royal Navy well resourced. It was in part to do with securing its expanding and troublesome empire and the continuance of its uneasy relationship with France. But another ominous imperative for pouring money into the seemingly bottomless coffers of the Royal Navy had become evident: the Kaiser. Britain's traditional enemy was France, who had long been a formidable maritime power, and she was still deemed by many as the most likely candidate for fresh hostilities. France had forged an agreement with Russia, which grew strained, but which at the time added to a prevailing consternation in Britain. The ingenuity of her submarine inventors who offered a variety of designs to the

French Navy, some of which were too ingenious to be practical, had given her the lead in technology and construction. It would also be the diversity of her submarines that would contribute to her eventual undoing. France and Britain had signed the Entente Cordiale in 1904, but it would take more than a flimsy political initiative to quell the clamour of anti-French sentiment in Britain and the generations of mistrust which still divided the two nations. The British attitude was that her oldest foe still had to be carefully watched.

In addition to suspicions about the French, the increasingly ominous antics of Germany's Kaiser Wilhelm II (1859–1941) were turning British apprehension into alarm. The German Navy believed that the key to military dominance lay in the control of the North Sea; to achieve its jurisdiction would necessitate building a fleet superior in number and efficacy to that of the British. To the prescient it had been clear from the moment that Wilhelm removed the German Chancellor, Otto Von Bismarck, in 1890, that Queen Victoria's rash and strong-willed grandchild was intent on war. After von Bismarck's demise the Kaiser had taken Germany on a thunderous and bankrupting ride, which could only lead to one outcome – war. The building of the Kiel Canal had sped up traffic between the Baltic and the North Sea; its completion ahead of schedule in 1895 was perceived as another powerful incentive to German military and naval ambitions.

Alfred Thayer Mahan

Before his accession the Kaiser had been consumed by a rabid nautical hunger, a craving fed by the scale and success of Britain's navy and which he was determined that Germany should match. Under his swaggering leadership Germany would follow the philosophy of the influential American naval strategist, Alfred Thayer Mahan (1840–1914), and Mahan's conviction that naval strength was central to the success of a nations' foreign policy. Mahan's philosophies had a palpable effect on naval thinking across the globe and, in particular, America, where administrations down the decades would subsequently give emphasis to the scale and potency of the US fleet.

Kaiser Wilhelm was convinced by the arguments of Mahan's seminal work, *The Influence of Sea Power upon History 1660–1783*. He arranged for its translation into German and its serialisation in newspapers. The Kaiser saw it as a persuasive tool in a propaganda campaign which aimed to convince Germany and its people of the need for an advanced navy and the wisdom of devoting to it huge amounts of public money.

Alfred von Tirpitz

The Kaiser began a total restructuring of the German Imperial Admiralty. The redoubtable Admiral Alfred von Tirpitz (1849–1930) was brought in as its principal architect. Wilhelm had an alarming impetuosity; though not a far-seeing strategist or reader of men, his appointment of Tirpitz was astute. With an innate naval flair, harnessed to energy and efficiency, Tirpitz was a formidable commander.

The Kaiser was consumed by his navy and its affairs: he catechised his naval chiefs, determined to learn each nuance of command, the ways of ships and the sea, the whole gamut of nautical subtleties and maritime lore. One is reminded of the young Winston Churchill when he was appointed First Lord of the Admiralty in 1911. Churchill ingested great quantities of facts and minutiae about the sea and its servants; he became a disciple possessed of an encyclopaedic knowledge. It was Fisher who had stoked Churchill's naval ardour, beguiling him with his energy, directness and charm – amid the clash and furore which attends Fisher, his charm is sometimes overlooked. Further comparison of Churchill and the Kaiser would be invidious, but fervour for the sea and their navies they certainly shared.

Tirpitz became a convinced advocate of submarines, though his initial response, characteristic of an officer whose career had been largely in the surface navy, was not one of great enthusiasm. Government monies were poured into building a new German fleet that would include versions of Fisher's big-gun dreadnoughts with which the Kaiser and von Tirpitz were enamoured. So much funding was allocated to the new fleet that it weighed further on the already stressed and heavily burdened German economy, in itself a contributory incentive for going to war.

Tirpitz, his avidity reminiscent of Fisher, was made Grand Admiral in 1911. At the start of the war in 1914 he was given command of the German fleet. Germany passed its First Fleet Act in 1889, sanctioning funding and support for the 'new' German Navy. A Second Fleet Act in 1900 imposed a seventeen-year deadline to build thirty-six battleships, two flagships and forty-five large and small cruisers. Though unrealistic, the German building target focused minds in the British Admiralty and prompted urgency in its own programme of naval modernisation. Thus it acted as a catalyst for an arms and naval race, a worrying possibility which was always inherent in following Mahan's creed. Mahan, a former US naval officer, believed that in building a strong navy a nation might fend off its enemies and thus avoid conflict; in the race to reinforce naval power in the years up to the First World War his theories seem to have misfired. It was not only Britain and Germany which chose to out-build each other;

other nations which joined in the navy race included Japan, her navy eager to enhance its potential.

Admiral Tirpitz's belief in submarines resulted in the building of a new submarine force. Germany had been late into the development of the submarine, but once started its progress would be impressive. His interest in submarines had been piqued when he served as commander of a torpedo flotilla, and was later put in charge of the German torpedo fleet. From being an avowed sceptic, Tirpitz had become a submarine disciple.[29] With the realisation that Britain's surface fleet remained the largest in the world, that in the skills of its sailors and experience of its commanders it more than matched that of Germany, Tirpitz's conversion from querulous to convert was complete. Exercised about Britain's navy, which still excelled despite Germany financing her extensive and expensive naval rebirth, he invested faith in submarine warfare. His reasoning was plain: at the start of the war Germany could muster twenty-nine battleships against Britain's forty-nine. As it transpired, the Battle of Jutland in 1916 was the only real 'open ocean' contest of the First World War. Had there been more, it still appears unlikely that Tirpitz and his fleet would have prevailed given the numerical superiority of the Royal Navy. Tirpitz could build a fleet of submarines quickly and cheaply if its assembly was compared to the cost and build time for a single warship. He aimed to sink as many ships as possible to achieve a level of equality between the number of British and German surface vessels.

Germany had launched its first submarine in 1906, at a time when America, Britain, France and others had already garnered comprehensive experience in their construction and operation. In Britain, Fisher was also impatient for more submarines and crews. He told Churchill his contacts in the industry had assured him that at least twenty new submarines could be laid down immediately and be completed within twelve months – Fisher's manner helped concentrate builders' minds. Days later he convened a meeting of shipbuilders and naval chiefs to discuss exactly how many submarines he wanted and when; if yards found they were stifled by bureaucracy he told them to short circuit the usual channels and deal directly with Sydney Hall. The pace at which boats

---

* Fisher succeeded Walter Talbot Kerr (1839–1927) as First Naval Lord. Kerr's career had included service in the Crimean War (1854–55) and the Indian Mutiny (1857). During his tenure as Admiral of the Fleet and First Naval Lord – the title was later changed to First Sea Lord – Kerr, unlike Fisher, had not been markedly supportive of submarines. With a whirlwind zeal, Fisher challenged the conservative approach of Kerr and his fellow naval grandees.

were built, and the speed with which crews and engineers were trained, is a mystery. In taking Fisher at his word, those involved dispensed with paperwork from which the detail of the programme could have been tracked. Historian Nicholas Lambert writes:

> The Admiralty archives contain only a handful of documents on the design and building of submarines during the First World War, and almost none on the wartime expansion and administration of the Submarine Service. Similarly, the surviving files created by the Commodore of Submarines and his staff hold few clues as to how they achieved a fourfold increase in submarine personnel without compromising the standards of crew efficiency that before the war were held to be essential to the efficient and safe operation of submarine boats.[30]

Fisher's urgent determination to ensure Britain had enough submarines for the Great War prompted him to open up production to British private builders, as previously production had been restricted to Vickers and naval yards. Secondly, he contacted an American, Charles Schwab (1862–1939), who had clout as a financier and industrialist.*

Fisher asked Schwab to supply the Royal Navy with American submarines. Nicholas Lambert:

> Schwab agreed and promised to deliver within eight months 20 craft of a type approved by the American Navy. Eventually the US Navy's *H-design* of 1911 was selected, not because it was the best available, but because the Navy Department [in America] objected to their more modern designs being given to the British. In any case this brought the total number of submarines ordered by the Royal Navy since the beginning of the war up to 63. In December [1914] preparations were made to build 42 more boats in the state-owned Royal Dockyards ... this number was curtailed, however, after Churchill questioned whether the Navy really needed so many.[31]

Despite engineering ingenuity, it is no exaggeration that, even by this relatively late stage of development, petrol-powered submarines were still – at

---

* Charles Schwab was president of US Steel from 1901 to 1903; chairman of Bethlehem Steel from 1904 to 1939; and Director-General Emergency Fleet Corporation from 1917 to 1918, when the German U-boat menace was at its peak.

their most primitive – underwater bombs waiting to explode. Some did. It is remarkable more did not. Labyrinthine electric wiring held huge dangers; exposed webs of wiring became white-hot, sparking and crackling; electricity circuits malfunctioned with alarming frequency, rendering boats dangerous, unreliable and subject to violent surges in power. Electricity and water is a lethal combination. Batteries which leaked or were invaded by sea water emitted toxic fumes. The B-class boats, as an example, had over 150 battery cells and carried 16 tons of petrol, the fumes of which could readily accumulate and ignite.

Improving British Submarines

Development had hastened across the globe. In Britain the badly hit A-class were followed by the larger B-class, of which eleven were built between 1904 and 1906. While an improvement on their forerunners, the B-class still had serious limitations: they were too slow; they could not stay out long, as they had no crew accommodation; internally they were of an open-plan design bereft of bulkheads, which exposed the crew to engine fumes and din and offered no defence against fire, explosion or inundation. Built by Vickers they cost in the region of £47,000 each and were intended as coastal patrol boats. At 142ft long and 12.7ft wide they had petrol engines. Though petrol units were hazardous, heavy oil engines were still insufficiently developed. Their engines were more powerful than the A-class: a 600hp petrol unit on the surface and a 180hp electric motor underwater. Their surface range was 1,000 miles and they could dive to 100ft, though operational experience as opposed to theoretical figures suggested that 50ft was more prudent – in the Great War, however, it is known that many dived close to 100ft. They had a crew of fifteen, displaced 287 tons on the surface and had twin torpedo tubes in the bows. Though still perilous, the B-class had a muscularity which the A-class lacked.

The A-class submarines were followed by the construction of the C-class. There were thirty-eight C-class boats built between 1906 and 1910. The C-class boats marked the conclusion of vessels which were seen as derivatives – though they were by now almost entirely British – of the *Holland* building programme. Most significantly the C-class boats were the last to be powered by petrol engines. They were followed by the much more potent D and E-class submarines, built specifically as long-range vessels and which had diesel engines and radio fitted as standard (see Appendices K and M).

A Slow Acceptance

Submarines and the service were growing up; the boats were becoming more formidable and technically able, and the service was establishing its own character and conventions. The submarine branch would not always be an errant child of the senior service, a cheeky upstart to be tolerated. It would grow into an exclusive club with demanding rules of admission and codes of behaviour. The sniping had lessened. Harsh critics had mellowed: even Admiral Wilson – old 'ard 'eart – would become a supporter, albeit a reluctant one. Better craft enhanced physical well-being and self-worth. Crews would grow proud of their once-derided trade. The lot of the submariner would remain damp to soggy, but it was preferable to be on a more business-like boat than one of John Holland's drenching tiddlers, the undeserving butt of jibes from naval panjandrums. The enlarged proportions of the boats made them marginally more seaworthy and compliant, though they were still capricious. But as any seasoned submariner would observe, find one that is not. This confounded the lugubrious and their insistence that size and weight would be fatal. The predictions were dire: bigger submarines would sink, be impossible to manoeuvre and be too heavy for their engines. It was all poppycock. Increased size gave boats greater stability and more buoyancy, though buoyancy was still insufficient, a weakness of the *Hollands* and subsequent *A*-class (Appendix K).

Flying the Flag

Three submarines, *C-36*, *C-37* and *C-38*, made a remarkable passage from Portsmouth to Hong Kong in February–April 1911. Such exploits were valuable in testing boats and crews, in garnering positive headlines and in confirming the worth of the submarine to naval chiefs. It was a way of flying the flag in distant corners where Britain had strategic and economic interests, and it was cheaper and less bothersome than committing warships with huge crews. The success and length of the *C*-class voyage confounded sceptics. It demonstrated the robustness of craft, the resolve of their commanders and crews, and the distances that could be covered. Accompanied by a mothership, HMS *Monmouth*, the trio of boats had to withstand cruel circumstances, including the weather. The skipper of one of the boats, Lieutenant Commander A.A.L. Fenner, wrote:

A strong NE wind turned the swell into a wicked waste of angry waters. The *Monmouth*, in spite of her 9,800 tons, was having a bad time, but her officers with anxiety watched the three little *C*'s battened down and once more taking it green. Indeed the cruiser's people marvelled that such a craft could stand so much. Frequently the boats would disappear under the waves, and the watchers never expected to see them again. Through forty-eight miserable hours this continued, with salt-water leaking down, wetting everybody's clothes and bedding.

The boats rolled and wallowed a great deal, spilling more acid from their batteries, and at the worst moment one of *C-37*'s men cut a vein while trying to open a sardine tin. Blood spurted all over the place and intensified the general adversity, until tourniquets were applied and the man could be given attention. It was a battered and rusty trio of boats which arrived in Hong Kong harbour on the morning of April 20, but they had proved to the world the ancient truth that small vessels will usually go through more weather than any human being has the heart to drive them. Everyone felt most trying the cramped space, lack of exercise and being battened down for hour after hour with little air and excessive heat. On a number of occasions it became necessary to stop all cooking, and in fine weather an electric boiler was rigged up abaft the conning tower.

For most of the journey *C-37* carried only two officers, which meant watch-and-watch, four hours on and four hours off by day, but at night three hours on and off. The seamen were in four watches likewise. In a surface ship, during almost any weather, you can at least walk about, but here in these boats no space was available, so that the personnel used to suffer a good deal from cramp.[32]

The traditional problem of hygiene was one of many difficulties. Submariners had become deft at innovation, as Lieutenant Commander Fenner described:

Bathing in tropical shark-infested waters presented a problem, but a canvas bag was rigged up on the upper deck and filled with fresh water.

The mothership supplied the submarines with provisions, the boats being too small to store food. Crews were each given 9.5*d* per day:

Every three or four days the parent-ship would stop and send along those articles previously asked for by signal; it was a novel method of deep-sea shopping. For the officers each boat began with six boxes containing everything to mess three persons during a week, apart from eggs, vegetables and fruit.

Staying healthy in such circumstances was something else to contend with:

> Very few incidents of sickness occurred during those weeks of varied temperatures, and notwithstanding all the dampness. Each evening the submarine's captain mustered his men, serving our pills, castor oil or quinine as required. In short the record voyage had been achieved not less by means of discipline and good organisation than by patient endurance with pluck.[33]

Fisher's Inshore Submarines

Fisher had suggested deploying submarines instead of laying mines to guard harbour entrances. It resulted in the construction of submarines designed primarily as inshore craft. Strategic implications, however, were only part of his thinking. He could also diminish the importance of the army – his old adversary – while strengthening his beloved navy. It was the practice that mines were laid by army engineers. If he could reduce the number of mines and the number of army engineers who laid them then the money saved could be allocated to the navy for building new submarines. At a stroke he would have diminished the role of the army and enhanced that of the navy. However, his plan had a damaging long-term effect. Insufficient consideration would be given to building submarines as long-range predators: a desideratum of its earliest creators that would allow it to achieve its full potential. The submarine was seen for too long as merely a fleet addendum. A distant role at this stage would, however, have been impractical because of the reliance on petrol engines. Though constantly modified and improved, petrol units in submarines would always be unreliable to dangerous and would inhibit operational value. Until a copacetic diesel was devised, the craft and its effectiveness would remain impaired.

The *D*- and *E*-Class

The birth of the British *D*-class marked a leap forward (see Appendix K). There were eight built between 1909 and 1912. Unlike their forerunners they were conceived as overseas boats. From the uncertainty that had presaged the arrival of the *Hollands* nine years before, the Admiralty had acted with surety. Its boldness was to do with Fisher's belief and a recognition by the Admiralty of civilian advances that could be turned to naval advantage.

The first of the *D*-class had been laid down in 1907 and commissioned two years later. They had two fundamental improvements: diesel engines and wireless. Experiments in telegraphy had met with mixed success on previous boats, but the ocean-going *D*-class were the first to have wireless as standard. Aerials were attached to a mast on the conning tower to be lowered before diving (see Appendix K). The *D*-class had double hulls like French craft and were heavier and bulkier than predecessor boats: *D*-class boats displaced some 500 tons, almost double that of the *B* and *C*-class vessels.

The ensuing *E*-class were highly accomplished submarines built, like the *D*-class, for distant offensives. By the start of the war in 1914 the navy had eleven of them. The *E*-class provided the mainstay for British operations during the Great War, with fifty-seven being built from 1913 to 1917. This included six minelayers, with two of the class built for the Australian submarine service. With a crew of thirty they were 181ft long and 22.5ft wide, displaced 660 tons on the surface, markedly more than the *D*-class, and had a surface speed of 16 knots and 10 knots if dived. They also had four 18in torpedo tubes for and aft. The *E*-class were the most reliable and potent submarines in the Great War. Naval leaders had finally begun to appreciate the full potential of the submarine. In 1912 John Jellicoe, the Vice Admiral of the Atlantic Fleet and later in command of the Grand Fleet said:

> What is it that the coming of the submarine really means? It means the whole foundation of our traditional naval strategy, which served us so well in the past, has been broken down![34]

Notes

1   Mercer, Derrick and Burne, Jerome, *Chronicle of the 20th Century* (Longman 1988), p.126
2   Williams, Archibald, *Victories of the Engineer* (Thomas Nelson and Sons, *c*. 1915), chapter 111
3   Mercer, Derrick and Burne, Jerome (eds), *Chronicle of the World* (Longman, 1989)
4   Hackmann, Willem, *Seek & Strike* (HMSO, 1984), p.23, 33, 119, 227; Black, Jeremy, *Tools of War: The Weapons that Changed the World* (Quercus, 2007), p.150–52
5   Marder, Arthur J., *From the Dreadnought to Scapa Flow: The Royal Navy in the Fisher Era, 1904–19, The Road to War*, vol. 1 (Oxford University Press, 1961), p.407
6   King-Hall, Commander Stephen, *My Naval Life, 1906–1929* (Faber, 1952), pp.97–98; Marder, *Dreadnought to Scapa Flow*, vol. 1, p.406
7   Marder, *Dreadnought to Scapa Flow*, p.332
8   Gough, Barry M., *A War of Combinations: First Lord of the Admiralty and First Sea Lord* (Churchill Archives)

9 Bacon, *The Life of Lord Fisher of Kilverstone*, vol. 2 (Hodder & Stoughton, 1929), p.181–62

10 Captain Edgar Lees was Bacon's immediate successor as Inspecting Captain of Submarines, 1904–6. In 1906 Lees retired from active service to become managing director of the Whitehead Torpedo Factory. He was followed by Sydney Hall as ICS, 1906–10. Hall was Keyes' predecessor and successor. Hall was well thought of by Fisher but Hall said his career suffered by being seen as a Fisher protégé and that when he arrived in submarines the service was 'hugger-mugger'. When Keyes left, the technically accomplished Hall was brought back into the service a second time, first as Captain Supervising Submarine Construction, 1914–15, being made Commodore of Submarines, 1915–18

11 Halpern (ed.), *The Keyes Papers*, vol. 1, 1914–1918 (The Navy Records Society, 1972, pp. xx–xxiv; National Maritime Museum, ref: 061.22NRS 1972 PBE1863/1)

12 Halpern (ed.), *The Keyes Papers*, p.xxi

13 Halpern (ed.), *The Keyes Papers*, p.xxi

14 Marder, Arthur J., *From the Dreadnought to Scapa Flow: Victory and Aftermath, 1918–1919*, vol. 5 (Oxford University Press, 1970), p.322

15 Halpern (ed.), *The Keyes Papers*, p.xxi

16 Halpern (ed.), *The Keyes Papers*, p.xxi

17 Gray, *A Damned Un-English Weapon*, p.23

18 Gray, *A Damned Un-English Weapon*, p.22

19 Everitt, Don, *K Boats*, interview with Layton, March 1961 (Airlife Publishing, 1999), p.11

20 Correspondence Hall to Keyes, sent from HMS *Diana*, Mediterranean, 7 October 1911, Keyes Mss 4/22, in Lambert, Nicholas (ed.), *The Submarine Service 1900–1918* (Ashgate for the Navy Records Society, 2001), pp.171–72

21 Lambert, *Submarine Service*, Hall-Keyes, 7 October 1911, p.171

22 Correspondence Keyes to Hall, sent from HMS *Dolphin*, Gosport, 19 October 1911, Keyes Mss 4/22, in Lambert (ed.), *The Submarine Service*, pp.173–78

23 Akerman, Paul, *Encyclopaedia of British Submarines, 1901–1955* (Liskeard Maritime, 1989), p.1

24 Akerman, *Submarine Encyclopaedia*, pp.176–77

25 Halpern (ed.), *The Keyes Papers*, p.xxi

26 Halpern (ed.), *The Keyes Papers*, p. xxii–xxiii; quoting Commander F.W. Lipscomb, *The British Submarine* (London, 1954), pp.79–82, 85–86

27 Akerman, *Submarine Encyclopaedia*

28 Marder, *From the Dreadnought to Scapa Flow*, vol. 5, p.334

29 Black, Jeremy, *Naval Power* (Palgrave Macmillan, 2009), pp.153–154

30 Lambert, Nicholas (ed.), *The Submarine Service 1900–1918*, p.xxxii

31 Lambert, Nicholas (ed.), *The Submarine Service 1900–1918*, p.xxxiii

32 Winton, John (ed.), *The Submariners* (Constable, 1999), p.27; extract from the private diary of Lieutenant Commander A.A.L. Fenner, commanding officer *C-37*, published in Keble-Chatterton, E., *Amazing Adventure* (Hurst & Blackett, 1935)

33 Winton, *Submariners*, p.28; diary Fenner

34 Memorandum in the papers of the British Admiral Jellicoe, 1912; quoted in Black, Jeremy, *Tools of War: The Weapons that Changed the World* (Quercus, 2007), p.146

Jacky Fisher, First Sea Lord 1904-10 and 1914-15.

7

Pioneers at War

Fisher had predicted with uncanny accuracy that the Great War would start by the middle of 1914, and that the prompt completion of the building of the Kiel Canal, allowing Germany to speed its warships with relative impunity from the Baltic to the North Sea, would hasten its coming. The double act of Churchill as First Lord and Fisher as his right-hand man – chairman and managing director – was powerful but explosive. Fisher had left the Admiralty three years earlier aged 70, a casualty of the poisonous Beresford affair (see Appendix G). He had been ennobled as the 1st Baron Fisher of Kilverstone. Kilverstone is in the county of Norfolk on Britain's eastern flank; an appropriate stomping ground for the mercurial Fisher, being the birthplace of Nelson. Fisher returned as the energetic and vociferous whirlwind he had been at his exit. But for a second time his appointment would end in resignation triggered by the Gallipoli – also known as the Dardanelles – campaign of 1915–16 in Turkey, then the Ottoman Empire (see Appendix L). The Dardanelles campaign was a joint British and French operation to seize the capital city of Constantinople and secure a sea route to Russia. It resulted in 130,000 dead and was a military debacle, apart from the role of the embryo submarine service. Fisher quit after volcanic rows with Churchill about the efficacy of the Gallipoli strategy.

By the start of the First World War in August 1914 the role of the submarine was still being decided. Britain's east coast would become busy with the establishment of nine submarine bases. Communications to and from the boats remained flawed; not all boats had radios and, in any event, the apparatus was still coarse. Surface vessels and submarines could not talk to each other; nor could submarines talk one to another; and trying to communicate with shore-based command centres would always be insecure and trepidatious. Poor communications subsequently led to chaotic and alarming events with Allied submarines and ships mistaking one another for the enemy.

Pigeon-Post

Lieutenant Cecil Talbot, mentioned earlier in the narrative as a young commander who went on to a distinguished career, was one of the first submariners to discover the danger of haphazard communications. By the time the war was declared the Admiralty had begun its fleet dispersal, although, given the protracted period the drums had been beating, the navy was not as ready as might have been thought. At the hour at which the conflict became official Talbot, the commander of the submarine *E6*, was in the company of two other submarines in the Heligoland Bight, off the north coast of Germany. Talbot was part of a naval force hoping to lure German surface ships out of their safe harbour. Talbot's son is quoted as saying:

> The German ships did not leave port but at one stage he did see, through his periscope, four large ships moving at full speed directly towards him.

One of the few ways a ship could attack a submarine was by ramming it, going full-pelt at a submarine in the hope of chopping it in two:

> He [Talbot] had received no information of any surface ships in the area and was justified in assuming that they were German. He therefore prepared to fire torpedoes. Only at the last moment did he identify the White Ensign and aborted the action. This avoided a potential disaster of huge possible consequence.[1]

Cecil Talbot was one of the first submariners in the Great War to use pigeons to compensate for the inadequacies of radio. In 1915, a year into the conflict, his submarine, on this occasion *E16*, had snared itself on a mine. Managing to free his craft, he released a carrier pigeon to warn the Admiralty about the whereabouts of the mine. Talbot's son continues the story:

> The pigeon flew to its owner in Essex who unwrapped the message and bicycled with it to the local post office, whence they tapped out a message

to the Admiralty. Wireless was in its infancy and communication with submarines was a real problem, except perhaps by pigeon, a clever ruse originated by my father.[2]*

The Terror of its Presence

Some in the Admiralty now saw submarines, despite their shortcomings and the difficulties of communication, as a triumph. Others remained unconvinced, partly out of prejudice but also through genuine concerns about reliability. Some early craft forced into service were inadequate: risky for crews, of dubious technology and devoid of bite. An *imagined* terror, however, is one of the submarines' strengths. Whether underwater attack dog or a toothless mutt in reality, its deterrent lay in its reputation as a bringer of mayhem. For a while two principal reasons kept submarines close to home: deployment to distant locations would have stretched still new technology to the limit; secondly, the threat of invasion was seen by many as a priority, though Fisher was steadfast that in the event of such incursion the surface marine would be sufficient to thwart it.

Devoid of Pace

The slowness of the submarine compared to surface ships posed problems. For a submarine to keep up with the fleet was arduous to impossible. The speed of the fleet required a submarine to set off in advance in the expectation it would be caught up by surface ships. It should have been a simple exercise, but it was complicated by the need for surface ships to maintain a high speed of 22–24 knots to outrun the possible presence of U-boats, whereas submarines did well to make 12–13 knots. Engines had improved but were not Herculean: to run for an extensive duration at maximum speed over great distances in order to stay abreast of the fleet would have been injudicious.

---

* Carrier pigeons were used by airshipmen who had learned from submariners and naval practice; early non-rigid (devoid of a rigid frame to support the envelope) reconnaissance airships had to let their stations know where they had come down in the commonplace event of a forced landing.

The Blockading Submarine

Despite its handicaps the submarine became especially important in three theatres: the North Sea, the Baltic and the Dardanelles. The *D*-class, the later *E*-class and German U-boats, were the first ocean-going submarines. In their design and purpose the future of the submarine was evident. In the way the surface fleet would reluctantly institute one of its oldest strategies to counter the U-boat threat, the convoy system, so the historic contingency of blockading an enemy, by using submarines, came into use. Its purpose was to pen in or tempt out the enemy's fleet. Secondly, it extinguished a nations supply lines. Either way, to box in or lure out the German fleet conceded control of the seas to Britain. If the German High Seas Fleet, which was modern but still no match for the British Grand Fleet, ventured from its well-defended corner of the Heligoland Bight, it faced decimation by the larger British fleet and, arguably, by its finer gunnery, of which Fisher had been a foremost advocate. Irrespective of its numerical superiority, any fleet which challenged that of Britain faced a daunting prospect: the British Grand Fleet arrived backed by centuries of naval prowess, a global reputation sufficient in itself to dent the morale of its foes, not that the officers and men in the German fleet lacked confidence. As well as stifling the German force, an effective blockade of its coastline and sea routes would be detrimental to its populace; it could result in civilian disquiet, with starvation being another of wars' hideous sideshows and one of its most effective.

As an instrument of blockade the submarine had inherent virtues. Surface ships effecting a blockade were vulnerable, not least from air attack; the ascendancy of the aeroplane had been swift, its advance spurred by conflict. No such vulnerabilities hampered the blockading submarine. Its clandestine characteristics of guile, concealment and its ability to slink away to a new location would come to the fore, the traits of the predator which critics still thought sly and improper. Queasiness about the ethics of the submarine played an immeasurable part in slowing its development; in the exigencies of war such qualms tend to be suspended. One by one different nations moved rapidly to bolster their submarine fleets, finally recognising the true value of the submarine as a deadly predator that could be deployed in distant theatres of conflict.

The First Attack

The first submarine attack of the Great War happened on 8 August 1914. A German U-boat, *U-15*, fired a torpedo at an *Orion*-class battleship, HMS *Monarch*, a ship of the Second Battle Squadron of the Grand Fleet. At the time of the assault the *Monarch* was engaged in gunnery practice off the remote Scottish island of Fair Isle, part of the Shetlands. There was comment that one might have expected the *Monarch* to be in a greater state of readiness, war having been declared four days before on 4 August. Others felt the dastardly Hun was not playing cricket; after all, the *Monarch* was quietly minding its own business in British waters while indulging in a spot of gunnery practice. The U-boat had fired a torpedo but missed, causing astonishment among those on the *Monarch*. The former submarine commander Richard Compton-Hall wrote:

> The *Monarch*, slowly working herself up to regal fury four days after war was declared ... the torpedo missed but the track put the British ships on their guard. The lookouts started to take a keen interest in affairs. Towards evening a periscope was sighted by both HMS *Dreadnought* and the flagship *Iron Duke*. Both put their helms hard over and sheered out of line to ram whatever lay beneath the slender glass-tipped tube; but the U-boat slipped down into the depths and easily escaped. The first attack and counter-attack had failed.[3]*

The next morning, as dawn broke over the mist-shrouded waters, the cruiser *Birmingham*, part of a screening force ahead of the battle squadrons, happened on a sight which sent frissons of excitement through the ship and its company: there in the fog lay the submarine *U-15*, exposed and vulnerable. Through the mist an incessant banging and hammering rang across the water. She had broken down and her crew had been trying with a growing desperation to repair their engine. The *Birmingham* spurted towards her, firing at close range, bearing down, ramming into her, her giant bows slicing her in half. The sinking of *U-15* endorsed the malaise of those who remained unconvinced about the dangers of the submarine: here was proof that a ship could easily despatch a flimsy U-boat. Such confidence was short-lived. Less than a month later, HMS *Pathfinder*, a scout cruiser, won naval immortality by becoming the first ship to be sunk by a self-guided torpedo.**

The loss of the *Pathfinder* on 5 September 1914, a sunny, peaceful Saturday afternoon, cost the lives of 259 – an estimate as the exact toll is unknown. She went down rapidly off the coast of Berwickshire. It is thought that a torpedo hit

---

* The *Iron Duke* won fame two years later in 1916 as the fleet flagship at the costly but inconclusive Battle of Jutland.

** The USS *Housatonic* was not sunk by a self-guided torpedo but by the Hunley's spar-torpedo in the American Civil War in 1864.

her magazine, causing the inevitable vast explosion of stockpiled ammunition. The kill was attributed to *U-21* under the command of *Kapitanleutnant* Otto Hersing (1885–1960). Its assault caused bitter recriminations.

The *Pathfinder*, part of the 8th Destroyer Flotilla, had been commissioned nine years earlier. Built by Cammell Laird at Birkenhead, an agile vessel at 385ft long, she was capable of 25 knots. But she had been travelling slowly to conserve her meagre stock of coal, her speed estimated at 5 knots; it made her an obvious target for a predator and brought criticism about parsimony in keeping her short of fuel.

Alarm was further heightened by the knowledge that *U-21* had earlier entered the Firth of Forth, the home of the Royal Navy base at Rosyth, Scotland. At one point shore batteries had opened up on her but to no avail. That a U-boat could reach so deeply into the homeland raised fundamental questions.

A Triple Tragedy

On 22 September 1915 an incident occurred which expunged nonsensical claims about Allied shipping being secure in so-called British waters. *Kapitanleutnant* Otto Weddigen (1882–1915), the commander of *U-9*, had stumbled on the German submariners' Holy Grail: three elderly, unguarded British cruisers, bereft of escort or protection, sailing off the Dutch coast. In an hour his torpedoes sank the Royal Navy's *Aboukir*, *Cressy* and *Hogue*, killing 1,459 officers and men. Compton-Hall:

> A loss of life greater than that suffered by the whole of Nelson's fleet at Trafalgar ... the British Admiralty was rudely shaken and alarmed.[4]

The watch officer on *U-9* was Johannes Spiess. He wrote of the *Cressy* going down:

> The giant with four funnels fell slowly but surely over to port and, like ants, the crew crawled first over the side and then on to the broad flat keel until they disappeared under the water. A tragic sight for a seaman.[5]

Until the triple sinking there had been as many submarine sceptics in Germany as in Britain; Weddigen's action helped muffle them. On 15 October 1915 he struck again, sinking a vintage cruiser, HMS *Hawke*, off Aberdeen, Scotland, at a cost of some 400 lives. Compton-Hall:

The Arte of ſhooting in great
Ordnaunce.

Contayning very neceſſary matters for all ſortes of
Seruitoures eyther by Sea or by Lande,

Written by William Bourne,
(∴)

IEHOVÆ
CANTABO QVIA BENEFECIT MIHI

Imprinted at London for
Thomas Woodcocke,
1587.

1 As well as envisaging early submarines, the prescient Englishman William Bourne produced erudite nautical manuals, covering topics from gunnery to navigation.

2 French steam engineer Denis Papin created numerous inventions and disguised a submarine design as a watering can, either as a joke or to stop plagiarism.

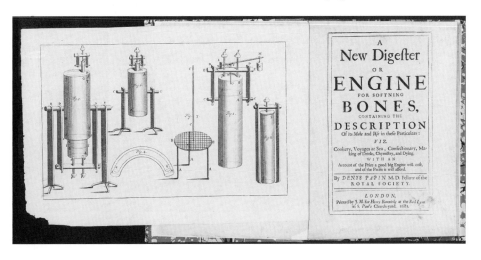

A
New Digeſter
OR
ENGINE
FOR SOFTNING
BONES,
CONTAINING THE
DESCRIPTION
Of its Make and Uſe in theſe Particulars:
VIZ.
Cookery, Voyages at Sea, Confectionary, Ma-
king of Drinks, Chymiſtry, and Dying.
WITH AN
Account of the Price a good big Engine will coſt,
and of the Profit it will afford.

By DENIS PAPIN M.D. Fellow of the
ROYAL SOCIETY.

LONDON,
Printed by J. M. for Henry Bonwicke at the Red Lyon
in S. Paul's Church-yard. 1681.

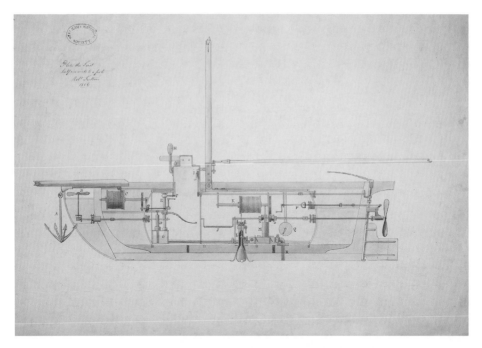

3 The talented American inventor Robert Fulton created the *Nautilus* submarine and went on to become one of the first commercially successful steamship operators.

4 Robert Fulton steam freighter photographed almost a century after his death. His *North River Steamboat* is acknowledged to be the first commercially successful steamboat.

5 Spanish intellectual Narcis Monturiol was an innovative engineer. He dived his fish-like 23ft-long *Ictineo* for the first time in Barcelona harbour in 1859.

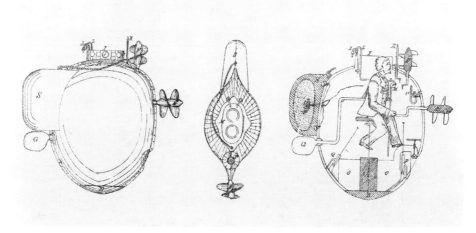

6 The brilliant American David Bushnell produced the innovative *Turtle* submersible in the 1770s to attack British warships in the American Revolutionary War.

7 The American War of Independence and American Civil War hastened submarine development, with a variety of underwater contraptions trying to sink surface ships. Cladding wooden warships in iron down almost to the water line reduced vulnerable target areas for primitive submarines. The original caption reads 'Infernal machine intended to destroy USS *Minnesota*'.

8 A memorial stone for those who died aboard the diminutive and ill-fated *Hunley* submarine when it made its attack on the USS *Housatonic*.

9 The distinguished Brooklyn navy yard, *c.* 1898. Submarine construction became faster as naval architecture, confidence and production techniques improved.

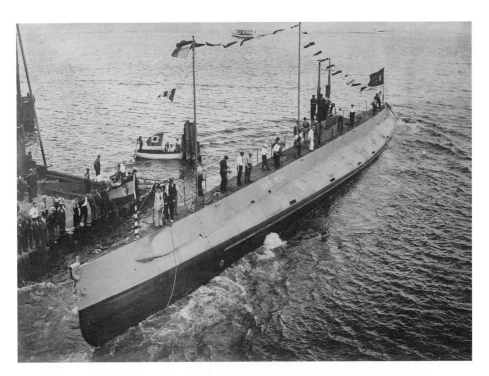

10 Isaac Peral was a brilliant Spanish engineer and naval officer who died prematurely and whose submarine endeavours were among the most advanced in the world.

11 The first US *A-1* submarine *Plunger* was laid down in 1901. For a time she came under the command of Chester W. Nimitz. President Roosevelt made dives on her.

12 The American Lewis Nixon and his highly regarded construction yard were eminent names in both surface marine and submarine construction.

13 At the US Naval Academy in Annapolis, students could familiarise themselves with the early versions of the still-strange contraptions which would change their world.

14 The American *B*-class *Tarantula* was laid down in 1905. She was 82ft long, had four torpedoes, an officer and a crew of nine and carried 1,880 gallons of petrol.

15 USS *Snapper* was launched at Fore River shipyard in 1909. Her first skipper was the legendary Chester W. Nimitz, who would command the Pacific Fleet in the Second World War.

16 Submarines were unreliable, uncomfortable and of limited range – as dangerous to crews as foes. Mother ships offered fuel, provisions, less Spartan living and some rudimentary repair facilities.

17 Admiral William Moffett, a lauded US naval aviation chief, was a persuasive, open-minded advocate of airships and submarines. He died in the 1933 *Akron* airship calamity.

18 Alfred Thayer Mahan, the cerebral American naval officer whose writings and strategic thinking influenced the Great War and helped trigger an arms race.

19 Mahan Hall at the celebrated US Naval Academy at Annapolis in America; a sign of the esteem in which the naval strategist and thinker Alfred Thayer Mahan is held.

20 USS *Seal*, laid down in 1909, was the first submarine Simon Lake constructed for the US Navy. Many regard American Simon Lake rather than the anti-British John Holland as the father of the submarine. Lake built a diversity of formidably advanced craft.

21 Simon Lake's submarines were John Holland's most serious competitors. Lake was a good showman and entrepreneur – at ease dealing with the press and the public.

22 The legendary *Holland* submarine, built by the Irish-American former monk John Philip Holland, on display in the United States at Paterson, New Jersey.

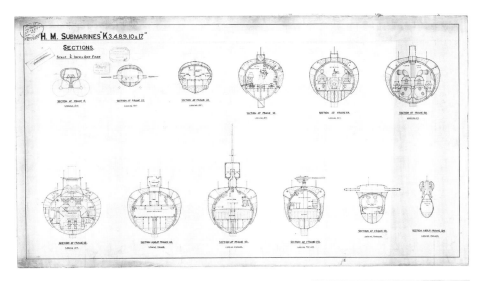

23 The clever ideas and ambitious naval architecture of the huge *K*-class submarines all came to naught in the calamity of May Island. © National Maritime Museum, Greenwich, London

24 Bowler hat, walrus moustache and wing collar: the stellar submarine designer John Philip Holland in one of his pathfinding creations.

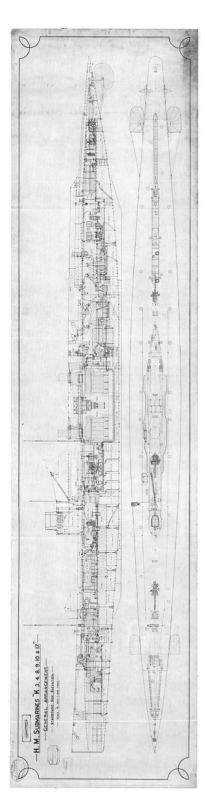

25 Plans for the *K*-class. Naval architects had to acquire new skills as submarines became more powerful and more potent. © National Maritime Museum, Greenwich, London

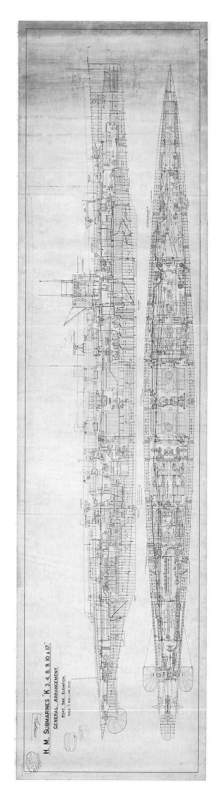

26 The giant *K*-class were designed as underwater battleships – as formidable on the water as beneath it. The concept was mongrelised and the *K*-class ended in ignominy. © National Maritime Museum, Greenwich, London

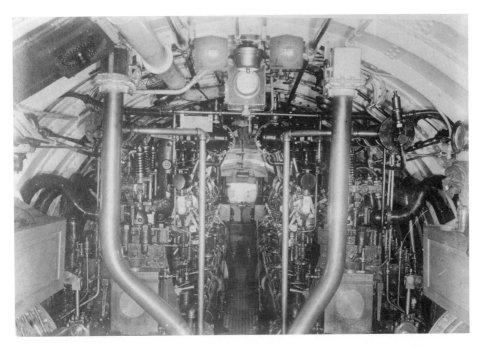

27 Unidentified American submarine photographed amidships, looking aft, between 1910 and 1915. Early craft were damp, dangerous, sometimes toxic and always insanitary.

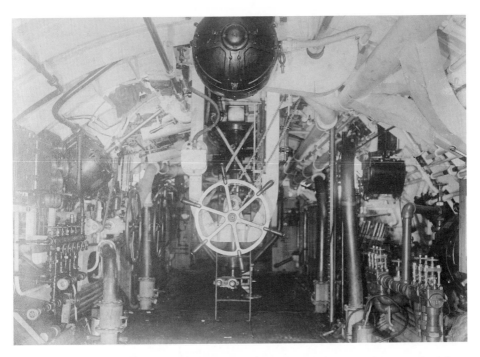

28 Only for the brave. The same unknown US craft looking forward. Constant noise, living cheek by jowl, crews tried to sleep between machinery and torpedoes.

29 The torpedo, released through tubes, made the submarine one of the deadliest weapons. Manning a submarine is mentally and physically exhausting. Trapped fingers, cuts, burned or bruised limbs were the least of the terrible hazards faced by pioneers submariners.

30 A flimsy submarine about to be crushed by a mighty surface vessel. Painters and propagandists often imagined such scenes in biblical David and Goliath terms.

31 France's *Korrigan* photographed 1910–15. French submarine dominance faded in part owing to an obsession with the novel and a refusal to standardise boats and equipment.

32 This powerful image of a British warship, taken around 1915, invokes the awful majesty of the ocean. Warships were faster and could ram and chop a surfaced submarine, or one near the surface, in half.

33 An ominous-looking *U-36* circles the Dutch steam packet SS *Batavier*, *c.* 1915. The sudden surfacing of a German submarine was frightening for unarmed craft.

34 Admiral Sir Martin Eric Dunbar-Nasmith VC, the commander of *E-11*, wreaked havoc in the Sea of Marmara in 1915 with a succession of daring attacks on enemy shipping.

35 Lieutenant Commander Geoffery Saxton-White VC, the commander of Boyle's former craft, *E-14*. He was killed by shellfire in the Dardanelles after one of his torpedoes exploded prematurely, forcing him to surface his craft.

36 A faulty gyro-compass caused *E-13* to run aground between Malmo and Copenhagen. Its crew had to abandon ship but fourteen were shot in the water. The atrocity caused worldwide outrage.

37 *E-13* survivors were given a heroe's welcome when they finally returned home to Great Britain.

38 The bodies of sailors killed in the *E-13* massacre were brought back to Hull, on the east coast of England, and buried with full military honours.

39 A German submarine's torpedo stranded on the French coast

40 *Deutschland* was privately built as a cargo-carrier. In the war, Germany used her as a blockade-buster and then converted her into a fighting sub with six torpedo tubes.

41 Newspapers portrayed the Kaiser and U-boat leaders as barbarous cut-throats. Victorious British submarines did actually fly the piratical Jolly Roger on their return to base.

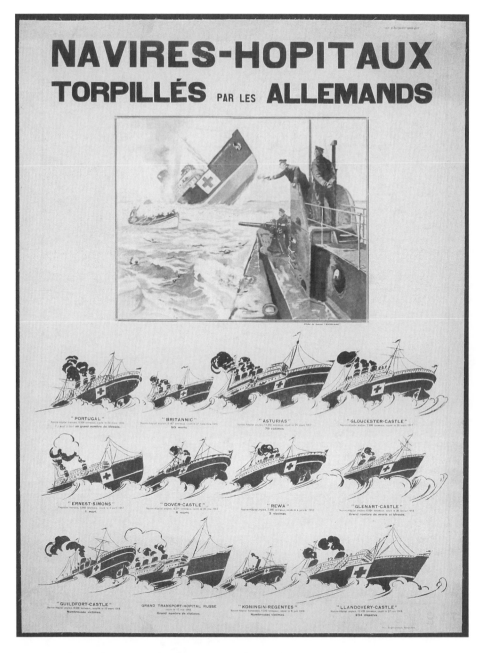

42 Out-and-out submarine warfare by Germany reaped worldwide opprobrium and cost Tirpitz his job. U-boats were accused of attacking defenceless hospital ships.

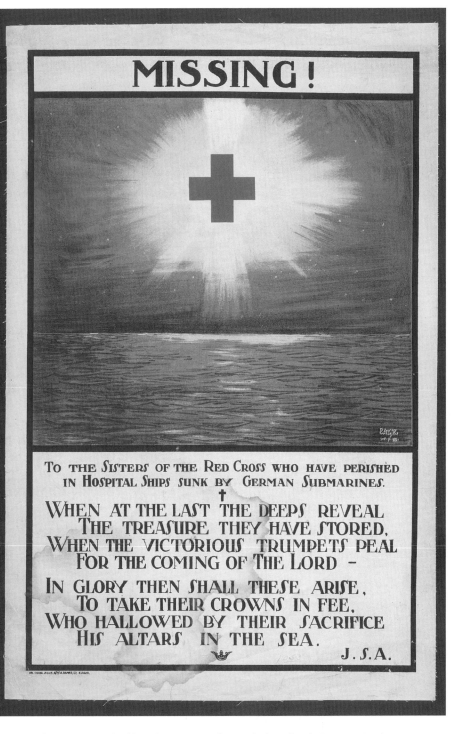

43 Hospital ships were sunk, although Germany vehemently denied such atrocities. Twelve, it was claimed, were reportedly sunk by mistake, because of unclear markings.

A MOVING PICTURE

44 A German commander
supposedly films the drowning
victims of a destroyed ship,
c. 1915. Unrestricted U-boat
warfare fuelled an imaginative
propaganda war.

45 An uncaptioned photograph
believed to be of the infamous
German *U-20*, which sank the liner
Lusitania. In 1916 *U-20* became
grounded off Denmark. Her crew
subsequently destroyed her.

46 Tirpitz as Blackbeard riding into New York harbour on a U-boat, 1917. Part of US Navy enlistment propaganda, as envisaged by the artist W.A. Rogers (1854–1931).

47 Germany and Tirpitz launched a fearsome fleet of submarines, in part to compensate for having a lesser surface fleet than that of Britain's Royal Navy.

48 Kaiser Wilhelm – old Bill – breaking his promises to the US to halt the unfettered U-boat campaign. His failure to comply helped hasten US entry into the war in 1917.

49 Other nations began building submarines ahead of Germany, but once started she swiftly assembled an impressive fleet and trained a cadre of skilful commanders.

Every LIBERTY BOND is a shot at a U BOAT

FIRE *YOUR* SHOT TO-DAY

BUY A LIBERTY BOND

SECOND LIBERTY LOAN

50 Wars are costly and tend to bankrupt participants. The US entered the Great War in 1917 and to finance its involvement, citizens could invest in patriotic saving schemes.

51 Some early submarines had sails; others used them to disguise themselves as yachts. All were subject to reconnaissance or attack by airship or fixed-wing aeroplanes.

RIGGED AS A SAILING-BOAT: A GERMAN SUBMARINE SUBMERGING, SAILS AND ALL, TO AVOID A BRITISH SEAPLANE'S BOMB.

52 American know-how came to the fore. A type of assembly line building developed, as used by Ford and the car industry and later, in the Second World War, for the super-fast construction of *Liberty* ships.

53 *Bremen*'s crew (*Deutschland*'s sister ship), *c.* 1916. Tirpitz had faith in his fleet of U-boats, which were reliable, had good range and highly capable commanders and crews.

54 Joseph Pennell (1857–1926) was among the war artists used by the US Division of Pictorial Publicity. His series of lithographs included *Submarines in Dry Dock*, 1917.

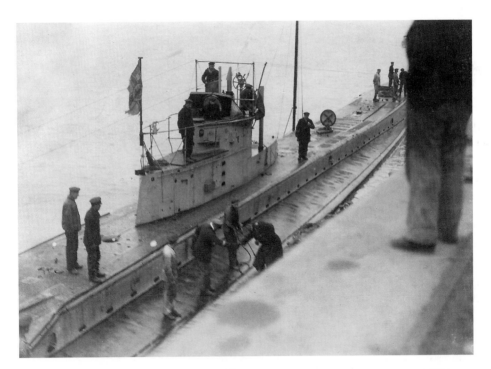

55 The Zeebrugge mole. The Zeebrugge raid was one of the most audacious of the war. Old, obsolete submarines were converted into underwater bombs.

56 Richard Sandford VC. One of a small band of astonishingly daring underwater warriors who played a key role in securing victory in the First World War.

57 Richard Sandford VC had his *C-3* submarine packed with explosives in the 1918 Zeebrugge raid. He rammed a viaduct and then had to leap for his life into a small boat

58 Royal Marines stormed defences at Zeebrugge on St George's Day 1918. Churchill
described the raid as 'the finest feat of arms in the Great War'.

59 Holbrook in Australia is far inland but boasts its own submarine. The town changed its German-sounding name to honour eminent submariner Norman Holbrook VC. Australian Navy submariners played a courageous role in the war against the Kaiser.

60 The crippled *UC-5* was displayed in London and New York. Mines she laid in the English Channel sank the steamship *William Dawson* and the cable-layer *Monarch*.

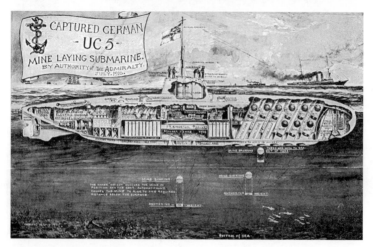

61 *UC-5* ran aground after planting mines in the English Channel; she had previously sunk twenty-nine ships. Her capture in 1916 was a propaganda coup for Britain and America.

62 The Pas de Calais. A predator from the depths lies beached and broken-backed. The death toll in submarines was horrendous. After the war scrap dealers cashed in.

63 After Germany's surrender, a U-boat stranded on Britain's south coast caused excitement for war-weary Englanders, who rowed out and clambered over it.

64 Captured enemy submarines were pored over by Admiralty engineers keen to learn their secrets. Their humbled presence in iconic British settings – such as Tower Bridge on London's River Thames – made for powerful propaganda.

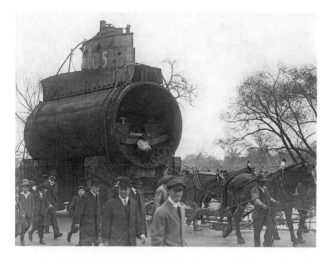

65 To the victor the spoils. The truncated carcass of a once-proud enemy submarine paraded in New York, 1918.

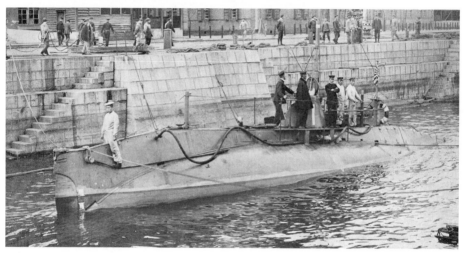

66 The Imperial Japanese Navy purchased its first submarine – one of the early *Holland* designs – from the United States.

67 Trials using *M*-class submarines as aircraft carriers ended in tragedy. In the years following the First World War, sixty crew members died when *M-2* sank off Britain's Dorset coast.

Armour plating against gunfire was, as Holland had foreseen, wholly ineffective against torpedo attack from below. Surface ships lacked any kind of defence against the submarine menace except, perhaps, high speed. Only warships had that capability and even they could not steam at full speed all the time. The slower merchant vessels appeared frighteningly vulnerable.[6]*

Loss of the First Civilian Ship

Five days after the disaster of the *Hawke*, a U-boat sank the first civilian, non-combatant vessel on 20 October 1915, the British commercial steamship SS *Glitra*, making passage from the port of Grangemouth, on the Scottish coast, to Stavanager in Norway. Though the death of the *Glitra* marked a turning point in the conflict, her denouement had been conducted with some decorum. The commander of *U-17*, *Oberleutnant* Johannes Feldkirchner (1884–1950), surfaced his submarine close to the *Glitra* and instructed her crew to depart their vessel. He was acting within the conventions, which governed at this early stage, submarine intervention in the free-flow of commercial traffic. Conserving his torpedoes Feldkirchner's men had clambered aboard the stricken ship and opened its seacocks, causing her to sink to the ocean floor. *Glitra*'s crew were put into lifeboats and towed by the submarine towards the sanctuary of the Norwegian coast.

A week later, without warning, the French ferry *Admiral Ganteaume* was torpedoed by *U-24* on 26 October 1915. There were 2,500 Belgian passengers aboard, most of them refugees. The torpedo missed but in the mayhem which enveloped the ship forty died. Lifeboats were dropped in panic, brawling breaking out on deck. Such was the horror of the submarine, its name alone being sufficient to cause abandonment and hysteria.

The *Lusitania*

Stray attacks by U-boats on civilian shipping were a portent of the unrestricted submarine warfare eventually endorsed by the German Navy. In 1915 it was one of the ten long-range German submarines, *U-20*, commanded by

---

* Otto Eduard Weddigen returned home to Germany a hero. Highly decorated he would later die at the age of 33 with his officers and crew in command of *U-29*, rammed and sunk by HMS *Dreadnought* in Scotland's Pentland Firth. He had killed some 2,000 men.

Kapitanleutnant Walter Schwieger (1885–1917) which caused international opprobrium by attacking a hospital ship on 1 February in the English Channel and which, three months later, on 7 May 1915, torpedoed and sank Cunard's passenger liner the RMS *Lusitania*.[7] In 1917 America came into the war three years after its commencement, drawn in by the sinking of the *Lusitania* and the Zimmerman Telegram.[*]

The sinking of the *Lusitania* marked a turning point. A total of 1,195 lives were lost on Cunard's 30,000-ton liner en route from New York to Liverpool. She was sunk in eighteen minutes by a single torpedo fired by *Kapitanleutnant* Schwieger, south of Cobh, Ireland.[9] The attack caused global outrage, significantly in America, marking the end of courtesies and lingering notions about honourable wars. The *Lusitania* had numbered American citizens among its passengers. Patrick Beesly wrote:

> [It] outraged a world not yet accustomed to the idea of total war involving innocent men, women and children. It seemed inconceivable … that the Imperial German Navy could be so ruthless, despite clear warnings that such behaviour was intended. It seemed almost equally unbelievable that one of the largest and most modern liners in the world, holder, with her sister ship *Mauretania*, of the Blue Riband of the Atlantic – a prestigious award for the fastest crossing of the Atlantic by a liner on a regular service – should go to the bottom far more quickly than the Titanic had done.[10]

A four-funnel liner, the *Lusitania* had been meticulously appointed: elegant, fast, romantic, a monarch of the seas. The menace of the submarine had been starkly demonstrated. The incident showed sceptics that if a submarine stalked its prey, if it was suitably armed with skilful commander and able crew, the length of a target ship increased its vulnerability and that its speed offered only an uncertain protection. The calamity would cost Tirpitz his job. Engulfed in worldwide acerbity his resignation in 1916 was accepted by the Kaiser. Tension rose further with the sinking of the Glasgow-built passenger-steamer the *Hesperian* – 10,920 tons – on 4 September 1915. The *Hesperian*, making passage from Liverpool to Canada, went down with the loss of thirty-two lives off the Fastnet, in the north Atlantic, off the south-west coast of Ireland. It was another kill for *Kapitanleutnant* Schwieger in his craft *U-20*, the commander and boat

---

[*]   The telegram was intercepted and decoded by Britain and passed on to the US. It appeared to suggest that Germany had incited Mexico to wage war on America and stated Germany's intention to commence unrestricted submarine warfare.[8]

which sank the *Lusitania*. In November 1916 *U-20* became fast on a sandbar off Denmark's Jutland Peninsula. She could not liberate herself or be towed free by German ships and had to be destroyed to prevent her from falling into Allied hands. Schwieger was seen as a hero in Germany and awarded the Iron Cross. He would, however, always be blamed for helping to bring America into the war by his assault on the *Lusitania*.*

With Britain trying to stifle Germany into submission by enforcing a blockade, Germany had for a period of some two years toyed with the idea of all-out submarine warfare. German navalists knew its High Seas Fleet was insufficiently muscular and numerically inferior to contest the superiority of the British Grand Fleet; the only way it could challenge the blockade, and Britain's surface fleet, was through a heavy reliance on its U-boats. But the effectiveness of its U-boat fleet was being neutered.

The U-boat Offensive

Under existing conventions, before destroying a ship, U-boats had to declare their presence; first surfacing and then safeguarding those aboard their quarry. Submarines were small and fragile and insufficiently capacious to accommodate survivors. In surfacing the submarine betrayed its greatest strength, that of stealth; it endangered itself from guns concealed on ships or risked being rammed, sliced apart and sent instantly to the bottom. Germany argued that Britain's blockade was an abuse of civilised behaviour: a policy to force it into capitulation by the starvation of its citizens, cutting off fuel, medicines and all other essentials. The German military knew if it failed to break the blockade it must concede the war. If Britain was permitted to pursue that which Germany thought barbaric, why should Germany not prosecute its own policy of unrestricted submarine warfare? Germany decreed, on a tit-for-tat basis, that it would establish a blockade of its own: any Allied ship in waters around Britain could be destroyed.

After the sinking of the *Lusitania* and other commercial vessels, and in spite of international criticism, the German position hardened. It led to an infamous period of maritime carnage. Over 100 U-boats devastated Allied shipping, a

---

* After the destruction of his *U-20*, Schwieger was given another command and was quickly back in action menacing Allied shipping. He perished with his entire crew on 17 September 1917 in command of *U-88* when it hit a mine off Jutland. He was 32. In his time he had wrought calamity, sinking over 190,000 tons of Allied shipping.

force which grew larger by the day with more U-boats being built and pressed into service than were being destroyed. It showed with a desperate clarity the impotence of Britain and the Admiralty to defend its surface marine. For Germany the strategy misfired: its stance galvanised its foes and strengthened their resolve; it incensed neutral nations, triggered global criticism and gifted Allied propagandists an opportunity beyond price. On the scales of demonic behaviour the imposition of a slow and often ineffectual blockade – *somehow* such essentials as food, fuel *et al.* would generally get through – failed to equate with the instant, merciless obliteration of hundreds of ships, crews and entirely innocent civilian passengers. Germany faced ruinous defeat and in its desperation had seen an unfettered U-boat campaign as the only way to salvage victory.

Division in the German Command

The writer Wolfgang Frank gives an insight into the chasm which opened up in the German naval command about the wisdom of an all-out U-boat offensive. In his book *The Sea Wolves*, the story of German U-boats – the volume is primarily concerned with the Second World War – he recalls:

> Their chief function [U-boats] was to attack shipping, but a violent difference of opinion soon arose as to the best way of using them for this purpose. No provision for this form of warfare had been in the articles of international law, for the clauses relating to war at sea applied only to surface vessels.[11]

Within a strict legal interpretation he was right: there were no written laws. But unrestricted submarine warfare constituted a brazen flouting of ethical considerations; the newness of the submarine could not excuse the breaching of infrangible conventions which for centuries had represented ethical maritime conduct. Frank wrote:

> The submarine's concentrated offensive, together with its extreme vulnerability, had never been the subject of study by international lawyers; as a result it was expected to wage war in a way which made nonsense of its *raison d'etre*. The existing rules of war required it to fight like a surface raider ... yet this method left the highly vulnerable U-boat an easy prey to the merchant ship's guns ... what the U-boat needed was the legal right to sink without warning any ship that entered a previously declared danger area. The blockade of Germany brought the issue of 'sinking without warning'

to a head. Anxious to evolve a direct counter-measure to the blockade, the German Navy demanded unrestricted U-boat warfare against all ships within a prescribed area around the British Isles.[12]

The German rationale for its all-out strategy met with universal condemnation. Stark divisions opened up in Germany about its propriety:

> Chancellor von Bethmann-Hollweg's government wanted to spare all neutral shipping and could not be dissuaded from this attitude despite persistent representations from the German Admiralty, in particular from Grand Admiral von Tirpitz. The U-boats had to fight with one hand tied behind their back. Thus they were not allowed to develop their full capabilities. When all restrictions were at last lifted in February 1917, it was too late; the U-boats were no longer in a position to win the war, for the enemy had grown too strong.[13]

Prevarication in Germany about sanctioning the unfettered submarine campaign gave Britain and its allies an opportunity to bolster flimsy anti-submarine measures. One might speculate about the impact on Britain had Germany begun its campaign sooner:

> Time was needed to create and develop the naval counter-measures [in Britain]. But political counter-measures could be commenced at once. Northcliffe placed his enormous propaganda-machine, with its world-wide connections, at the disposal of Britain's politicians and launched an unparalleled Press campaign to bring the U-boat war against Britain's merchant shipping into disrepute. He achieved his aim, but it was clear for all to see that for the first time in her history, Britain's very survival was threatened ... shipping losses were rising week by week. The U-boat was quickly eating away not only the lifeline of the British Isles but the whole foundation of the Allies' strength. The danger of complete collapse lay dark and menacing on the horizon.[14]

Wolfgang Frank over-eggs his case. Alfred Charles Harmsworth, 1st Viscount Northcliffe (1865–1922), was a powerful press baron, but not *that* powerful; the policy would have *still* been judged abhorrent without rabid editorials; nor was it the *first* time in Britain's long and turbulent history that its survival had been threatened. Without quibbling, however, his central argument is right: the U-boat threat had made Britain's situation grave. By 1917 Germany's downfall was becoming evident. Its ground forces had failed to achieve anticipated victories. German protests that it had warned ships about the perils of venturing into disputed waters appeared cosmetic; as the slaughter gathered momentum, self-justification was drowned out by a roar of global outrage. Shipping losses at the close of 1916 and the beginning of 1917 were 300,000 tons a month, twice the figure of the previous year. By February 1917 nearly 470,000 tons had been destroyed. In March the figure rose to 500,000 tons. In April it leaped: 350 ships sunk, representing nearly 900,000 tons.

The Convoy System

Neutral shipping was turning away from England, as the risk for merchantmen reaching Britain had grown too severe. It was a determined effort to starve Britain into submission.[15] With little choice the Admiralty turned to the convoy system. With destroyers providing protective screens to merchant ships the casualty rate fell dramatically.[16] One of the earliest outcomes of the convoy system was a cessation of daylight U-boat attacks for fear of being out-gunned or rammed by a surface protector; lurid accounts tell of submariners staring up from their tiny craft as the giant bows of a ship bore down. The convoy strategy also made it hazardous for a U-boat to 'pick off' a merchant ship; a fast destroyer, dispensing depth charges, could chase its quarry by speeding along tell-tale tracks left in the water by a submarines' torpedo. As the submarine writer Edward Horton commented:

> Counter-attacks achieved only modest success in terms of U-boats destroyed but they did make life a great deal more hazardous for the marauders.[17]

Given the size of the world's oceans and that communications were coarse, Horton makes another valid point:

> A flotilla of twenty-five ships is more conspicuous than one ship alone – but only marginally. It is nothing like twenty-five times as conspicuous. Even without armed escorts ships are less at risk if they sail in groups ... shipping lanes are not like highways ... the Atlantic ocean is vast and U-boats had no hope of forming even a loose net across the Western Approaches to the British Isles. A U-boat might certainly wreak havoc with a convoy but first it had to find one, and it was this comparative elusiveness of ships in convoy that proved their greatest salvation.[18]

The Exploits of Submariners

British submariners in the First World War showed astonishing courage and audacity. Their craft were used correctly if deployed as offensive weapons. The potency of the submarine was diluted when engaged as a defender of a shoreline, kept at its station to picket an enemy fleet or used as bait to tempt a foe from a safe anchorage. The submarine was at its deadliest when it lurked at sea waiting to pick off a target, or slid quiet as a snake into enemy waters to unleash its venom. The submariner ventured in fragile craft into uncharted seas, to confront mines, protective netting, warships dropping depth charges and keen to ram predators into oblivion. Protected only by a depth of water, virtually blind to that which lay above, and able only to squint through a misted tube by nearing the surface and risking exposure, it was no trade for the faint of heart, the squeamish, the claustrophobic or those who spent morbid hours imagining their end on the seabed, helpless in a steel coffin, suffocating, gasping their last. No fewer than five Victoria Crosses were awarded to British submariners in the Great War. A sudden strike – surprise and stealth being chief among the advantages of the submarine – caused carnage and spread a contagion of panic.

A Town Named Holbrook

The first naval VC of the Great War, and the first awarded to a submariner, went to Norman Douglas Holbrook (1888–1976), who not only won Britain's highest medal but had a town in Australia named in his honour. Like many of his fellow officers Holbrook had graduated from the training college at HMS *Britannia*, Devon. By the age of 26 he was a lieutenant in the submarine service. He was in command of the obsolete *B11* which had been dispatched to the Dardanelles, comprising a treacherous 38-mile-long Strait which was barely 4 miles wide in north-west Turkey. Linking the Aegean Sea to the Marmara Sea, the Strait is notorious for its unpredictable currents. It presents the submariner with more daunting challenges than swift-running tides: an alarming mix of salt and seawater, it holds special difficulties, the type which John Holland encountered when he had first floated his *Fenian Ram* and watched it sink unceremoniously to the bottom. Holland had been tricked by one of the submariners' pet hates, a perilous concoction of fresh and salt water. A submarine set up for fresh water sailing, or in the jargon one which is appropriately 'trimmed', has less buoyancy and is more prone to dive. If a boat is trimmed for fresh water, and experiences heavy water of a greater density which contains salt, it will rise. If the salt content is severe a submarine may inadvertently bob to the surface in hostile waters, greatly adding to the burden on its already overstretched commander.

This then was Holbrook's lot: an obsolescent machine, swift tides and a swirling cocktail of fresh and salt water. There were yet more hazards: the *B11*, built in 1906, was hardly as fast as the current. How then to make headway? The answer: with strong nerves, great patience and enormous difficulty. The Strait is achingly narrow and twisting, and, another factor high on a list of submariners' dislikes, it is desperately shallow in places. The Turks had also sown lines of mines in the water and positioned powerful guns and artillery batteries on each bank and shore. In short, the fortified Dardanelles was a nightmare for a submarine and especially so for one which should have been pensioned off long before. It was for his courage on 13 December 1914 that Holbrook was decorated. British submarine operations in the Sea of Marmara began well in advance of the major land and naval push in the weeks which followed.

Holbrook had set sail in his small and elderly *B11* to try and interrupt seaborne Turkish supply lines to the Gallipoli Peninsula; such an assault would benefit Allied land forces. Holbrook left Tenedos, the small island near the entrance to the Dardanelles, which the British had commandeered as a supply base for the Gallipoli campaign. He had to negotiate lines of mines, diving beneath them, and navigate the pinched Narrows, a stretch of water under constant surveillance, patrolled by gunboats and guarded by batteries of guns and searchlights. Throughout the mission *B11* unwittingly rose and dived, called 'porpoising' in the trade, as Holbrook gingerly negotiated swift tides of salt and fresh water. Of his boat he recalled:

> Often she came up as far as forty feet then went down again without altering speed or helm. When I wished to bring her up I had to give her full helm and speed for up to 500 [rpm] on two [motors] and even then sometimes remained at twenty feet for a quarter of an hour or more, before she would come up the remaining twenty-five feet to see [using the periscope].[19]

The *B11* had only limited dive time before its batteries became flat, so he had resisted diving his craft until the last moment. For much of the time he was only just below the surface with the tell-tale conning tower poking above the water, making a tempting target for shore-based batteries which subjected the vessel to a continuing barrage for the duration of the operation. Through his periscope Holbrook had spotted an elderly Turkish battleship, the *Messudieh*, lying at anchor. In the melee, enduring a ceaseless hail of bullets and shells, he pressed on, determined to close on his prey. Holbrook continued:

When I sighted [the *Messudieh*] I altered eight points to starboard to attack her, and the boat [his submarine] immediately sank to eighty feet and remained there, and nothing would bring her up till I blew two auxiliaries for five minutes [author's note: the auxiliaries were ballast tanks blown by compressed air to make the craft lighter and more buoyant]. I think the cause of this was the sudden change of tide [current] from ahead to the beam. At the time of firing the diving was very erratic, the depth varying from fifteen to forty feet. On firing the boat sank to forty feet. I made men run forward and took some time on three [motors] before she came up, then she refused to dive till I flooded the auxiliaries I had previously blown.[20]

It was a remarkable feat of seamanship and boldness by Holbrook and his crew. It is difficult to achieve accuracy in firing a torpedo if a submarine is stable; when it is bouncing around, pitching up and down, stubbornly refusing to answer its helm and being blasted by bullets and shells, to fulfil such a feat was astonishing. The release of a torpedo impaired stability, a boat becoming instantly lighter by the weapons' sudden exit. It had been frustrating in the past trying to comprehend why torpedoes consistently missed their target. Once revealed the explanation seemed obvious: real and mock warheads were of a different weight and ran at different depths. The early boats were prone to all manner of weight considerations, as Holbrook alludes to in instructing his crew to go forward. For his torpedoes to be effective he had to judge distance and depth with minute precision; to achieve a spot from which he could fire with any hope of success he had to dive beneath another line of five mines. Having done so he fired two torpedoes and sank the aged *Messudieh*, a 9,000-ton coastal defence ship. Many of its 600 crew were trapped but later escaped; thirty-eight died.

Holbrook and his crew had to make their own escape with *B11*, on occasion grounding in shallow water, chased by patrol boats and subject to gunfire. Julian Thompson, the military historian, notes:

When he arrived at Tenedos, he had been submerged for nine hours with almost dead batteries, and only the fact that he had the current with him allowed him to make it.[21]

Holbrook's success echoed round the world. *The New York Times* wrote:

… a thrilling achievement … the boldest exploit of the war … little craft runs gauntlet of guns and is submerged nine hours in attack on battleships.[22]

For a small farming town in Australia, 250 miles from the nearest seaport, Holbrook's accomplishments held a special resonance. The submarine service of the Australian Navy would forge its own distinguished history in the Great War and the Second World War. Ten Mile Creek, as it was called, is a little community in the south of New South Wales, situated midway between Sydney and Melbourne on the Hume Highway. In 1840 a German immigrant settled there and, as the years passed, the town would eventually become known as Germanton. In the fervour of the Great War its name was thought unpatriotic, so it was changed it to Holbrook, in celebration of Norman Holbrook and his Victoria Cross.*

Henry Stoker: Actor-Submariner

Another of the pioneer Australian submarines, *AE-2*, saw action in the Dardanelles in the days which followed Holbrook's exertions; *E*-class boats were more capable than the *B*-class, though their superiority in no way diminishes the courage shown by their commanders. By April 1915 four *E*-class boats were in the Dardanelles. The story of the *AE-2* is remarkable, as is that of actor Lieutenant Commander Henry Hugh Gordon 'Dacre' Stoker (1885–1966), born in Dublin. He was a cousin of Abraham 'Bram' Stoker (1847–1912), the Irish writer who created the 1897 Gothic nightmare, *Count Dracula*.**

The submarine *AE-2* had been constructed at the Vickers yard in Barrow-in-Furness and commissioned into the Royal Australian Navy at Portsmouth in

---

* To honour its namesake in 1997 the town acquired part of a submarine which had been decommissioned in 1995 by the Royal Australian Navy. The town subsequently organised a drive to buy the entire submarine, raising $100,000, nearly all of it donated by Lieutenant Holbrook's widow, Gundula. The amount, however, was insufficient for the town to purchase the entire submarine. After negotiating with a Sydney scrap yard it managed to acquire the boat's upper casing, which now sits proudly, if a little incongruously, in Germanton Park, in the centre of Holbrook. The submarine on show is HMAS *Otway*, an *Oberon*-class submarine. The town also boasts a scale model of Holbrook's *B11*.[23] The *Otway* (*S59*) was larger and more threatening than Holbrook's valiant little *B11*. Built by Scotts Shipbuilding in Greenock, Scotland, she had been commissioned in 1968. At 295ft long and measuring 26.5ft in the beam, *Otway* had eight officers, a crew of sixty and a range of 9,000–10,000 miles.

** Bram Stoker was also the assistant to the legendary Victorian thespian Sir Henry Irving (1838–1905) and the manager of London's Lyceum Theatre which Irving owned. Lieutenant Stoker's theatrical pedigree was secure; after his exploits with *AE-2* he would build his own successful stage and film career.

February 1914. Based at Sydney with her sister craft *AE-1*, the two submarines had made a record-breaking voyage to Australia, partly under their own power and partly under tow. Her crew comprised members of the Royal Australian Navy and the British Royal Navy. With *AE-1*, the first Australian navy submarine, commanded by Lieutenant Commander Thomas Fleming Besant (1883–1914), *AE-2* had helped in the occupation of Rabaul in German New Guinea, Southeast Asia. Thomas Besant, born in Liverpool, had joined the Royal Navy in 1905 at the age of 15. As a young midshipman he had served in China during the Boxer Uprising, transferring to the Royal Australian Navy in 1913. On 14 September 1914, Besant and his command, *AE-1*, were lost in mysterious circumstances while on patrol in Rabaul's Cape Gazelle: thirty-five men were posted missing, including Besant and his fellow officers, Lieutenant Charles Lewis Moore, 26, and Lieutenant the Honourable Leopold Florence Scarlett, 25.*

Stoker's objective in *AE-2* was to negotiate the Straits and break into the Sea of Marmara to attack Turkish ships. One of many problems, as Holbrook had found, lay in coping with the rapid currents of the Narrows. Though the *E*-class were better than Holbrook's *B*-class, the batteries were still incapable of holding a charge for a lengthy period. To make realistic headway against the fast-flowing water, it was necessary to keep the boats at maximum speed: this, again, would help to quickly flatten submarine batteries. Irrespective of their class, all submarines of the period, and much later, were inhibited by having to charge their batteries. They could only be charged by engaging the diesel engine when a boat ran on the surface; in war the only time a submarine would dare break the surface was at night. In negotiating the Straits a submarine had to regularly surface, not simply to replenish its batteries but to allow its commander and crew to get a navigational fix; this, of course, had to be undertaken in daylight, a highly perilous procedure which, inevitably, would activate artillery batteries waiting on shore.

The submarine *E-15* had tried on 17 April 1915 to break into the Marmara while under the command of Lieutenant Commander Theodore Brodie. The mission had ended in calamity. Brodie's craft had been hit by swirling tides and swept ashore. The shore batteries had opened up. Brodie and six of his crew

---

* One of the myriad tragedies of the Great War would be the toll of young submariners whose experience was needed in 1939 at the start of the Second World War. Their first-hand knowledge would have been of incalculable value. Lost in the Great War their absence held a special keenness; by 1939 there survived a cadre of seasoned submariners, though one depleted by the initial conflict.

were killed by a Turkish shell while the rest of the crew were captured. The British had been forced to shell and sink the grounded hulk to stop it falling into enemy hands. Once dived it was almost impossible for a commander to tell where his craft was being taken by errant currents, and where, as a result, he might surface. There were few mechanical or electrical aids; the location where a submarine emerged, and when, were largely of God and luck.

The courage displayed by crews and commanders such as Brodie, Stoker, Holbrook and Besant won laurels for the infant service and their oft-derided craft. The naval leader Rosslyn Wemyss (1864–1933) pointed out that the Dardanelles campaign was the event which brought the submarines to prominence, confounding sceptics and giving the service a dangerous chance to demonstrate the effectiveness of its vessels and the intrepid nature of its commanders and crews:

> By their assaults on the enemy's shipping [they] created a veritable panic in these waters, hitherto regarded by him as safe. Battleships, cruisers, gunboats, transports, supply vessels of every description, all were attacked with a cool courage and calculated audacity unsurpassed in the annals of our naval history. Only in this theatre of war did these officers find a full outlet for their prowess and initiative.[24]

Wemyss was among naval chiefs who stressed the importance of trying to observe the proprieties of war:

> They [submarine officers] proved that this latest weapon of maritime warfare could be effectively used in a manner very different to that exercised by the Germans in their merciless campaign against allied and neutral shipping, for though our officers did not hesitate to sink enemy's vessels they never did so without ascertaining that they were legitimate targets, whilst they scrupulously respected the lives of non-combatants.[25]

Six days after Theodore Brodie's catastrophe, Henry Stoker's *AE-2* began its mission. Stoker had set his heart on a naval career at the age of 12. He had been 'blooded-in' at HMS *Britannia*, the Royal Naval training college, and undergone further training at the illustrious Royal Naval College, Greenwich, London. By the age of 19 he was a sub lieutenant and, at 23, had been promoted a lieutenant in command of a submarine. His first posting was to Gibraltar in the Mediterranean where Britain had established a submarine base. Stoker was a gifted athlete and had supposedly transferred to the new Royal Australian Navy Submarine Service in the hope that he would be able to play polo.

In 1913 he was given command of the submarine *AE-2*. Its first foray in the Dardanelles on 23 April 1915 had to be aborted because of an engineering malfunction; though the *E*-class boats were an improvement on their predecessor craft, they were still pioneering contraptions and subject to breakdowns. Undaunted, Stoker set off again the next day, 24 April 1915, a few hours before the Allied landings were due to take place.

In the early hours of 25 April, as the ships of the invasion fleet were ferrying the Anzac Corps to land on Gallipoli's west coast, Stoker's submarine sailed quietly into the Dardanelles. A moon and searchlights played across the surface, mines lay strung across its depths. Trying to conserve his batteries – as Holbrook had done – Stoker had delayed diving his vessel until the last moment. On being spotted by a shore battery he had to immediately submerge, negotiating a minefield as he went, hearing the heart-stopping scrape of mines bumping along the length of his submarine's hull as he inched through the water. As dawn broke he brought *AE-2* up to periscope depth. He had spotted a Turkish cruiser, the *Peykisevket*, which he managed to badly damage with a torpedo. Once more he had been seen and forced to crash dive as the shore batteries got a fix on him. Patrol boats and warships raced across the water to sink him, and he narrowly avoided being cut in half by the bows of a Turkish destroyer.

As a consequence of Stoker's assault, another Turkish destroyer, which had been successfully shelling the invading Anzac forces, had to abandon its barrage and make a swift retreat, alarmed by Stoker's presence; invading soldiers on that hellish night would have been grateful that Stoker and his crew had drawn the warship's fire. For hour upon hour his little submarine ducked and dived, bobbing and weaving to avoid its tormentors. Sometimes it ran aground in the swirling shallows, Stoker and his crew desperately trying to free it, running and jumping up and down its length to alter its balance, putting its engines into reverse at full power; above them circled gun boats and destroyers hunting down their quarry. Forced to surface, Stoker encountered two Turkish vessels which had stretched a containment wire between them, hoping that it would catch on the *AE-2*'s conning tower. Again he had to hastily submerge. In the chaos of the chase his submarine had been damaged, springing oil and water leaks. If the oil which had gathered in the bilges had been pumped out in the ordinary way it would have risen to the surface and betrayed the craft's position.

For several hours Stoker kept his boat silent and motionless on the ocean floor, trying to fool his pursuers into believing that he had made his escape, while giving his vessel and its exhausted crew a chance of rest. After more than sixteen hours underwater he nervously brought the boat to the surface on the evening of 25 April 1915. His luck was in. It was dark and no Turkish ships were evident. His batteries were flat, so he had to start his diesel engine to replenish them and to make headway. The air in the craft had become dangerously fetid, the crew gasping for fresh air. Instead of turning for home Stoker pressed on into the darkness, finally succeeding in his determination to enter the Sea of Marmara.

From 26 to 30 April he played a hazardous game of cat and mouse, deliberately showing his presence to fishing boats on the surface, sailing into the quieter, upper reaches of the Marmara, diving and reappearing at different locations, raising his periscope above the waterline. His plan was to cause panic in the Turkish command by giving the impression that more than one submarine had entered the waters; if successful the subterfuge might have dissuaded the Turkish Navy from sending more ships into the Dardanelles as reinforcements. In the event, unbeknown to Stoker, a second submarine, *E-14*, under the command of Lieutenant Commander Edward Courtney Boyle (1883–1967), had managed to get through. For what must have seemed an interminable period from 27 April to the night of 29 April, *E-14* came under almost continual shelling from shore batteries, having to surface to charge its batteries, swiftly diving to elude its foe, hampered throughout by a damaged periscope. As Stoker had done, for several hours Boyle kept his boat silent and hidden on the ocean floor, resting crew and craft in the hope that the Turks would think he had evaded them.

At one point Boyle torpedoed and sank a Turkish transport ship and by chance, on the evening of the 29th, he met up with Stoker's *AE-2*. For Stoker and his crew, exhausted by days and nights of nerve-wracking combat, hour upon hour being chased and harried at every turn, it was joyous to discover that they were not alone. Their travails, however, were not at an end. The following day the damaged *AE-2* refused to maintain a level plane, rising to the surface in spite of frantic efforts to the contrary by Stoker and his men: she was either refusing to answer her helm, because of being damaged, or had encountered inappropriate water, the traditional problem for submariners operating in the Dardanelles. At one point Stoker had been forced to put his craft into a deep and violent dive, venturing to a dangerous depth where she could have been crushed by the weight of water, the boat creaking and groaning in its agony.

The doughty *AE-2* had finally had enough; she rose to the surface, out of control, battered and bruised, almost willing herself to be sacrificed. She rose up into the morning light, dangerously close to a Turkish torpedo boat which immediately opened fire, thrice holing her engine room. Determined that the Turks would not capture his vessel Stoker had no choice but to scuttle her. He blew the main ballast tank, ordered the crew on deck and helped by his fellow officers, Lieutenant John Cary and Lieutenant Geoffrey Haggard, opened the remaining tanks to flood the craft. She sank at 10.45 a.m. on 30 April 1915.

Stoker and his crew were taken prisoner and would be held in captivity by the Turks for the next three and a half years, though for a time Stoker managed to escape, before being caught again. The crew were decorated and Stoker given the Distinguished Service Order (DSO). Stoker and his crew had shown the utmost courage and fortitude. He was promoted to commander in 1919 and offered other positions in the service, but he retired from the navy in 1920, later making his name as an actor, director and writer. At the outbreak of the Second World War he returned to naval duties, being given command of a submarine base, and helped in the planning of D-Day. Four years before his death in 1966 he became, in 1962, the Irish national croquet champion at the age of 77. Stoker characterised an iron resolution which ran through the submarine service. If the boats were remarkable, they were matched only by the spirit of their personnel.

Edward Boyle: Chameleon Submarine

The *E-14* persisted with her voyage, causing mayhem in the Marmara, sinking two ships, one of them a transport vessel bound for Gallipoli with 6,000 men and field guns aboard. The Turks were a persistent enemy, constantly chasing the submarine, once nearly cutting it in two with the bows of a destroyer; in that moment Boyle and his craft were within seconds of disaster. Though down to just one torpedo, *E-14*'s patrols disadvantaged Turkish shipping, inhibiting and altering its deployment, causing chaos with its communications and disrupting vital supply routes. Instead of urgent Turkish supplies being ferried quickly and easily by sea, they had to be transported overland on a time-consuming and difficult journey.

Again it was the fearful reputation of the submarine, its sometimes imaginary presence, which had helped to give the Allied forces a tactical advantage. To compensate for his lack of armaments, Boyle had devised a range of ploys to make the enemy think he was not alone. He dived, hid, laid low and used the sea as his cover. Then, after a suitable interval had elapsed, he would reappear in a different spot, his tell-tale periscope clear of the surface for all to see, causing massive alarms and diversions to shipping. Such capers convinced his foe their waters had been seized by more than a lone predator; in the Turks' more fevered reckonings they would have thought a marauding nest of submarines had gathered.

Boyle even rigged up a gun on his boat to help disguise it, making its profile appear that of a different craft; he would then remove it, dive and reappear, his craft devoid of the device. His subterfuge helped scare at least one or more Turkish steamers into making a sudden and hasty bolt for the safety of the shore.

The submarine has inherent guile. If a commander could summon up an equal cunning then the combination could wreak havoc. On 17 May, after being at sea for twenty days, Boyle departed, surfacing off Cape Helles, the south-western tip of the Gallipoli Peninsula, and escorted to Turkey's Imbros Island in the Aegean Sea, and to safety by a British destroyer. The crew were decorated and Boyle awarded the Victoria Cross. Boyle's illustrious career would continue, eventually retiring from the Royal Navy as a rear admiral.[26]

The Role of the Public Schools

As with several of his brother officers, Boyle was a former public school boy; in his case Cheltenham College, which in its time produced a plethora of surface, submarine and other military commanders. A public school background instilled in its pupils a sense of duty to crown, country and ones' fellow man. Christian principles were *de rigueur*. If not quite born to rule, there was a tacit understanding they would take a lead. Courage was *expected*: it would not have been manly to demonstrate a lack of nerve. Had counselling or psychiatric analysis existed, it is unlikely any would have agreed to it. Public schools ran army and navy cadet forces; it was beholden on pupils to enrol. It represented their first taste of the services, though some were of military families, dynasties which went back generations, be it army or navy, its members serving in Britain or its dominions. Sport was a priority: it encouraged, supposedly, a sense of team spirit. Young public school men were raised in the belief that they had a responsibility towards those less fortunate than themselves and a duty of care to those in their charge. Boarding schools and dormitories taught officers about the pressures of communal living, no mean consideration in the cramped, highly charged confines of a primitive First World War submarine. For younger crew members it would sometimes be the first time that they had been away from home; the officer corps were more used to being estranged from the familiar security of hearth, home and parents. They could cope with the miseries of a pioneer submarine having, after all, survived the rigours and deprivations of an English, Scottish or Irish public school. They were appropriately institutionalised from a tender age, having left home as children to first enter naval college and then the navy. Officers were generally resilient: capable, patriotic, of moral fibre. They had initiative and learned years before how to fend for themselves. Those insufficiently resourceful were weeded out. In surface ships the incompetent might hide their inadequacies in a large vessel amid the presence of a sizeable complement, for a while at least. With a small crew in a little boat there was never anywhere to hide.

Geoffrey Saxton-White

Torpedoes were dangerous, and not only to the recipients. As the war moved to its bloody denouement Lieutenant Commander Geoffrey Saxton-White (1886–1918), in command of Boyle's old submarine, *E-14*, left the Greek port of Mudros on the Mediterranean island of Lemnos on 28 January 1918. His mission was to try and force the Dardanelle Straits and attack the German battlecruiser the *Goeben*, which was said to have run aground after being damaged in one of her sorties in the Dardanelles. White would be another of the Great War submariners to be awarded the Victoria Cross. *E-14* had scouted for the warship but failed to find her. When she turned for home she encountered another enemy ship and fired a torpedo. Instead of reaching its target the torpedo suddenly exploded within yards and seconds of exiting the submarine. The size of the detonation and its close proximity badly damaged the craft. Inside the boat the crew were cast into darkness, the electrical circuits having malfunctioned. The blast had sprung the fore-hatch and water was pouring into the submarine. With its stability wrecked the submarine immediately rose in the water, attracting heavy shelling from the shore batteries. White dived his boat and managed to make headway, but the vessel and its systems had been mortally damaged. It became uncontrollable and, with the air supply close to exhaustion, White had no choice but to bring her to the surface, trying to make for shore to give his crew a chance of being saved. For more than half an hour she came under heavy fire. Throughout the bombardment White stayed on deck, directing as best he could his crippled vessel towards land. She sank, however, and White and his crew were killed. He was 32. Nine months later, in October 1918, the Armistice between Turkey and the Allies was signed at Mudros, from where White and his men had set off on their fateful voyage.

Martin Nasmith: Swimming with Torpedoes

In a roll call of daring men who witnessed action in the Dardanelles, other names stand out. And none more so than Lieutenant Commander Martin Eric Dunbar-Nasmith (1883–1965) of the submarine *E-11*. Nasmith – he was later knighted and added the Dunbar to his name in 1920 after marrying Beatrix Justin Dunbar-Rivers – achieved a formidable tally of kills in the Dardanelles. After the Royal Naval College in Dartmouth, he had joined the navy in 1896 at the age of 15. On 19 May 1915, in his submarine *E-11*, built by Vickers at Barrow and launched a year before, he left for what would become the most successful mission to the Sea of Marmara. Nasmith and his craft departed quietly in the dead of night, slipping away from the Allied submarine base on the Aegean island of Imbros. His tour of duty would last until 7 June.

The Straits and the treacherous Narrows were mined, protected by batteries of powerful guns, netting threaded across the waters to entangle and snare invaders. Gunboats and destroyers kept a ceaseless vigil and spotlights pierced the darkness. Despite the perils Nasmith got through to the Marmara where he and his crew in *E-11* ran amok. Though constantly harassed and attacked – he lost his periscope in one assailment – he sank or crippled eleven ships, including an ammunition carrier, a sizeable gunboat, transport and store ships. The naval historian Peter Kemp wrote:

> Since these submarines could carry only a limited number of torpedoes, he [Nasmith] evolved a means of making every one of them tell by setting them to float at the end of their run and recovering all that did not hit their targets. This involved following up the track of the torpedo, and, when close enough, swimming off to it and removing the firing pistol before manoeuvring it, tail first, through the rear torpedo tube back into the submarine, a particularly dangerous operation as a single false move in the removal of the pistol could detonate the warhead. It was typical of Nasmith that he always insisted in swimming off and removing the pistol himself when a torpedo was to be recovered ... throughout his naval career Nasmith was a man of great courage, modesty and integrity; the beau ideal of a naval officer.[27]

Nasmith won the VC and his crew were decorated. He went on more successful operations in the Marmara: in three missions he sank or disabled fifty-eight smaller ships and a diversity of twenty-seven larger steamers. In 1932 he was knighted and in the Second World War made commander-in-chief at Plymouth and the Western Approaches, charged with defeating the Atlantic U-boat menace. Of Turkey, Edward Horton wrote:

> Rarely can a nation at war have suffered such depredations at the hands of a small number of foes in its midst ... the Turks were desperate to obtain some means of combating the marauders, but in the absence of really effective anti-submarine devices there was little they could do. They appealed to their German allies for naval help and they got it.[28]

Introducing Silas Q. Swing

Submarine commanders had to be resourceful, innovative and audacious. Martin Nasmith, on 21 May 1915, overhauled a small Turkish sailing ship. Instead of sinking it he lashed his submarine to its side and, thus disguised, cruised all day off Constantinople on the look out for enemy ships. As it transpired he failed to find any, but it was a novel guise. There were moments of merriment as well as bravery. Nasmith came upon a small steamer which, on examination, was found to be carrying guns. He ordered her crew to abandon the ship, having decided to blow it up. The crew of the steamer were in a state of understandable panic and, in the chaos, some of the boats into which they had tried to jump and scramble were capsized. In the midst of the melee and confusion, with participants screaming and shouting, there suddenly appeared a figure on the upper deck of the steamer proclaiming to be called Mr Silas Q. Swing, a correspondent of the *Chicago Sun* newspaper. Admiral Wemyss recalled:

> He [Mr Swing] assured the somewhat astonished submarine commander that he was pleased to make his acquaintance! Nor was this the only instance of absence of hostile feeling encountered, for with the crew of a sailing vessel whose cargo was found to be innocent Nasmith relates that 'they parted with many expressions of goodwill on both sides'.[29]

Snared by a Mine

Submarines would frequently bump along the bottom or scrape against unidentified and unexpected objects. On 7 June 1915 Nasmith was in the Narrows at a depth of 70ft when his boat appeared to have hit heavily either the bottom of the channel or an object in its path. While trying to investigate the problem, Nasmith gingerly brought his boat up to 20ft – any more and it would have been rammed or shelled by the enemy. A large mine had come loose and was found to be hanging by its mooring ropes from the stern of the submarine. It was impossible for the boat to free itself of the floating bomb while it remained submerged. But to have risen higher in the water would have exposed it to the shore guns and to Turkish patrol boats. For more than an hour Nasmith continued his passage beneath the water, throughout which the mine tapped and knocked on the hull of his boat. Finally, in a more remote corner of the waters, Nasmith risked coming to the surface where, by clever manoeuvring – and luck – he somehow managed to free it of the explosive.[30]

The Intervention of *U-21*

Submariners who had managed to inveigle their craft into the Marmara proved that, even if in treacherous and confined waters, heavily mined and under round-the-clock surveillance from surface protectors and a phalanx of powerful shore batteries, a well-run and fortunate boat could cause mayhem. Today such intrepid raids would be impossible, given the advances in submarine detection. Germany, in coming to the assistance of the beleaguered Turks, sent one of its most formidable submarines, the *U-21*, to the Aegean. Its passage had been long and arduous, from the Kiel Canal, round Britain and through the Straits of Gibraltar; a perilous voyage which had demanded stamina and cunning in her commander and crew, and a significant reliability and capability from the submarine. The *U-21* arrived in the Dardanelles in late May 1915. While en route to the Dardanelles her sister craft, *U-20*, was operating elsewhere and, on the afternoon of 7 May 1915, altered the course of the war by attacking, as mentioned previously, the *Lusitania*, 8 miles off the Irish coast.

When *U-21* reached her destination in the Dardanelles she quickly put an end to the relative freedom which the Allies had enjoyed. Within two days she had torpedoed and sunk HMS *Triumph* (1903) on 25 May, and HMS *Majestic* (1895) on the 27th. The *Triumph* lost seventy-three men; the *Majestic* forty-three. Both were pre-*dreadnought* battleships.

Max Horton: North Sea and the Baltic

In the different theatres of combat the North Sea and the Baltic campaigns brought more submariners to the fore: among them the redoubtable Max Kennedy Horton (1883–1951), the commander who had initiated the tradition of flying the Jolly Roger pirate pennant from victorious submarines. He was of the elite who built reputations in the Great War and performed sterling service twenty years later in the Second World War.[*]

Horton made his mark as a resolute warrior skippering HMS *E-9*, in which he torpedoed and sank the German cruiser *Hela* on 13 September 1914 while

---

[*] During the second half of the Second World War Horton became the commander-in-chief of the Western Approaches, a classic example of hunter turned gamekeeper. He was axial in the Allied campaign – but not before considerable losses – to rid the Atlantic of the German U-boat menace which, as in the Great War, posed one of the greatest threats of the conflict.

on patrol off Heligoland. For the rest of the day he was pursued and harried, but managed to get back to his base in the British east coast port of Harwich. On 6 October 1914 he sank a German destroyer, the *S116* – later re-numbered *T116* – and was awarded the DSO, the first in a clutch of decorations in recognition of his fearlessness in a series of hair-raising encounters.

Geoffrey Layton: The Flouting of International Law

Other names would achieve glory, among them Lieutenant Commander Geoffrey Layton of *E-13*, destined to be knighted and made an admiral. En route to the Baltic, on the night of 18–19 August 1915, the young Layton's boat ran aground in Danish territorial waters. Germany had established substantial commercial links with neutral Sweden, as its purchase of Swedish iron ore was vital to the German war machine. The sea traffic in iron ore in the closed waters of the Baltic had to be stopped and British submarines were dispatched to impede it. Layton's craft had suffered from a malfunctioning gyrocompass. His boat had become fast in the shallows of Saltholm Island, in the Oresund, the strait which lies between Sweden and Denmark. To sailors the area is one of enormous peril, with fickle tides and strong easterly winds sweeping in from the Baltic. After a cold and miserable night, failing to budge their craft, Layton and his crew were confronted the next morning by a Danish torpedo boat, the *Narhvalen*. Its captain informed them that under international law they would have to shift their vessel within twenty-four hours or the Danes would be obliged to intern both it and them. Layton sensibly dispatched his first lieutenant to the Danish warship, telling him that, on reaching Copenhagen, he had to inform the navy of his boat's plight. Some time later a German torpedo boat, *G-132*, arrived. It steamed away when the Danish torpedo boats *Soulven* and *Storen* appeared, and which were joined later by a third Danish torpedo boat, the *Tumleren*.

In the meantime, *Oberleutnant zur See* Graf von Montgelas, the commander of *G-132*, had reported the presence of the grounded submarine to the commander of the German Baltic Coast Defence Division, Rear Admiral Mishke, who ordered that the vessel, still stuck fast, be destroyed. The torpedo boat *G-132* returned, accompanied by another torpedo boat, and opened fire, first unsuccessfully with a torpedo, and then with continual shelling, hitting the submarine repeatedly, ceasing only when the Danish *Soulven* manoeuvred into a position where it placed itself between the German attackers and their quarry. Fire broke out on the submarine. The batteries had been hit and poisonous chlorine gas had contaminated the boat. Layton and his men had to quickly abandon their craft. Some tried to swim to the shore, but half the boat's company, fifteen men, were drowned. The rest were interned in Denmark, Layton among them, though he eventually escaped to Norway with his first lieutenant and then home to resume the war. As the naval historian Paul Halpern wrote, the incident was:

> ... a brutal violation of international law [and] a clear indication of just how seriously they took the threat of British submarines.[31]

There were charges and counter-charges that the Germans had shot crew members while they were trying to swim to safety. Halpern:

> The Germans claimed the submarine had fired back and hotly denied firing at the men in the water. The Danes protested strongly. *E-13* was subsequently refloated and interned ... for the duration of the war.[32]*

Francis Cromie: A High Tally

On 4 September 1915 another important name in submarine annals, Lieutenant Commander Francis Newton Allen Cromie (1882–1918), set sail for the Baltic in his craft, *E-19*. He was accompanied by *E-18* under the command of Lieutenant Commander R.C. Halahan. By September 1915 the Royal Navy had five submarines operating in the Baltic, those of Cromie and Halahan among them. The Russian submarine fleet was beginning to take effect in the Baltic; a construction programme had begun in 1912 and, by 1915, submarines of the Russian *Bars*-class were filtering through.**

---

* When Layton escaped his internment in Denmark he had disguised himself as a Danish seaman and left a decoy in his bed to fool his guards. He had exited the building in which he was being held by using a classic escapee technique: climbing out of a bedroom window by tying together and clambering down hammock lashings. After various other disguises – in one he posed as a Finnish seaman, in another as an American – he eventually succeeded in getting back to England, where he was arrested before the Admiralty was able to confirm his identity.[33]

** Less sophisticated and agile than the British *E*-class, the *Bars*-class carried a more formidable range of armaments. The *Bars* had torpedoes mounted externally, which added to drag, impairing smoothness of line and reducing hydrodynamic efficiency. The engines, too, were prone to breakdowns.

Until the Armistice and the Russian Revolution, British submarines had used Allied-Russian naval bases, their task being to sink enemy ships which voyaged between Germany and Sweden, many loaded with valuable iron ore. Cromie's submarine, commissioned in 1914 and built by Vickers, scored significant victories. On the morning of 11 October 1915 it began its patrol in the south Baltic by intercepting the *SS Walther Leonhardt*, a German steamship carrying Swedish iron ore.

Cromie and his men ordered the crew into lifeboats and sank the carrier with explosives. Another German ship, the ore carrier *SS Germania*, witnessed the explosion and subsequent sinking, and later that morning made a run for it. Cromie gave chase, racing his submarine on the surface, trying to keep up with the steamer, firing at it with his deck gun. In its haste and panic the ship ran aground and was later destroyed by Cromie and his crew using dynamite charges.

The next to be sunk by Cromie and his men boarding the vessel and opening its valves was the German *SS Gutrune*. There was more to come. The elderly *SS Director Reppenhagen* was sunk in the same manner as the *Gutrune*, its seacocks and valves opened. Next came the German *SS Nicomedia*. There is a story that the *Nicomedia*'s crew gave Cromie and his men a barrel of beer; fable or not Cromie sent it to the bottom like the rest. In just one day Cromie had sunk four German ships and crippled another – the *Germania* refused to sink and was later salvaged. They had inflicted the losses without expending a single torpedo, which was just as well as they had been plagued by carrying faulty torpedoes.*

Days later Max Horton was back in action. Between 18 and 19 October 1915 his *E-9* lurked between Landsdort and Haradskar, south of the Stockholm archipelago. He attacked four German ships carrying coal and wood; three sank, the fourth was crippled, their crews put into lifeboats or their safety otherwise assured. Though conventions of decency were observed by the British, the actions of Allied submarines in the Baltic were disputatious: iron ore had not been listed as contraband under the 1913 Declaration of London and there were incidents which angered Sweden about sinkings being in or close to neutral or territorial waters. The German Navy always presented robust counter-charges to suggestions that they had breached international law.

---

* On 31 August 1918, Cromie, by then a naval attaché, was murdered in the British Embassy in Petrograd (formerly St Petersburg). He was shot by the Cheka (Bolshevik secret police) for his alleged role in an anti-Bolshevik coup. Britain was backing the 'White Russian' forces of Tsarists and anti-Bolsheviks. The Cheka killed more than 6,000 White Russian supporters.

Francis Goodhart: The Sinking of the *Prinz Adalbert*

Francis Goodhart, the commander of *E-8*, was another who caused havoc in the Baltic. Built at Britain's Chatham naval yard, *E-8* had been launched in 1914. She sailed for the Baltic on 15 August 1915. Her passage had been difficult; she was harassed by German patrol craft and had suffered damage to a propeller. A week later *E-8* joined up with *E-9* and they sailed into Revel harbour – now Tallinn, Estonia.*

In the Baltic Goodhart struck a devastating blow. On 23 October 1915, approximately 20 miles off Libau, once an important Russian port on the Baltic – now Liepaja in Latvia – he engaged the SMS *Prinz Adalbert*, an armoured cruiser escorted by two destroyers. His torpedo wreaked huge damage, causing the *Prinz Adalbert*'s magazines to explode. Named in honour of Kaiser Wilhelm II's third son, Prince Adalbert of Prussia, and commissioned in 1904, the craft had been built as a gunnery vessel at the German naval shipyard in Kiel. In 1914 she had been attached to the Scouting Group III of the High Seas Fleet and had later joined German operations in the Baltic. When Goodhart made his strike the *Adalbert* had just undergone an extensive refit, having been damaged by a torpedo attack three months earlier by *E-9*. After Goodhart's attack she sank immediately with the loss of 672 lives. There were only three survivors. It was Germany's worst Baltic disaster.**

British submarines in the Baltic vitiated the German military campaign. Germany was debilitated by having only a few ports and outlets in the Baltic, which made it more feasible for a limited number of submarines – which because of assiduous tactical manoeuvrings the enemy thought part of a greater fleet – to conduct a blockade.

The important naval base of Kiel could be readily patrolled. The ferrying of critical cargos such as iron ore dwindled to a trickle as submarines raised their game. Max Horton raided Kiel harbour, causing panic in the German fleet and

---

* The Revel harbour area had long been familiar with conflict: it was the scene of a Russo–Swedish naval battle in 1790. Struggles for control of the Baltic were nothing new. They stemmed from the sixteenth and seventeenth centuries when Sweden gradually usurped the declining Hanseatic League, a hangover from medieval days, and Denmark, its neighbour and occasional foe, as the foremost Baltic power.

** Goodhart would later perish in one of the contentious steam-driven *K*-class submarines (see Chapter 8).

obliging commanders to move warships into what they thought safer waters; ships which could have been used more productively elsewhere by the German command had to spend time and fuel trying to catch him. Such exercises tied up German capital ships and were costly in both economic and strategic terms. For the German fleet fuel had become scarce and expensive. Provisioning and fuelling any fleet at war at sea had for centuries been difficult. Baltic hostilities were no different, complicated by the knowledge that submarines were in the vicinity. Though trying to hunt them down was expensive, the German fleet had no choice: a lone craft – let alone a flotilla, as some imagined – could herald catastrophe. Horton's raid on Kiel harbour and the German hunting party which pursued him was another example of the psychological impact the real or imagined presence of a submarine could cause, the threatened surface ships assigning to it awesome abilities often beyond the reality – not always, as the sinking of the *Adalbert* had shown. Ships heavy with iron ore sat in port, frightened to venture out. Such raw materials had to be acquired from elsewhere, necessitating slow, costly and vulnerable overland journeys.

The way in which Allied submarines frustrated German operations was evident in the planned German attack on the Russian city of Riga, now the capital of Latvia. Germany intended a land assault reinforced by a powerful naval presence. A formidable fleet had been mustered under the command of Admirals Franz Ritter von Hipper (1863–1932) and Erhard Schmidt (1863–1946). En route from Danzig to Riga on 19 August 1915, Lieutenant Commander Noel Laurence's submarine *E-1* torpedoed and damaged the battlecruiser *Moltke*, a powerful big-gun ship (1911) which would see action in the Battle of Jutland the following year. Later in his career Laurence was knighted and made an admiral. Had he sunk the *Moltke* (23,000 tons) with 1,000 crew and forty officers it would have been a major trophy for the Allies – as it turned out, she was scuttled in 1919 to stop her falling into Allied hands. But a screen of protective destroyers had prevented him from following up his attack. However, after Laurence's assault, Hipper and Schmidt ordered their ships back to base, alarmed by the presence of a submarine, or submarines, aware that their vessels were virtually helpless in combating them. Devoid of naval enforcement the land assault on Riga failed; for the Allies it was only a temporary victory, with German forces making a successful occupation weeks later. As with Great Britain, Germany would eventually adopt convoy screening to deter Allied submarines. Her reluctance was rooted, in part, in the cost and the strategic compromise in tying up scarce capital ships whose presence was always urgently needed elsewhere.

A Sad Conclusion

The German occupation of Tallinn in 1918 and the signing of the Brest–Litovsk peace treaty between the Central Powers and Russia's new Bolshevik government on 3 March 1918, which put at end to Russia's participation in the conflict, forced the British submarine flotilla to move to Finland. There, however, Germany became embroiled in the Finnish Civil War, leaving the British with no choice but to scuttle their eight-strong submarine flotilla and their three support ships, the *Obsidian*, *Emilie* and *Cicero*, near Helsinki harbour, to stop the craft falling into German hands. It was a sad and unsatisfactory conclusion to the heroic efforts which had been made by the infant submarine service. The treaty increased German influence in Estonia, Latvia, Lithuania, Poland, Finland, Belorussia and the Ukraine. Effectively it deprived Russia of 30 per cent of its imperial population.[34]

Richard Sandford: Zeebrugge

The fifth VC awarded to a Great War submariner went to Richard Douglas Sandford (1891–1918) in a different theatre of conflict. Sandford had been part of a force which played a role in the Zeebrugge raid in Belgium on 23 April 1918. German U-boats were stationed at Zeebrugge and had proved a menace. The idea was to sink obsolete British ships at the entrance to the harbour in order to block it and pen in German submarines and other vessels. An ambitious and dangerous operation, it had been approved by the audacious Roger Keyes (see Appendix H).

The plan met with a large number of casualties. A fleet of seventy-five ships and some 1,700 men participated. Two obsolete submarines, *C-1* and *C-3*, were packed with explosives; manned by volunteer crews the two craft were effectively transformed into floating bombs. *C-1* broke down and was unable to take part. *C-3*, under the command of Sandford, continued with its mission. The submarine was supposed to destroy a viaduct, the plan being that under cover of darkness and a smokescreen the submarine would aim directly at the viaduct, before ramming and wedging itself into its girders and steel work. The submariners would then set the timer to detonate the explosives a few minutes hence and make their escape as best they could in a small boat just before the submarine, and hopefully the viaduct, were blown to pieces.

In its daring, some might say madness, it could only have been a plot sanctioned by Keyes. In the event, the wind changed and the smoke screen disappeared, leaving Sandford and his crew exposed to heavy artillery fire.

There was still 1½ mile to be covered before the submarine reached its target. It is astonishing it was not shelled out of the water, but it seems the German gunners were distracted by explosions and gunfire elsewhere: the mayhem was being caused by surface ships and 200 marines who were trying to get ashore and who were coming under a heavy and merciless bombardment. Sandford steered his craft at the viaduct, ploughing it into the steel work. Having set the timer he and his men took to a small boat. Within a moment there was a mighty roar and debris rained upon them. In the chaos they were thrown into the water and miraculously rescued by another small boat. The crew were decorated and Sandford won the Victoria Cross. Sandford died at the age of 27, a few days after the Armistice was signed, not from wounds or enemy action but from typhoid.

Tricks and Ploys

A combination of the submarines' inherent guile, matched by the cunning and courage of its commanders, gave the submarine a special terror. The captain of a surface ship had no such advantage: beyond the vastness of an ocean its bulk could rarely be concealed. Playing to the strengths of their submarines, commanders would engage in tactics based on subterfuge and disguise. Some of the tricks became known as the 'tethered goat' ploys. This comprised a submarine hiding beneath an Allied mercantile ship which appeared, in its lack of armaments, to be easy prey for a U-boat predator. A U-boat might then be tempted to the surface with the intention of boarding and sinking its prey, rather than wasting one of its torpedoes; it would then either hole it beneath the water line with its deck gun or have its crew open its seacocks. Once the U-boat had surfaced the British submarine would break cover, rising from the water to make its challenge. It worked only until U-boat commanders became familiar with the strategy.

The year of 1915 was the most productive for Allied submarines: their blockade had exacerbated Germany's internal pressures; the limited number of Baltic outlets had become dangerous to inoperable, which had contributed to food and fuel costs rising in Germany. For the Allied submarine service, buoyed by victories and hungry for more, it became a duller, less fruitful period. There were fewer easy targets for the Allies because Germany had instituted the convoy system. German commercial traffic was now chaperoned by warships and naval targets had become increasingly rare.

The Independent Submarine

The Allied submarine campaign left an indelible imprint. For more than 300 years warships had ruled the seas. Within fifteen years of John Holland's creation, however, the submarine had become one of the navy's most potent weapons. Its technology was still lacking: communications, propulsion, weaponry; its 'blindness' when submerged and its need to surface to charge its batteries; in the years ahead there would be ceaseless refinement. Despite its shortcomings it had shown it did not have to be under the custodianship of the surface fleet. It could operate alone and in distant oceans for relatively long periods with a reasonable degree of reliability. By 1915–16 it had begun to usurp the role of the battleship as the capital vessel of the Royal Navy. It did not have the battleship's majesty, but would achieve its own glory. At the outbreak of hostilities in 1914 the outspoken and distinguished surface commander, Admiral Sir Percy Scott, one of the Royal Navy's experts on gunnery, said:

> As the motor vehicle has driven the horse from the road, so has the submarine driven the battleship from the sea.[35]

To Blockade and Spy

The submarine had established its prowess and near – at the time – invincibility. That is not to claim that in axial terms of losses and gains, victories and defeats, the First World War was an unadulterated success for British and Allied submarines. Far from it. At war's end, fifty-four British boats and, in most cases their entire crews, had been lost: the figure represented over three boats lost each quarter. Nor for those in the service did the war represent four years of buccaneering heroics and unremitting excitement. While often in the grip of terror and dread anticipation, much time was spent on thankless patrols in the inhospitable Baltic or the grey waters of the North Sea. Though the submarine is at its most potent as a predator, the Admiralty's recognition that surface ships were vulnerable as blockade vessels gave it a new distinction. To those who had watched its progress with moral disdain or strategic disbelief, it finally dawned that with its ability to hide from aerial or ocean marauder, and to move quietly to a fresh location, a submarine could be more effective than a blockade warship. During the hours and weeks on patrol, submariners became the ears and eyes of the surface navy. Their vital, often nerve-wracking, sometimes interminably tedious patrols, allowed the submarine to demonstrate another virtue: that of spy, messenger and communicator. Again, its approval rose, even among hardcore sceptics.

New Developments

Submarine development did not cease with the *E*-class, however. Before the war ended several new types were built: some capable, others less so, and some of them unmitigated disasters. Three *F*-class submarines for coastal patrol work were built by three different yards: the Chatham naval dockyard, Thornycroft and White's yards.[36] A total of fourteen *G*-class (1914–17) boats were modelled closely on the successful *E*-class. Constructed by Scotts, Vickers, Armstrong Whitworth and at the naval yard in Chatham, their fitments included an electric cooker and a Fessenden oscillator, a device devised to send signals from one submarine to another. Experiments to improve communications involved several foremost scientists, including Ernest Rutherford, the first person to split the atom (see Appendix M).

The struggle to find a way of containing the submarine menace continued throughout the war. Though some submarines were in themselves useful layers of mines, in different forms it would be the mine and the depth charge which would rank among the submarines' greatest perils. After the *G*-class a large number of *H*-class vessels were produced, forty-two in all, with the first batch of ten boats built in Vickers' Canadian yards in Montreal. With the urgencies and unusual demands of war, British yards had become too hard-pressed to take on further work. The *H*-class were smaller than some predecessor boats. Built in three batches, those in the first two batches were 150ft long, while craft in the third batch were 170ft. The second group of submarines comprised another ten boats built at the Fore River Yard (1883–1986) at Quincy, Massachusetts.*

Fore River's eminent history failed to stop it being caught in a diplomatic row about its construction of *H*-class submarines; their building had begun in 1915 when the US was still neutral. Consequently, under international duress, America impounded the craft and would not release them until 1917 when it had finally entered the war. The remaining twenty-two *H*-class craft were constructed by Vickers and three other foremost British yards: William Beardmore (1890–1930) of Glasgow and the Clyde; Cammell Laird (1828–1992) of Birkenhead and the Mersey; and Armstrong Whitworth (1847–1927) when the company merged with Vickers to become Vickers-Armstrongs of Newcastle and the Tyne. Little

---

* Fore River had an impressive reputation. Its importance as a builder of US Navy submarines, battleships and aircraft carriers grew in the Second World War. In 1902 it had constructed the giant and legendary 475ft, seven-masted sailing schooner, the *Thomas W. Lawson*; built to carry 11,000 tons of coal she went down with the loss of seventeen men in a storm off the Isles of Scilly in 1907.

but national ruination is the standard outcome of war, but Britain's shipyards, at times employing as many as 40,000 people, were galvanised by such orders; Great War commitments, though, failed to stave off eventual calamity in the industry which succumbed to a wave of mergers, state intervention and closures which devastated Britain's once all-conquering shipbuilding sector.[37]

Swiftness: A Constant Quest

A continuing problem for submarines was that of speed. They had become faster but it was impossible to keep up with surface ships, either the ships of the Royal Navy, or in its role as predator or surveillance craft if stalking an enemy warship. When the *H*-class boats were being built, the Admiralty were informed, wrongly as it turned out, that Germany was building a new generation of exceedingly fast submarines. If anything was guaranteed to imbue urgency at this time it was a suggestion that Germany was to acquire a weapon more potent than anything in its own arsenal. The Admiralty had wanted a submarine flotilla which it could deploy for reconnaissance in the Heligoland Bight. The new boats, the *J*-class, would be fitted with the latest long-range radios to report movements of the High Seas Fleet back to London. The *J*-class boats would need to be swift in their role as scouts in order to keep up with German warships. They were powered by three 1,200hp Vickers diesel engines which produced 19.5 knots, making them among the fastest boats in the world, though not quite as swift as some warships. Seven *J*-class submarines were built, and their success encouraged the Admiralty to strive for an even quicker and more ambitious class. With the benefit of hindsight it is almost a pity the *J*-class were so accomplished. They acted as an incentive for the Admiralty to strive for an even better and swifter craft, an ambition which would end in disaster. The *J*-class led to the construction of the vast steam-powered *K*-class. Intended as fast and formidable, they become infamous, effectively scuppered before they had even departed the drawing board by the Admiralty's insistence on achieving impossibly ambitious levels of scale and speed.

Notes

1 www.maritimequest.com, quoting Talbot's son
2 www.maritimequest.com, quoting Talbot's son
3 Compton-Hall, *Submarine Boats*, p.172
4 Compton-Hall, *Submarine Boats*, p.174
5 Compton-Hall, *Submarine Boats*, p.178; from USN Office of Naval Intelligence document 'for official circulation only', dated February 1926
6 Compton-Hall, *Submarine Boats*, p.174

7 Howarth, David, *British Sea Power*, p.415

8 Beesly, Patrick, *Room 40: British Naval Intelligence, 1914–1918* (Hamish Hamilton, 1982), pp.206–7, 216

9 Beesly, *Room 40*, chapter 7

10 Beesly, *Room 40*, p.85

11 Frank, *The Sea Wolves* (Rinehart, 1955)

12 Frank, *The Sea Wolves*, p.6

13 Frank, *The Sea Wolves*, p.7

14 Frank, *The Sea Wolves*, pp.7–8

15 Black, *Naval Power*, p.156

16 Black, *Naval Power*, p.157; Black, *Tools of War*, pp.147–48

17 Horton, *The Illustrated History of the Submarine* (Book Club Associates, 1974) p.103

18 Horton, *The Illustrated History of the Submarine*, p.103

19 Thompson, *The War at Sea 1914–1918*, p.268; quoting from a letter Holbrook sent to Roger Brownlow Keyes, in Lambert, *The Submarine Service*, pp.300–301

20 Thompson, *The War at Sea*, p.269; from Holbrook–Keyes letter in Lambert, *The Submarine Service*, p.300–1

21 Thompson, *The War at Sea*, p.269

22 *The New York Times*, 15 December 1914

23 Green, Brett, *HMAS Otway of Holbrook*; Webby, *Musings on Holbrook (or Germanton)*

24 Wemyss, Admiral of the Fleet, Lord, *The Navy in the Dardanelles Campaign* (Hodder & Stoughton, c. 1918), p.152

25 Wemyss, *The Navy in the Dardanelles Campaign*, p.152

26 Australian Government Department of Veterans' Affairs: http://www.anzacsite.gov.au/5environment/submarines/AE-2.html; Commander H.G. Stoker's biography *Straws in the Wind* (Herbert Jenkins Ltd., 1925)

27 Kemp, Peter (ed.), *The Oxford Companion to Ships & the Sea* (Oxford University Press, 1976), p.574

28 Horton, *The Illustrated History of the Submarine*, p.86

29 Wemyss, *The Navy in the Dardanelles Campaign*, p.154

30 Wemyss, *The Navy in the Dardanelles Campaign*, p.154–55

31 Halpern, Paul, *A Naval History of World War One* (US Naval Institute, published in UK by UCL Press Ltd, 1994), pp.200–201

32 Halpern, *A Naval History*, p.201

33 Balsved, Johhny, *Fladens Historie*, www.navalhistory.dk/english history/1914-1918/E13-Escape.htm

34 Pope, Wheal and Robbins, *The Macmillan Dictionary of the First World War*, p.83

35 Admiral Sir Percy Scott, letter to *The Times* newspaper, 5 June 1914

36 Colledge, J.J., *Ships of the Royal Navy*, vols 1 and 2 (Greenhill, 1969)

37 Richie, L.A., *The Shipbuilding Industry: A Guide to Historical Records* (Manchester University Press, 1992); Burstall, A.R., *Shipbuilding in Liverpool: Sea Breezes*, vol. 20, April–May 1936 (Mersey Docks and Harbour Board Estate Records); Moss, Michael S., *Oxford Dictionary of National Biography: Beardmore, William, Baron Invernairn (1856–1936)* (Oxford University Press, 2004); Colledge, *Ships of the Royal Navy* (Casemate, revised edn 2010, first edn 1970); Perkins, J.D., *The Canadian Submarine Service in Review* (Vanwell Publishing, 2000)

The huge K-class: 'too many damned holes'.

8

The Ill-fated *K-class*

The only way the Admiralty could exceed the swiftness of the *J*-class was to build a class of vessels which were propelled by steam. No diesel unit, or any engine imagined in the future, could provide the requisite degree of power. Experts, including Jacky Fisher, vehemently rejected the idea. With his characteristic bluntness, Fisher informed a leading steam proponent, the commander of the Grand Fleet, Admiral Jellicoe, that to put a steam engine into a submarine would be madness. Memories were stirred of problems encountered in the past with steam-powered submarines: impossibly hot temperatures in craft; the difficulty and slowness in extinguishing boilers – and relighting them – when a submarine dived, making it vulnerable on the surface; tell-tale smoke trails which compromised stealth; inundation through leaking chimneys and a plethora of apertures. Speed became a flawed and dangerous preoccupation: the attainment of swiftness through the use of an inappropriate engine. The Admiralty could be obdurate and pressed on with building the ill-fated steam-powered *K*-class.

The *K*-class were giants: their silliness would end in calamity and extract a dreadful toll. Despite widespread reservations, the navy commissioned seventeen *K*-class boats between 1916 and 1918. Submarine author Don Everitt writes:

> No class of modern warship in the Royal Navy, or in any other navy, has ever suffered so much calamity as the *K-boats*. They were involved in sixteen major accidents and countless small mishaps. One sank on her trials. Three were lost after collisions. A fifth disappeared. Another sank in harbour. The loss of life was appalling ... the *K-boats* became the object of much superstition, hatred and contention. They were frequently described as the 'suicide club' ... [1]

Everitt also states that the *K*-class were:

... the products of bad design and bad strategy and that their continued use in the face of many accidents typified the bigotry of many naval and military minds of that era. [But] there were many who regarded them with affection and pride ... brilliant in conception and performance, years ahead of their time, but unhappily pursued by ill-luck.[2]

The concept of the K-class was not that of a submarine but an underwater warship. The navy expected it to do everything a surface destroyer could do. It had failed to understand that hybrids, mongrel weapons, do not work. The Admiralty had committed similar blunders with airships, seeing them as flying warships (see Appendix C). Built by Vickers-Armstrongs the K-class were 339ft long and 26ft wide, almost twice the length and width of the successful E-class boats. The K-class displaced 1,980 tons on the surface and 2,566 tons if dived, some three times heavier than an E-class vessel. On the surface they were super fast, 24 knots, driven by twin 10,500hp Yarrow boilers which powered geared turbines, made by Parsons or Brown-Curtis, two names with proud histories. The engineer and aristocrat, the Anglo-Irish Charles Algernon Parsons (1854–1931), had invented the steam turbine. With a Cambridge First in mathematics to his name he had founded the Parsons Marine Steam Turbine Company in Newcastle. He found fame gate crashing the Spithead Review in 1897, Queen Victoria's Diamond Jubilee Fleet Review at Plymouth. In his spirited *Turbinia* (1894) he could reach 34 knots. The tiny *Turbinia*, a gentleman's yacht, had sped and weaved through the vast Spithead assemblage of ships, clad in bunting and finery. Naval chiefs gasped; never had they seen such a swift craft. As well as finely tuned turbines its hull was elegantly slender, helping it slice through the water, enhancing its speed; a feature submarine engineers noted with interest.

The quality of the engineering pedigree in the K-class was high, though the design was criticised as convoluted. Maritime historian Christopher Chant:

> [The K-class's] faulty tactical origin was matched by the complexity of the K-class design's propulsion arrangement, which was based on two steam boiler units each with its own funnel and air inlet. Before the boat could dive, therefore, the boiler had to be damped down, the funnels retracted, and all openings sealed against water ingress. It was, as one observer of the time said, a question of 'too many damned holes'.[3]

Powered on the surface by oil-powered steam turbines the K-craft had an auxiliary diesel generator of 800hp. Built by Vickers it drove a dynamo and charged banks of batteries when the vessels were on the surface. Though its propulsive power was limited, the generator could be used to drive the craft if it was hampered by problems which might result from its use of steam boilers. Julian Thompson noted:

> Like many dual-purpose weapons systems, in this case boats that were devised to operate with the fleet like destroyers on the surface, yet have the characteristics of submarines when dived, the design contained flaws, which gave them a reputation for bad luck. The *K-boats* had funnels and watertight hatches that could be closed in thirty seconds. But small obstructions could jam these open.[4]

The *K*-class had eight torpedo tubes: four in the bow and four in the beam. Originally they had two tubes on the deck which were mounted on a swivelling apparatus; they were found unsatisfactory and subsequently removed. They had deck armaments and an additional eight torpedoes, as well as the eight in the tubes. The crew numbered fifty-nine, six being officers. Surface range was said to be 12,500 miles at 10 knots. But dive times could take five minutes, a serious drawback. From the start the vessels were cumbersome and difficult to handle: it was inevitable that problems would stem from their scale. They could dive to 200ft but were 339ft long. At maximum depth they had to be careful not to expose their stern; having to worry about having their boats' bottom in the air was an additional worry for a commander forced on occasion into a crash dive. Other limitations were both comedic and perilous: heavy seas could wash into the boats' two chimneys and extinguish the boiler fires. As critics had prophesied, when the boilers were aflame temperatures in the craft became Saharan. Chimneys looked fine on grand liners which bestrode oceans, but unaesthetic and top-heavy if poking from a submarine. As appendages they were vulnerable as well as unappealing.

French ardour for steam was unabated. Its navy had at least one submarine whose folding funnel had been so badly buckled by violent seas that it was too bent to be closed or retracted; the damaged funnel leaked water into the boat and stopped it diving, leaving it exposed to attack on the surface and with no choice but to make a swift run for home. Numerous changes were made to the initial *K*-class design, among them radical alterations to the bow to try and make it more hydrodynamic; the changes succeeded in making its front end bulbous and ungainly. Instead of a modest conning tower, on earlier boats swathed in removable waterproof curtaining, a vain attempt at protection from angry seas, the *K*-class had a full-blown deckhouse which incorporated the conning tower. John Phillip Holland, with his contempt for fussiness and his insistence on an uncluttered, clean profile, would have been scathing. Admiralty chiefs, nevertheless, were enamoured: at least *K*-class boats *looked* like one of their own, with some of the scale and presence of a traditional surface warship. In truth it was neither fish nor fowl. The *K*-class had few of the virtues of a purebred submarine and on the surface could never properly compete with a warship. Where the Admiralty had in the past been un-ambitious about submarines, now it had become ridiculously so.

The Submarine *K-13*

The stories of heartache and disaster are manifold. One involved the newly launched *K-13* on the early morning of 29 January 1917. Tugs had towed her from Fairfields yard down the Clyde. She was impressive to look at, but size and looks belied competence. In speed the *K*-class were years ahead: no submarine twenty years later during the Second World War was faster. But the quest for power and speed came at a shocking price. Fairfields was a yard of pedigree. Its foundations had involved legendary shipbuilding names Robert Napier (1791–1876) and marine engineer John Elder (1824–1869), whose premature death robbed shipbuilding of a noble talent. The business had been formed from previous companies in 1888. In the years which led to the Great War, it was one of the Clyde's foremost yards, building as many as twelve vessels simultaneously, from liners to warships; as with many other yards, though, it collapsed in the 1960s.

Fairfields had invested *K-13* with a high level of skill. A trial dive would be held in Gare Loch, which at its southern end opens into the Firth of Clyde. Her commander was Lieutenant Commander Godfrey Herbert. There were eighty aboard, fifty-three of them officers and crew. The rest were directors and employees of Fairfields, sub-contractors, Admiralty officials, a Clyde pilot and two more officers, the engineer and commander of *K-14*, also built at Fairfields. On 28 January 1917, *K-13* completed her trial dive in the loch, being submerged for an hour. On the 29th, during her final trial dive, something went terribly wrong. Vents had not been closed properly and she sank, hitting the bottom, bows up, at a depth of 55ft. Her design incorporated an astonishing number of 'holes': nine watertight doors, torpedo hatches, twelve more hatches, valves, manholes, inspection vents, apertures and other openings. Mercifully, bulwarks that sealed off sections of the craft to safeguard it from total inundation had been built into her design. The other submarine commander aboard, the commanding officer of *K-14*, was Charles Goodhart, the former commander of *E-8* which had sunk the *Prinz Adalbert* in the Baltic.

The rescue for those who had survived on *K-13* was delayed and disorganised; inside the boat, Herbert and Goodhart decided that one of them should try and exit the boat to direct the rescue. It was somehow determined that it would be Goodhart. He would attempt to reach the surface, passing through a hatch which gave access to the flooded conning tower. Goodhart rocketed up, but Herbert could not close the hatch and was also sucked out. Herbert, not Goodhart, reached the surface and helped to direct the rescue. A hole was cut in the bows through which forty-six survivors were eventually pulled to safety. Goodhart's body was found in the bridge, having shot upwards, his head being smashed on a steel obstruction. The remaining thirty-three bodies were found in the hull. The survivors had been underwater for fifty-seven hours.[5] Desperate for air, virtually comatose, the survivors felt as if their chests and lungs would collapse; a medical expert on the surface had calculated at the start of their nightmare submersion that there was only enough air for eight hours.

In addition to his DSO, Goodhart was posthumously awarded the Albert Gold Medal. *K-13* was salvaged and later rejoined the fleet as HMS *K-22;* another example of sailors having to put aside their suspicions and distaste about serving on a boat in which others had perished. As with Commander Norman Holbrook of HMS *B-11,* the recipient of the Victoria Cross, the story of the stricken British *K-13* would have a curious echo in Australia. In the New South Wales city of Sydney, in the suburb of Carlingford, is a striking memorial, set in a pool of water, to those who died aboard *K-13.* It was financed by the widow of Charles Freestone, his rank that of a leading telegraphist aboard the craft. Mr Freestone was among those who had managed to escape. He subsequently emigrated to Australia where he made a prosperous and successful life, and built a sizeable business. Originally from Chelmsford, Essex, after surviving on *K-13* he transferred to the Royal Australian Navy in 1921 and served another five years before his discharge at the age of 30. The memorial bears the inscription:

> In memory of those officers and men of the Commonwealth who gave their lives in submarines while serving the cause of freedom.[6]

The commander of *K-13* Godfrey Herbert had an adventurous, incident-strewn career, one involving Q-boats, which were an attempt at subterfuge by the Admiralty to lure enemy submarines to the surface (see Appendix O).

The May Island Catastrophe

From a catalogue of disasters in which the British *K-boats* were ensnared, the most notorious became known as the Battle of May Island, an incident which became a monumentally tragic farce. It occurred in the final year of the Great

War on the evening of 18 January 1918, off the Isle of May at the entrance to the Firth of Forth in Scotland. A grandiose fleet exercise, it involved a large number of blacked-out battleships, cruisers, destroyers and K-class submarines. What followed was a series of collisions. They were caused in part by poor communications and hampered further by the blacked-out lighting and strict radio silence that a realistic wartime exercise demanded. The hazardous proximity of submarines to one another and to the various surface craft involved in the manoeuvres added to the dangers. How much of the catastrophe which ensued was due to human error is impossible to judge.

K-14's rudder had become stuck and in her plight she was struck by K-22, which in turn was hit by the battlecruiser HMS *Inflexible*. Other submarines and ships turned back to help. In the chaos there were a number of narrow misses. The destroyer HMS *Fearless* hit K-17, which sank. The submarine K-11 hit K-6, which in turn rammed K-4, cutting her almost in half and causing her immediate sinking: there were no survivors. While desperate rescue attempts were being made to pluck the men of K-17 from the sea, a posse of destroyers, unaware of the presence of the submarines and the tragedy which had befallen them, ploughed through the scene, vastly increasing the devastation and killing most of those who had survived. In an hour and a quarter 105 seamen were killed. It brought the total dead, in a diversity of K-class incidents, to 270; all the accidents were as a result of 'friendly' rather than enemy or 'in-action' incidents.

It is extraordinary more submarines were not sunk at May Island. If the submarines involved in the exercise had been of a smaller and more conventional type a greater number of lives would have been lost; it says something ar least for the strength, size and build-quality of the K-class. Though the K-class had numerous faults, the debacle at May Island was not caused by their inadequacies. It resulted from submarines and surface ships being operated too closely together; compounded by the circumstances of a wartime manoeuvre which necessitated the imposition of radio silence and a lighting black-out. Operating the K-class in close proximity to surface ships was madness. Submarines as big as the K-class did not have the agility or nimbleness of smaller boats. Though vast by the standards of a conventional submarine they were still fragile in comparison with a surface ship; the smallest collision could mean disaster.

In war the presence of a submarine was so alarming, and communication so wretched, a warship was prone to immediately open fire, worrying later whether the boat was friend or foe. There are parallels in the way navies used airships. The US Navy built the world's largest and most advanced airships and persisted with dirigibles longer than most – the *Akron* and *Macon* were designed as giant aircraft carriers – and would on occasion sail their airships too close and too low to warships, a habit which sometimes met with catastrophic results. Proximity to surface warships and dense, heavy air encountered at low levels, increased perils for an airship (see Appendix C)

A total of twenty-one K-class submarines should have been built, but the order for the last four was cancelled and replaced by a quartet of M-class boats. These were diesel-electric craft which, in effect, were monitors, vessels whose genealogy could be traced back to the American Civil War and before. Some M-class submarines were developed as aircraft carriers. It was an interesting notion but one which proved largely unsuccessful, as did other attempts at turning submarines into transporters of aircraft (see Appendix J).

From various types created during the Great War, the outstanding submarine remained the E-class; encouraged by its competence the Admiralty sought to emulate its strengths in an improved craft. The modifications saw another new category of submarine, the L-class, and twenty-seven boats were built; the majority were introduced too late to have much effect during the years of hostility, but the original ambition of the Admiralty had been to build more than seventy such craft. A number were used as minelayers.

L-Class Submarines

The L-class were fast, capable and well-armed. The second in the series, L-2, which had started life as E-58, had been commissioned in 1917. She had been built by Vickers at Barrow. In February 1918 she had a remarkable escape from a depth charge attack made by three American warships which had mistaken her for an enemy submarine. The first depth charge had caused the craft to bed her stern into the sea floor, her bows pointing upwards towards the surface at a steep angle. More depth charges were dropped which nearly shook her to pieces. Miraculously she managed to blow her ballast tanks and surface, whereupon the destroyers began shelling her; with her crew waving the white ensign L-2 and her crew were fortunate to survive. A minute or two longer and she would have been sunk by the Americans who had holed her superstructure. It was only in her last remaining moments that they ceased firing on realising their calamitous mistake.[7]

The submarine L-10 was the only one of the class lost in action during the Great War. Newly built by one of the premier Scottish yards, William Denny & Sons (1844–1963), on the River Leven in Dumbarton, she had been on patrol in the North Sea. On 4 October 1918 she torpedoed one of a group of four German destroyers laying mines in the Heligoland Bight. For unexplained reasons, on unleashing her torpedo she suddenly shot to the surface, being spotted and chased by the other ships which rapidly sank her with her complement of thirty-eight.[8]

The submarine *L-12* was another built by Vickers. With *L-11* she had been converted into a minelayer. On 16 October 1918, *L-12* torpedoed and sank the German submarine *UB-90*. Eleven years later, on 9 June 1929, she was involved in an accident off the Pembrokeshire coast, Wales, with the British submarine *H-47*, built by William Beardmore of Glasgow, Scotland. *H-47* sank with the loss of nineteen lives; three survived. *L-12* was damaged but survived, being broken up in 1932. *L-12* had been on an officer training exercise and ahead of *H-47* when the collision occurred.

A Surface Attack

As the war ground to its conclusion the German submarine *UB-16*, converted into a minelayer, set off from Zeebrugge to patrol the waters of the North Sea off Harwich on England's east coast. For reasons known only to her commander, she was on the surface on 10 May 1918; it seems likely that she had suffered some form of malfunction. Whatever the reason for her lack of concealment she made a seductive target. The British submarine *E-34* could not believe her luck. She fired two torpedoes, sinking the U-boat; of sixteen aboard only her commander, Vicco von der Luhe, survived. Rescued by the *E-34* he later died of illness while a prisoner of war. From her launch in 1915, *UB-16*, under different commanders, had sunk twenty-three merchant ships, many of them fishing vessels. She had also sunk the British destroyer, HMS *Recruit*, with fifty-four casualties, on 9 August 1917.[9] Once the pride of the north-east, the *Recruit* now lay a hulk on the ocean floor, coated in rust, another barnacled victim of *UB-16*.

By the Armistice, after four years of hostilities, Great Britain, the world's leading seafaring nation, had lost 90 per cent of its maritime tonnage. Enemy submarines had wreaked havoc, as had British submarines on German shipping. At the end of the Great War Germany surrendered 176 submarines, with more than 100 handed to the British and the rest shared among the Allies.

In the inter-war period strides were made by Britain, America and Japan. New types of submarines were developed and finessed in readiness for a central role in the coming conflict, in which German U-boat wolf-packs in the Atlantic would again imperil Britain. Submarines were versatile, quicker, cheaper to build, run and man, than surface vessels. Such considerations encouraged Holland, which would be particularly inventive, as well as Denmark, Norway, Sweden and Poland to build up their own submarine fleets.

In the years immediately after the First World War, Russia, by then the Soviet Union, was effectively bankrupt – as were other participants – and concentrated on its air force and army, leaving its major submarine development until the 1930s. By 1939 and the start of the Second World War the USSR had a diversity of submarine classes. Germany, under the Versailles Treaty, had been forbidden from building U-boats but had kept abreast of technical breakthroughs through clandestine links that it had forged with countries such as the USSR, Spain and the Netherlands. With the ascendancy of the Nazi Party, the building of a new and highly formidable U-boat fleet began again in the mid-1930s.

Notes

1 Everitt, *K-Boats*, p.9
2 Everitt, *K-Boats*, pp.9–10
3 Chant, Christopher, *Submarines of the 20th Century* (Tiger Books International, 1996), pp.28–29
4 Thompson, *The War at Sea*, pp.210–11
5 Garland, Pauline, librarian of the Submarine School Library, HMAS *Platypus*: members. optusnet.com.au/ord 4/k13submarinememorial.htm; Thompson, *The War at Sea*, pp.210–11
6 www.navyhistory.org.au/sydney-memorial-to-hm-submarine-k13/
7 Colledge, J.J. and Warlow, Ben, *Ships of the Royal Navy: The Complete Record of all Fighting Ships of the Royal Navy*; Gardiner, Robert (ed.), *Conway's All the World's Fighting Ships, 1906–1921* (Naval Institute Press, Annapolis, 1985), p.93; Hutchinson, *Jane's Submarines: War Beneath the Waves from 1776 to the Present Day*
8 Hutchinson, *Jane's Submarines*
9 Kemp, Paul, *The Admiralty Regrets: British Warship Losses of the 20th Century* (Sutton Publishing, 1999), p.55

Epilogue

The key moment in the submarine campaign in the Great War came in February 1917 when it was agreed in Germany, fiercely resisted by some, that unrestricted submarine warfare should be pursued against Allied shipping. Historian Christopher Chant:

> During April 1917 the shipping tonnage lost to submarine attack increased to 881,000 tons, representing one ship in every four bound for a British port. The effect of the campaign was so profound that it was calculated at this time that the UK had food reserves for only six weeks, and the country therefore faced the prospect of starvation or an accommodation with the Germans.[1]

The irony is that the German decision to sanction unrestricted U-boat sorties saved Britain and its allies by being a catalyst that helped bring America into the conflict. In turn it persuaded the British Admiralty to authorise the convoy system, about which it had been reluctant, concerned that it tied up too many ships and assisted the foe by its bunching of vessels, which concentrated targets for U-boat attack. Chant:

> It was soon proved that the concentration of defence provided by the escort warships was greater than the concentration opportunity offered to the German submarines, and sinkings soon declined to a significant degree.[2]

The hecatomb of the Great War brought impetus to submarine development, as had previous hostilities; it gave the submarine an opportunity to prove its worth, which it did in bloody theatres where the clash of armies failed and surface navies were inappropriate or could not reach, the Dardanelles being a prime example. In eighteen years, from John Holland's creation at the turn of the century to the conclusion of the war which was supposed to end all wars, the submarine had usurped the centuries-old might of the battleship as the capital vessel of any surface fleet. By the beginning of the Second World War, twenty-one years later, hoary jibes about the submarine being a vulgar toy had been consigned to history. Alongside the advance in aircraft it had matured to become cardinal to victory.

At its most potent it was never seen. Nor at its most impotent, when inanimate and crippled on an ocean floor. The heroism of its personnel occurred in dark anonymity, unwitnessed. The world could learn the fate of a surface ship through pictures and by newsreel. In a submarine whose crew would never see daylight again, trapped in black and airless coffins fast on a seabed, anguish and death went unseen. The final throes of a stricken submarine and its crew were played out unobserved beneath the waves. Lives were snuffed out in an instant in a flash of flame, others stolen by arbitrary inundation, the choking seep of gas, the torment of air expiring, of lungs imploding.

Muscle to steam, petrol to diesel, through the heroism and horrors of two world wars, the submarine is today a nuclear leviathan patrolling the seas, her passage a carefully guarded secret. She lurks in sunless depths, torpedoes charged, rockets aimed at land-locked targets: despots in palaces, street fighters in tenements, babies who scream and mothers who weep; they know little of her presence in her ocean lair. A grey mammoth, steel-skinned, slowly nosing through quiet waters, brushing aside dark forests of weed, hidden for months, a shark among fishes, only signalling her existence with a sudden spurt of carnage. This then is what the creation of an Irish monk who resented the British has become. A sentinel of stealth, keeper of peace, bringer of apocalypse. Once blind, now all-seeing; once deaf, now sharp-eared. Her command centre a continent away. Always ready, listening for that which lies above, the cry of a desperate world.

Notes

1   Chant, *Submarines*, p.36
2   Chant, *Submarines*, p37–38

Appendix A

Airships and Submarines

The characteristics and principles of the airship applied to the submarine. They were both mongrels, strange hybrids: the submarine was a boat but sailed *beneath* the water; the airship sailed the skies but flew *without* wings.[1] They would confront similar difficulties: to progress, each had to push aside a great weight of water, or that which is unseen, the density of air. Where the submarine pushes aside water, the airship, relying on the same principles of buoyancy as the submarine, cut through a volume of air, which though intangible, at lower levels is heavy and dense. The early versions of both craft were cramped, uncomfortable, dangerous. Each was subject to deep scepticism. Both had crews drawn from other services – mainly navy, but in airships also from the army and embryo air force. Each depended on untested technology. They shared their greatest strength: stealth, floating silently in cloud or water. They were related as allies in arms or as enemies, airships being used as submarine spotters in the Great War. Submarines tended to dive slowly, operating just below the surface, their shadow identified from an airship gondola. Airships dropped smoke flares to mark the presence of a hostile submarine; surface ships then made pell-mell to engage it, or steamed rapidly away if the ship's captain thought it the safest course. On occasion airships rained small bombs on submarines, usually missing, their aim being generally woeful. There was an extensive interchange of personnel between the submarine and airship service. Sueter, Bacon, Burney, each knew about both submarines and airships. They contributed to what the author has called the 'new arsenal'. Murray Sueter had trained as a torpedo officer on HMS *Vernon* and subsequently joined Reginald Bacon's HMS *Hazard*, the submarine mothership. It was Bacon, the father of British submarines, who later moved into matters aerial and recommended that an airship similar to a German Zeppelin, whose achievements had been noted by the Admiralty, be built by Vickers at Barrow. Nine months later Bacon's plan was approved. Sueter, who by then had become the Inspecting Captain of Airships, supervised its build, airship control coming under the aegis of the ordnance department of the Admiralty. The airship to be built was the *Mayfly*, which didn't. It broke in half while being pulled from its shed, prompting an outburst from Admiral Sir Arthur ''ard 'earted' Wilson, the naval grandee who had been scornful of submarines and their 'piratical' crews. Wilson proclaimed *Mayfly* such a calamity that the entire airship building programme must be abandoned, conveniently overlooking that *Mayfly*'s collapse was caused by his Admiralty colleagues dispensing with its keel in defiance of all expert opinion. His demands contributed to a hiatus in airship development, the first of many which hindered its advance and saw Britain trail in the technology in the ensuing decades. Though in charge at the time of the *Mayfly* fiasco, it did not stem Sueter's ascendancy: three years after the debacle he was given command of the Navy's air department and oversaw the birth of the Royal Naval Air Service.

Notes

1 Swinfield, *Airship*

Appendix B

Charles Dennistoun Burney

Admiral Sir Cecil Burney's son, the naval officer Commander Sir Charles Dennistoun Burney (1888–1968) had inherited his father's interest in submarines and underwater hostilities. Dennistoun Burney invented the paravane when he was a young naval officer.[1] Towed by ships it was designed to cut the wires of tethered mines. It saved countless hundreds of lives and made him a fortune. In 1930, under the auspices of the engineering and armaments conglomerate, Vickers, Dennistoun Burney built Britain's most successful airship, the giant *R-100*. In August 1930 it sailed 3,364 miles from Britain to Canada, sister ship of the doomed state-built *R-101* which crashed en route to India in Beauvais, northern France, hours after lift-off from Cardington, Bedfordshire. The *R-100* had been designed and built at Howden in East Yorkshire by Sir Barnes 'bouncing-bomb' Wallis at an early stage in his stellar career, assisted by Nevil Shute Norway, later internationally acclaimed as the best-selling novelist Nevil Shute. Dennistoun Burney was energetic, entrepreneurial, a determined salesman and highly inventive. He also created the Burney Streamline Car; an ambitious, highly advanced and bizarre-looking affair, its shape not unlike that of a small airship on wheels. He later became a Member of Parliament. Through his father, Sir Cecil, the sometimes strange and costly paths of the airship and the submarine had crossed once more.[2]

Notes

1 Cornford, L. Cope, *The Paravane Adventure* (Hodder & Stoughton, c. 1919)
2 Swinfield, *Airship*

Appendix C

Flying Warships

In seeing airships as 'flying warships' the Admiralty had made creations based on strict principles of lighter-than-air unworkably heavy by loading them with accoutrements which were weighty and, in some cases, unnecessary; it was a costly madness which had led in part to the *Mayfly won't Fly* fiasco of 1911, two years before the *K*-class submarine designs were drawn up.[1] In fairness, early dirigible calamities were not the sole fault of the Admiralty; the embryo air force must also accept its share of blame, especially in the case of the airship *R-38* disaster over the River Humber in Hull on 23 August 1921, in which perished forty-four of the forty-nine aboard.

Notes

1   Swinfield, *Airship*

Appendix D

John Arbuthnot Fisher

Fisher's role in submarines would be axial. Having joined the navy at 13 on 12 June 1854, Fisher was first assigned to HMS *Victory*, Nelson's flagship at Trafalgar. He went on to a brilliant, all-encompassing career of more than sixty years, holding a clutch of senior appointments and seeing service in a diversity of postings: China, Istanbul – then Constantinople – North America, the West Indies, the Mediterranean and the Baltic.

An expert in torpedoes and gunnery, Fisher had been at HMS *Excellent*, the naval gunnery school, and HMS *Vincent* with its emphasis on mines and torpedoes. His expertise was amply demonstrated by the accuracy of his guns when in command of the new battleship HMS *Inflexible* during the bombardment of Alexandria in the Anglo–Egyptian war of 1882. The *Inflexible* was a confusing cocktail of the outmoded and the advanced: modern fixtures included torpedo tubes, electric light, a hull more thickly plated than anything before. But she still had sails – never used to propel her – and cumbersome muzzle-loading guns which infuriated the impatient Fisher. He won kudos in Britain on a mission ashore in Egypt, planning to armour a train with guns and plating to assist a reconnaissance mission. In 1863 he was made Gunnery Lieutenant on HMS *Warrior* (1860), Britain's first all-iron warship, the jewel in Queen Victoria's fleet. Fisher was correct in his conviction that a key to naval dominance lay in the excellence of a ship's guns and the adroitness of her sailors in handling them; a belief manifest in his famous creation, the revolutionary all big-gun dreadnought battleship. Though the anti-submarine crusade was tenacious, the likes of Bacon, Keyes and the indomitable Fisher would remain unflinching. Fisher had been made the First Sea Lord on Trafalgar Day, 21 October 1904. He had been brought back from Portsmouth by the Liberal Unionist statesman William Palmer, the 2nd Earl of Selborne (1859–1942). In

1900 Selborne, under the prime minister, the 3rd Marquess Salisbury, had been appointed a member of the Privy Council and the First Lord of the Admiralty.

The Unionist government, comprising the Liberal and Conservative parties, had assumed power in 1895. Lord Salisbury was the Conservative prime minister, but many top jobs went to the Liberals. At the turn of the twentieth century things were done differently, with nepotism taken for granted: Salisbury's son-in-law was the Liberal Selborne and Salisbury's nephew, the Conservative Arthur James Balfour (1848–1930), the leader of the Commons. In a seventeen-year period Salisbury was prime minister three times: 1885–86, 1886–92, 1895–1902. It was Balfour who would succeed his uncle in 1902 as prime minister, though he had to relinquish power to the Liberals in 1905 when the party split; in 1915 Balfour returned to Cabinet as First Lord of the Admiralty.

Some of the virulence directed at Fisher was unjust, stemming from those who were embittered, whose careers he had thwarted. Others were antagonised by his abrasive manner and his far-reaching changes. Some opprobrium he heaped upon himself by inviting, as an example, junior ranks to openly criticise and upbraid their superiors. He conducted debates publicly, sometimes in the press, brazenly encouraging those such as the Navy League to lobby for his policies of naval expansionism and reform. He would also present arguments to his political masters which were so exaggerated that they were plain silly, claiming quite spuriously that Britain would be entirely naked and defenceless if his policies were not implemented in their entirety and that her opponents were already Atlas-strong and free to command the world's oceans without hindrance. For Fisher everything was black and white: a realistic but a duller tone of grey held little appeal. Mercurial and quixotic he was magically gifted; but, equally, unceasingly combative and compelled to pick needless arguments.

Appendix E

Louis Mountbatten

Returning as First Sea Lord, Fisher had taken the job held by Lord Louis Albert Francis Victor Nicholas George Mountbatten, the 1st Earl Mountbatten of Burma (1900–79), his roots being considered too German. The name Mountbatten had a good ring but was bogus: a stylish handle adopted by the Battenberg family. Mountbatten had cut a dash. Popular but controversial, some claimed reputation exceeded ability. With anti-German sentiment at fever pitch he had to go. Born in Austria, eldest son of Prince Alexander of Hesse, he had been raised in England and married his cousin, Princess Victoria, a granddaughter of Queen Victoria. He later become a naturalised British subject. Mountbatten's exit was a blow to the navy. His rank had been achieved more by ability than connections, though the latter would not have stalled his climb. Among influential admirers was the historian Arthur Marder:

> Though handicapped by his German ancestry and by his gout, he was a first-rate, all-round seaman, a born leader, an efficient, even brilliant tactician and strategist ... he looked the beau ideal of the British naval officer.[1]

In terms of European royalty the Great War was a monumental family spat. It is interesting to speculate on how naval strategy and reform would have differed had it been Mountbatten alongside Churchill rather than Fisher.

Notes

1 Marder, *From the Dreadnought to Scapa Flow*

Appendix F

The Torpedo: A Musical Interlude

There is a fascinating aside to the Whitehead torpedo story. Robert Whitehead's eldest daughter, Agathe, married a young officer in the Imperial and Royal Austro-Hungarian Navy, *Kapitanleutnant* Georg Ritter von Trapp. They met in 1908 when he had been sent to the Whitehead factory in Fiume to study submarines and torpedoes. In 1909 Agathe had launched the submarine *U-5* and in 1911 she married Georg. Georg was given command of *U-5* but his naval career ended in tatters when Austria lost the war and surrendered her coastal provinces to Italy and Yugoslavia. With no coastline to defend, Georg was unemployed, with five children to feed and clothe. In the midst of adversity calamity struck when, in 1922 Agathe died aged 32 of diphtheria. Georg engaged a governess, Maria Augusta, to help raise his children. He later married her and she, too, bore him several children. Among other things, Maria taught the children to sing.

Before long the musical talents of the family brought them worldwide fame as *The Trapp Family Singers* and their unusual story, recounted by Maria von Trapp in her book of the same name, became the basis of the Hollywood film *The Sound of Music*, five of the children being, of course, great-grandchildren of Robert Whitehead. Made in 1965 the film starred Julie Andrews and Christopher Plummer. With music by Richard Rogers and lyrics by Oscar Hammerstein, it was the last musical the legendary pair would make; Hammerstein died nine months after the original stage version had premiered on Broadway in 1959.[1]

Notes

1   Gray, *The Devil's Device*, pp.184–186

213

Appendix G

Bacon, Fisher and the Beresford Affair

On removing Bacon from leadership of the submarine service, Fisher had appointed him his naval assistant, putting him to work on the design committee of his pet project, the radically advanced all big-gun *dreadnought* battleship and, too, design work on the construction of the fast new battlecruisers which were intended to provide the navy with the vital agility and speed lacking in its older vessels; somewhat ironically, as it transpired, battlecruisers would prove themselves suitably nimble but too light and vulnerable to withstand the onslaught of long-range heavy-guns with which the new generation of battleships would be equipped. For Bacon's career to prosper it was important to enhance his surface time in 'big ships'. He had been Inspecting Captain of Submarines from 1901 to 1904 and private secretary to Fisher 1904–05. Consequently he was appointed commander of HMS *Dreadnought* from 1906 to 1907 and captain of HMS *Irresistible* from 1907 to 1908. Bacon's command of the much-vaunted HMS *Dreadnought* exacerbated ill-feeling about Fisher's marked preference for promoting those officers he judged 'progressive' and who had paddled happily in his 'fish-pond' (see Appendix D).

While serving with the Mediterranean Fleet, Bacon had ingenuously sent Fisher letters which commented on its utility and the reaction of those at sea to Fisher's startling innovations; in the ensuing viperous Fisher–Beresford feud the inadvertent leaking of the supposedly confidential missives led to a scandal about spying in the navy which engulfed the protagonists and blemished Bacon's reputation. The allegation that an officer snooped on his fellows while sneakily passing on confidentialities to his protector, the First Sea Lord, smacked of a discourteousness and impropriety that would reap opprobrium today, let alone in the Victorian navy, heavily overlaid with its own moral code and conventions about what constituted acceptable behaviour.

The charges weighed on Bacon and bore on his decision to quit the navy in 1909 to become the managing director of the civilian Coventry Ordnance Works. His observations, in truth, had been relatively circumspect but blown out of all recognition by the Beresford camp in its campaign to hound Fisher and his acolytes from office. Nevertheless, the correspondence was an embarrassing indiscretion by Bacon and its exposure proved disproportionately costly.

In addition to being an admiral, Beresford was also a Member of Parliament. Though popular, with a network of influential friends which had been galvanised into an anti-Fisher lobby, he could be gaseous and a bore; he and his compatriots had been ruthless in trying to see off Fisher. For his part, Fisher was provocative and unbending. Beresford personified much about the navy of the time that Fisher loathed; for Fisher, needling Beresford was irresistible. Had the combatants sought compromise then the matter might have been settled more amicably; pacific, however, was not in either man's lexicon. Bacon would always be subject to the jealousy of rivals, an envy exacerbated by his prudent coddling of the infant and resented submarine service. Unimaginatively nicknamed 'Porky', he was also dubbed, with more justification, the 'Father of the Trade'. The Fisher–Beresford debacle gifted Bacon's opponents an incident with which to sully his reputation. For a clever and committed officer who had distinguished himself in the service of the nation and the submarine service it was a deeply wounding affair; the misfortune and calamities which had plagued the A-class and their personnel appeared to be a contagion which at this unfortunate juncture had now spread to their mentors.

The Coventry Ordnance Works comprised a consortium of shipbuilding companies: Fairfield, Cammell Laird, Yarrow and John Brown. Its creation in 1905 had been nurtured by the government, which had shown itself keen to break the duopoly of the ubiquitous Vickers and Armstrong Whitworth. There was disquiet in government about a dependence on only two suppliers in a critical sector. It was felt that the birth of the Coventry Ordnance Works would stimulate competition and drive down prices. Roger Keyes encountered the 'Vickers problem' when he assumed the leadership of the submarine service and bought foreign boats. Bacon was recalled by the navy at the start of the Great War in 1914, and by its end had been promoted to admiral. In his post-navy years he became a prolific author and naval historian. His biographies included that of his mentor Fisher and he was a stout defender of Admiral Jellicoe, whose credibility fell after the inconclusive Battle of Jutland in 1916, in which Germany and Britain each claimed victory and which was horrendously costly in lives and ships.

Bacon's supposed Olympian aloofness garnered few friends and guaranteed a squadron of detractors, though some were hardly the shiniest buttons on the poop deck. Lesser critics seem to have been largely motivated by spite. He had rare gifts and had long been a favourite of Fisher; the First Sea Lord's patronage was sufficient in itself to make Bacon a 'marked man' by those who would never test the waters in Fisher's pond, of which there were many. He also had more influential opponents whose track records lent credence to their reservations. Among them was Maurice Hankey (1877–1963). Ennobled in 1939, Hankey was an adviser to the Cabinet and a succession of prime ministers. For an extraordinarily long twenty-six years he was Naval Secretary to the Committee for Imperial Defence, whose deliberations were critical and decisions far-reaching. Hankey was of *real* as opposed to imagined influence. While itinerant and usually ill-informed politicians came and went, genuine power lay in a closed cadre in which Hankey was pivotal. Another Bacon critic was Admiral Reginald Yorke Tyrwhitt (1870–1951), commander of the east coast Harwich Force in the Great War. Aspersion centred on Bacon's supposed remoteness; centralism, or closeness to the Admiralty; his unwillingness to heed advice and, in the Great War, his caution which, it was alleged, prevailed over boldness. Yet, earlier, had his custodianship of the embryo submarine flotilla been other than cautious he would have been condemned as reckless.

His autocratic reputation followed him into civilian life. At Coventry Ordnance Works, which struggled in the post-war recession, ceasing to trade in 1925, his command-style leadership style irritated seasoned managers. In truth, Bacon was probably just too bright, his reputation scarred by fall-out from the Beresford debacle. Britain's Victorian navy was stuffed with well-connected dunderheads whose careers had been brutally truncated by Fisher. Fisher quit the navy twice. In his absence those officers he had favoured were left exposed to recrimination and an accumulated bitterness.

Appendix H

Roger Keyes

Keyes was born into an army family in India, one of seven children. His father became General Sir Charles Keyes. From an early age Roger Keyes had wanted to be a sailor, to his father's chagrin. In 1884, aged 12, he joined the navy training college at HMS *Britannia* in Dartmouth, Devon. Adventure and courage run in the Keyes' family genes: later on, Roger Keyes's son, Lieutenant Colonel Geoffrey Charles Tasker Keyes (1917–41) of the Royal Scots Greys (2nd Dragoons) won a posthumous Victoria Cross, Britain's highest award for gallantry, for his astonishing bravery in North Africa in the Second World War, in which he led a suicidally dangerous mission, and in which he was sacrificed, breaking into General Rommel's headquarters in North Africa.

Roger Keyes' first postings were on ships in Africa on anti-slaving duties. For a young man it was an exciting time with gun fights, river chases in small craft and daring rescue missions. He was stationed for four years in South America before returning to England and taking command of the destroyer HMS *Possum*. In 1898 he went to China as commander of the destroyer HMS *Hart*, switching soon after to HMS *Fame*. He went to China as a lieutenant and emerged a commander after a catalogue of excitements, his promotion in recognition of his boldness and leadership.

In China, during a tumultuous period, Keyes was embroiled in the Boxer Uprising (1898–1900), in which British citizens and Western interests were threatened, and became immersed in several hair-raising exploits. In one, in which he and his complement were heavily out-gunned and outnumbered, he managed to seize four Chinese destroyers and take many prisoners. It was the stuff of legend, with piratical British raiding parties brandishing swords and handguns. More was to come with the capture and destruction of a heavily armed fort. In another episode, Keyes helped save the beleaguered Admiral Edward Hobart Seymour (1840–1929) and his men, the commander-in-chief of the China Station. Keyes recalled such incidents in his book *Adventures Ashore and Afloat,* which through modern eyes offers an unintentionally Bertie Woosterish peek into just how privileged a navy officers' circle could be: derring-do at sea, on land bagging grouse on Norfolk shoots, glittering soirées in grand country piles at weekends, then rushing back to one's ship for more acts of selfless bravery.[1]

Keyes' rollicking China stay was followed by a clutch of other appointments, which included serving in Portsmouth; in the Intelligence section of the Admiralty; as naval attaché in Rome; and as commander of HMS *Venus* in the Atlantic Fleet. He left the submarine service to become, in 1915, the Chief of Staff for Naval Operations at the Dardanelles. He went on to a glittering career – though he always had detractors – one which spanned the Great War and, in the Second World War, was appointed Director of Combined Operations 1940–1. He was also the Conservative MP for Portsmouth from 1934 to 1943.[2]

Notes

1 Keyes, Sir Roger, *Adventures Ashore and Afloat* (George G. Harrap & Co. Ltd., 1939)
2 Lambert, *The Submarine Service*, pp.383–5

Appendix J

Submarines as Aircraft Carriers

Governments experimented with the seemingly bizarre notion of using submarines as aircraft carriers; if perfected they could have combined the two wonders of the age and added a formidable entrant to what the author terms 'the new arsenal'. A lack of range was among the many limitations which hampered early aeroplanes. Submarine range, however, had improved in later models, especially if vessels were used primarily as surface craft. The idea would also be investigated with airships, small fighters being slung beneath the belly and released over or close to the target: in the 1930s the Goodyear Tire & Rubber Company developed the *Akron* and *Macon* dirigibles for the US Navy, in which batches of fighters were held in hangars built inside the airship's envelope.[1]

The submarine *E-22* underwent the necessary modifications. Built by Vickers at Barrow she had been laid down on 27 August 1914 and commissioned on 8 November 1915. The aeroplane to be strapped to her deck was a converted version of the successful Sopwith Camel; though tricky, in skilled hands it was a useful dogfighter, matched only by the DR1 triplane of Manfred von Richtofen (1892–1918), the famed Red Baron. The changes necessary to its design would have impaired its aerodynamics so it was decided, instead, to use two Sopwith Schneider seaplanes perched in an ungainly and uncertain manner on *E-22*'s upper casing. Theoretically the idea seemed plausible; it was less so in practice. The intention was for the submarine to gently submerge, leaving the seaplanes afloat, ready to take off and engage the enemy. On completion of its mission an aeroplane could then return to the North Sea east coast docks of Felixstowe, which is today Britain's leading cargo port. After liberating their aircraft the submarine would dive to safety to avoid the slim chance of being hit by retaliatory bombs from Zeppelins – their aim was generally poor, though

221

such events were not unknown – or attacked by German aeroplanes which were used later and with greater success. The chances of an attack on a British submarine by a German surface ship were considerably more grave. Zeppelins would sometimes drop flares alerting a warship to the presence of a submarine. The ship could then turn and flee, or race to the scene, whichever seemed the most wise in the circumstances. If the latter, the warship would speed to the location, especially if the submarine was on the surface – with frequent breakdowns it was always possible – to ram or fire upon it with its heavier and superior guns. The Sopwith Schneider experiments were not a success and were abandoned. The extra weight of the aeroplanes hindered the submarine. From sea or air points of view, it was an awkward caboodle, even before the palaver of separation. Detaching the seaplanes proved slower than imagined. Trying to gently lower the submarine to the point where the seaplanes were afloat was risky. Choppy or violent seas would have imperilled both aeroplane and submarine. The seaplanes were reconnaissance aircraft, rather than fighters, and thus less suitable to address the Zeppelin menace and the later threat of invading Gotha bombers.

Later, *E-22* became one of many submarine tragedies of the Great War. While she was conducting surface exercises, in a rare incident involving submarine versus submarine, she was torpedoed by the German vessel *U-18* while off Great Yarmouth, on Britain's east coast, on 25 April 1916. Thirty-one of thirty-three aboard were lost.

In Germany, experiments with submarine–aeroplane carriers were being conducted prior to those in Great Britain. They involved two legendary submariners of the Kaisermarine. The first was the Prussian aristocrat *Oberleutnant* Lothar von Arnauld de la Perière (1886–1941), the commander of the Imperial German Naval Air Service, who became the most successful U-boat commander of all time. He sank 194 ships totalling 454,000 tons in the Great War. The second was the highly accomplished *Kapitanleutnant* Walther Forstmann (1883–1973) and his submarine *U-12*. Forstmann, too, would become one of the most highly decorated and successful U-boat skippers. Their high number of kills could be attributed to their targets being largely unarmed mercantile vessels. Perière would surface – the sudden and frightening appearance of a U-boat causing alarm and panic aboard her prey – order his target to halt and have the personnel put into small boats. His crew would then board the vessel and scuttle it, opening seacocks or blowing it up. It saved wasting expensive torpedoes. Torpedoes were not only costly, they were heavy, cumbersome and consumed precious space; boats could only carry a few. At this early stage in the conflict submarine warfare had a semblance of propriety, with submariners expected to adhere to prize rules to ensure the well-being of civilians and non-combatants. Such civilities were cast aside when Germany later pursued its policy of unrestricted submarine warfare

Perière was in command of two reconnaissance sea planes, Friedrichshafen FF29s, based in the occupied Belgian port of Zeebrugge, situated on the North Sea. Zeebrugge had been occupied by Germany in the opening months of the war. Being within striking distance of Britain it was an important naval and air base for Germany. The Kaiser had been encouraged by the actions of Forstmann and Perière in 1914 when they had modified an FF29 seaplane so that it could carry bombs. It had flown up the Thames and over London, dropping its load of 12½lb bombs. Though the sortie caused little damage, it had shown the vulnerability of London's defences and highlighted the closeness of Zeebrugge to England: the limited range of the seaplane could be overcome if a submarine were appropriately adapted. Forstmann's *U-12* submarine was prepared.

A relatively small submarine, it had been designed for coastal or inshore use; its sea-keeping abilities, even free of its inappropriate cargo, were far from exemplary. The seaplane was balanced precariously on its deck, held by fitments intended to allow easy detachment, which they did not. Its wings poked from either side of the submarine. The vessel and its aeroplane made an ungainly and unseaworthy lump; neither would have survived in heavy seas. In January 1915 Forstmann set sail. Roughish water made him submerge his boat earlier than had been planned. Nevertheless, the seaplane floated on the surface and took off, flying down the English coast and returning safely to base, without dropping its bombs. It was an interesting experiment, but in the clamour of war it proved too arcane and the tests were shelved until 1917 when more experiments with largely unsuccessful results were tried with smaller planes on long-range submarines.

Notes

1   Swinfield, *Airship*

Appendix K

M-class; *Surcouf*; Specifications

The *M*-class were a type of submarine monitor designed at a time in the Great War when torpedoes were considered inaccurate beyond close range; in addition to torpedoes, the *M*-class boats were armed with a 12in gun in a turret mounted forward of the conning tower, and were also fitted with an anti-aircraft gun. The original monitors were turreted iron-clad warships. Their most outstanding characteristic was a formidable degree of armament, the most famous of the early period being the USS *Monitor* (1862). With a plentiful supply of shells it was imagined the *M*-class submarines would be able to surface, or rise to periscope depth, and then bombard ships with shells from its deck armaments. There was also a notion in the British Admiralty that the *M*-class boats could assail coastal locations, perhaps seaboard towns held by the Germans in occupied Belgium; bombarding shore targets had been a function of the original surface monitors. Such thinking was understandable, but another reminder of the way the Admiralty persisted in seeing submarines as warships. The initial role envisaged for the *M*-class changed as the conflict continued. Whether the shells would have been sufficient to inflict serious damage on seaside towns, or to penetrate plating on ships' hulls, is unknown. The submarine had to surface to reload its guns; theoretically this could be done quickly, though in reality it was laborious and left the boat exposed and vulnerable to attack. Of the four craft ordered, three were built and only the first entered service before the war ended. For some of its trials *M-1* came under the command of the celebrated submariner Max Horton, a hero of the Baltic and other campaigns. Again, tragedy would strike. Five years after the war had ended *M-1*'s gun was rendered ineffective by an inundation of seawater and, two years later, on 12 November 1925, while on exercises in the English Channel off the Devon coast, she was lost while submerged with sixty-nine men aboard, following an accident with the Swedish freighter, the SS *Vidar*. The collision partly detached the gun from its mounting, the hull was pierced and it is possible that her magazine had been flooded.

Her sister boat, the *M-2*, was converted into an experimental aeroplane carrier, the gun turret being removed and replaced with a small hangar. The Admiralty had hankered after a reconnaissance vehicle of the air: the idea of an aerial scout was the *raison d'être* for the small early naval airships. A little seaplane, the two-seater *Parnall Peto*, was specially designed for *M-2*. With folding wings she could be tucked inside the submarine's miniature hangar. Parnall & Sons, based in Bristol, had begun as a shop-fitting and weighing scales company. By the Great War it had branched out into making aeroplanes. The *Peto* was its most difficult project. The final model had metal floats and a five-cylinder 169hp Mongoose engine made by Armstrong Siddeley, the renowned British car and aero-engine maker formed in 1919. During the First and the Second World War Parnall made several hundred aeroplanes and seaplanes. In a hair-raising procedure the little *Peto*, made of wood, fabric, aluminium and steel, could be fired by catapult from the deck of the submarine. A crane installed on top of the hangar winched her from the sea following her sorties; lifted from the water onto the deck, sailors folded her wings back to her fuselage and pushed her back into her hangar in readiness to dive. The stability of the vessel was affected by it being turned into a lumpen concoction; it made a juicy target on the surface and had dubious hydrodynamics beneath the water, which resulted, inevitably, in a deleterious effect on handling. *M-2* left her Portland naval base on the morning of 26 January 1932. She sank with the loss of her entire crew of sixty on manoeuvres in West Bay, formerly Bridport harbour, on the Jurassic Coast in Dorset, England. There was speculation that the stern hydroplanes had malfunctioned or that the hangar doors had been inadvertently left open; when found days later the doors were ajar with the *Peto* fastened inside. The accident ended aeroplane-carrying development by the Royal Navy.[1] *M-3* was used in 1927 for minelaying experiments and *M-4* was never completed. The costly saga of the *K*-class and its derivatives had drawn to an inauspicious close.

The French *Surcouf*

In 1934 France commissioned the 4,000-ton submarine *Surcouf*, an enormous boat by the standards of the day. It was an albatross, less accomplished than the

King of the Corsairs, Robert Surcouf (1773–1827) whose name it bore; as a privateer authorised by letters of marque, Surcouf had captured nearly fifty ships. The *Surcouf* carried a spotter plane in a hangar, which was built to the rear of its conning tower. The vastness of the *Surcouf* broke the London Naval Treaty of 1930, the signatories being Britain, America, Italy, Japan and France. A League of Nations agreement, it limited the scale of submarines and the size of their guns. The British *M*-class were 'big-gun' submarines which also infringed the spirit of the treaty. Loftily described as an underwater-cruiser, the *Surcouf* was designed to cause as much damage on the surface as beneath it. As a submerged aeroplane carrier its ambitions exceeded capabilities, a megalomania not unknown in submarine history. Another example of a mongrel vessel, it was expected to fulfil too many roles and consequently performed most of them badly. The *Surcouf* was an example of *folie de grandeur* and its end was inevitable: an inelegant mountain of scrap. Other nations, including Japan and Italy, conducted submarine-aeroplane trials. A fleet of submarines which emerged and disappeared after disgorging a squadron of aeroplanes was a beguiling notion which in the years ahead enticed strategists –and dreamers – and which resulted in diverse development programmes. Further experiments included the utilisation of small 'folding' aircraft or kit-planes, which could be more readily accommodated and assembled while the submarine was at sea.

Fleets and Specifications

Great Britain

C-class boats marked a halfway point between the raw *A* and *B* boats and the far more advanced *D*- and *E*-class vessels. Progress had been made in the use of hydroplanes, the diving planes which act like elevators on an aeroplane. Normally fitted in pairs to either side of bow and stern, diving planes pitch the bow up or down. When the *B*-class were being built, some had diving planes fitted to conning towers. After experimentation it was found unsatisfactory and they were then re-positioned at the bow. The finessing of diving planes and a growing dexterity in their use helped diving, surfacing and in keeping boats stable on a level plane. The *C*-class vessels displaced 288 tons on the surface and 318 tons submerged. A sizeable fleet of thirty-eight were built in two batches, the second group being marginally more powerful and of a greater range. The first batch were capable of 13 knots on the surface and 7.5 knots when dived. They had a range of 1,500 miles on the surface at 7 knots and 50 miles at 4 knots if submerged. The *C*-class boats which were built in the second batch had a range of 2,000 miles at 7 knots and 55 miles at 5 knots if dived. At 143ft with a 14ft beam they had a crew of sixteen. Spindle-shaped hulls made them difficult on the surface, though when dived their performance was in advance of the B-class. They lacked buoyancy, having a marginal 10 per cent reserve over surface displacement, and this was a conundrum with which architects would wrestle. As with all complicated contrivances, apparent solutions spawned new problems. One could search for greater buoyancy in the existing configuration, but submarines are cramped and restricted; in the early ones there was hardly room for the crew. Boats were packed with paraphernalia, every centimetre of space being utilised. One could bolt on inelegant and voluminous tanks which held nothing but air to enhance buoyancy, but the increased size and weight impaired performance, economy and handling; imagine forcing oneself under water clutching a beach ball. A seaworthy vessel needs width or 'beam' with v-shaped hull and deep keel. Early submarines were narrow, bereft of conventional hull or keel. Others had keels which proved too shallow to glue them into the water to keep them stable and upright. Boats heaved and rolled like corks. Archimedes' principle always posed problems: 'Any object, wholly or partially immersed in a fluid, is buoyed up by a force equal to the weight of the fluid displaced by the object.' That was fine for Archimedes of Syracuse, who espoused his principles 2,000 years before submarine designers tried to come to terms with the physics of buoyancy in which a submarine that floats has positive buoyancy; that which sinks is described as negatively buoyant; and that submarine which remains stable and level is known as being in a state of neutral buoyancy. Even in today's leviathans the physics of buoyancy, achieving more air while not compromising handling, line, hydrodynamics and space, raise daunting questions.

As the First World War neared Britain had fifty-seven boats, of which forty were the older, limited, but vaguely competent – if compared to some obsolete types deployed by other participants – B- and C-class boats, used mainly on coastal duties. The remaining seventeen were more potent long-range D- and E-class vessels. Eight D-class boats were produced, and these were specifically designed for long-range use. They had three torpedo tubes instead of two: two in the bow, a third in the stern; because of the vessels' size it was thought they might not be able to turn rapidly enough to engage the enemy but could, perhaps, fire a stern torpedo. The two bow tubes were sited one above the other instead of in the conventional side-by-side position. This allowed the boat to be more pointed at the bow; being less stubby and more streamlined improved its hydrodynamics and helped it cut through the water more easily. Saddle-tanks were also fitted for greater buoyancy. At 163ft, with a beam of 13.6ft, the D-class displaced 483 tons on the surface and 595 tons dived. They had a crew of twenty-five and were more habitable, allowing them to stay out longer. Surface speed was 14 knots and 10 knots if dived. The long-range capability was an impressive 2,500 miles at 10 knots on the surface. The first was built by Vickers at Barrow in circumstances of great secrecy. They bristled with innovation, and a policy of confidentiality and discretion seemed prudent. The most important developments were the twin diesel engines and the radio, which was fitted as a standard component. The diesel engines were sufficiently light and compact to be squeezed into the limited confines. *D-1* had a 1,200hp engine, while later craft had 1,750hp engines installed. If submerged they used an electric 550hp motor. Diesel engines had a safer flash point, making them less hazardous than petrol. The *E*-class provided Britain's submarine spine and, by 1917, another forty-six had been built. Swift production continued until the end of the war and, by then, another eighty-eight boats, of different types and not all successful, had been constructed. At war's end Britain had 137 boats with a further seventy-eight being built; the figure represented the largest and most successful submarine fleet in the world.

Germany

The first German submarine, *U-1*, was built by Krupps at its Germaniawerft yard at Kiel, northern Germany. The second half of the nineteenth century became a hot-house of engineering invention. It spawned technology barons who founded engineering and science-based businesses which came to dominate markets in Britain, Europe and America. This frenzied epoch of capitalism bred German companies that would grow into foremost contenders on the world stage. The years up to the Great War were lucrative for August Thyssen (1842–1926) and his conglomerate, which embraced iron ore, steel, coal mining and the accomplished Kiel shipyard. By 1904 Thyssen was the largest producer of rolled steel in Germany. With Tirpitz and the Kaiser overseeing a rebirth of the German Navy and its military, Thyssen's clout and coffers burgeoned. The defeat of Germany, however, brought it to the brink of collapse: properties were seized and others fell under French control; margins shrank on diminished trading, further eroded by the hyperinflation which blighted the post-war years.

The German *U-1* was an experimental coastal craft, as were the seven boats which followed in her class. She was launched on 4 August 1906. On 14 December 1906 she became a test and evaluation boat for the German Navy at its base in Eckernforde, Schleswig-Holstein, on the Baltic Sea near Kiel. Coming late to submarines, Germany had avoided the travails which beset petrol-powered British boats. *U-1* had a 400hp Korting heavy oil engine, but it emitted a plume of tell-tale white smoke which at night made the craft dragon-like. Billowing smoke, fire and sparks poured into the sky from a deck exhaust: so much for stealth. She had a single torpedo tube in her bow, two spare torpedoes and also carried a mine. At 139ft long and 12ft wide she displaced 238 tons on the surface and 283 tons submerged. Surface range was 1,500 miles at 10 knots and 50 miles at 5 knots. She had a crew of twelve which in later models increased to twenty-two. Boats after *U-1* grew larger: *U-5* to *U-8* were 188ft long and 18ft wide, weighing 506 tons on the surface and 636 tons submerged. *U-I* had a single heavy oil and electric engine, whereas later boats had twin engines. Armaments also increased: *U-2* to *U-8* had four torpedo tubes.

Five of the submarines were built at Germaniawerft in Kiel, with boats *U-2* to *U-4* constructed at Kaiserliche Werft Danzig shipyard. The Danzig yard, on the Toten Weichsel (Vistula River) on the Baltic, became a premier centre of construction, with forty-six vessels built there between 1906 and 1917. *U-1* undertook ambitious trials in 1907, journeying 600 miles in stormy seas from Wilhelmshaven on the North Sea to Kiel.[1] Germany's late entry allowed it to copy successful British and European designs, utilising the best and rejecting the inappropriate. From the outset, U-boat designers could concentrate on building craft propelled by diesel engines. Germany specialised in long-range U-boats for distant offensives. Britain wanted long-range vessels but needed inshore boats to defend its extensive island coast. Germany's more limited seaboard posed fewer problems. By August 1914 and the start of the Great War, Germany had twenty-eight boats: of those, eighteen were for training and defence. The other ten had greater power, range and armaments. In the war Germany built an additional 134 U-boats, 132 *UB*-class and 70 *UC*-class vessels. UBs were small submarines of the component type sent to Pola on the Adriatic: despatched by rail in bits they were an artful design and relatively easy to assemble. The initial batch of seventeen UB-1 boats were used on inshore operations, freeing up larger craft for more ambitious roles. In 1915 another thirty boats, *UB-II*-class, were bigger, faster and punchier. By war's end Germany had built eighty-five *UB-III* boats which displaced 500 tons on the surface − *UB-1s* displaced 127 tons − with five torpedo tubes and 105mm surface armament.[2] Germany also built minelaying *UC* submarines; small and prefabricated they were used first in the English Channel. A later class, operational from 1916, had three torpedo tubes and eighteen mines.[3]

The United States

America, Russia, Italy, France and Austria-Hungary had assembled their own submarine fleets, all being less formidable than those of Germany and Britain. The United States, largely through the tortuous endeavours of Simon Lake, John Holland and *Holland VI*, enjoyed a temporary headstart in submarines and their technology. She slipped behind Germany and Britain as their own refinements were perfected and the race to build bigger and more competent vessels quickened in the years leading up to the Great War. Between 1900 and 1903 America had seven *A*-class boats, which were bigger and more competent versions of *Holland I*. In the opening years of the Great War three of the class were refurbished and used for training purposes. They were inordinately primitive and described by a medical officer as virtually unfit for habitation. With a seven-man crew all activities took place in a cramped single space: cooking, sleeping, eating, defecating in an open lavatory, in boats which were notorious for their violent pitching in even relatively calm waters. The attainment of a degree of civilised habitation became something of an obsession for designers of subsequent classes. Three *B*-class boats comprised *Viper (B-1)*, *Cuttlefish (B-2)* and *Tarantula (B-3)*. They had a distinguished role in the Great War, being largely deployed as patrol vessels, much of it in the strategically important Philippines.

Five *C*-class craft were built. The first, *Octopus (C-1)*, constructed by the Electric Boat Company, was the first designed by L.Y. Spear after John Holland's acrimonious exit from the business. The final vessel in the class, *Snapper (C-5)* in 1911, was used for experimental work which included exercises with surface ships and aircraft. These were some of the earliest explorations in naval aviation. Development was undertaken into battery types and communications, and radio and signalling tests were conducted. *Snapper* was fitted with a bell, operated by compressed air, used for signalling while the craft was dived. *C*-class boats were some 23ft longer than *B*-class, measuring 105ft in length with a beam of 14ft. Their crew of fifteen was five more than on the *B*-class. The *B*-class displaced 140 tons on the surfaced, while the *C*-class displaced 230 tons.

Three *D*-class boats were built, the first being constructed in 1908. In the *D*-class emphasis was on safety, with internal configurations offering different layouts. Dividing craft into compartments was tried: the idea being that if one compartment flooded, its inundation would not necessarily imperil the entire boat. However, the programme met with only partial success. Dividing the craft increased weight, reduced already limited space and made access and moving about more difficult.

The *E* and *F*-class boats were a major advance on predecessor craft. The first, *Skipjack (E-1)*, was commissioned in 1912. Its name came from a small tuna fish and a fishing sloop, used in oyster dredging and found in the Chesapeake Bay. *Skipjack* was the command of an officer who became legendary in the US Navy and submarine service, Lieutenant – later Admiral – Chester W. Nimitz (1885–1966). *Skipjack* was used for far-reaching experiments, including underwater radio transmissions and use of the first ballistic gyrocompass, a device which became the subject of a legal wrangle. It was developed from the gyroscope invented in 1852 by the Frenchman Leon Foucault. In 1903 the German scientist Hermann Anschutz-Kaempfe (1872–1931) built a functioning gyrocompass and secured its patent. In 1908 the American inventor Elmer Sperry (1860–1930) acquired a patent for his own gyrocompass. In 1914 Sperry tried to sell his compass to the German Navy and was sued by Anschutz-Kaempfe, who won his case in 1915 by claiming Sperry had infringed his patent rights.

Skipjack, one of two in its class, had an illustrious career. In 1917, when the US entered the war, she left America to be deployed as a U-boat patrol vessel in the Azores. The first *F*-class boat – one of four – was commissioned in 1912. During exercises she and *F-3* collided. *F-1* suffered a gash in her port side and sank in ten seconds. She had a complement of twenty-two men, of which nineteen died.

The ensuing G-class were used as educational vessels. In 1915, after her record-breaking dive, USS *Seal* (*G-1*), designed by Simon Lake (see Chapter 1), was used for tuition purposes. Experiments conducted by her concentrated on sound and detection tests. She spent time patrolling and listening for U-boats thought to be in the Nantucket area, south of Cape Cod, Massachusetts. Towards the halfway mark in the war there persisted a lingering resentment towards the submarine; to the prescient its promise was patent and its role important if the US became a participant, which it did in 1917. Two developments reflected an increased emphasis on the submarine and, too, a growing certainty that the war which had subsumed Europe was contagious. The first was the establishment of a submarine base and submarine school; the second, in 1920, two years after the end of the war, was the founding of a listening and hydrophone school. Both were in New London, the best deep harbour in Long Island Sound. Once famous as a whaling port, it had secured its naval credentials during the American Revolutionary War. The G-class boats were used as tuition craft at the new schools. *G-1* was a crucial boat: she was Lake's first vessel for the US Navy, a pathfinder which pointed the way to future designs. She was decommissioned in 1920 after being towed to the Philadelphia Navy Yard. Sadly she was not preserved for posterity, an exhibit to entertain and inform future generations – the same could be said of other submarines and surface craft. Her end was undignified: a target for depth charge attacks. She sank in 1921 when assailed by experimental bombs.

When America entered the war her H-class submarines patrolled the east coast. It was off California, however, that two encountered difficulties. *H-3* met thick fog and became stuck on a sandbank, being refloated a month later. *H-1* suffered a similar though more calamitous fate: stuck fast on a sandbank in 1916 she sank after being towed free, an accident which cost the lives of four personnel, including that of her commanding officer, Lieutenant Commander James Webb. The K-class boats took part in experiments with far-reaching consequences: advanced testing on torpedoes, batteries, listening and detection devices. The class, comprising eight boats, was assigned to wartime patrol work off the Azores. Submarine types grew in range, potency and the way designers strove to safeguard crews by judicious compartmentalising. During these formative years there was a determination to create boats which were safer and more habitable.

The L-class, 167ft long and 17ft wide, had a complement of twenty-eight. Eleven were built. On the surface they could attain 14 knots and 10 knots if dived. Powered by a 900hp diesel engine and, beneath the waves, a 680hp electric motor, they had four tubes and eight torpedoes. On the surface they displaced 436 tons and 530 tons submerged. After service in the Azores, L-class boats crossed the Atlantic to Bantry Bay, County Cork, Ireland, a deep and natural harbour. Their task was vital: to support Allied shipping menaced in the Atlantic by U-boats.

Only one boat comprised the M-class and it was used largely for experimental purposes. Seven N-class boats were built, used mainly for training. A fleet of twenty boats, including those of the O-class, set off in 1918 for the Azores. But the Armistice was signed before their mission began, which prompted their return to the United States without seeing action. A number of O-class vessels were stored, refurbished and pressed back into service in the Second World War. In 1917 a sizeable twenty-seven R-class boats were laid down. Peace made them obsolete; as with the O-class, R-class craft were mothballed and saw heroic action over twenty years later in the Second World War.

Russia

Russia had been crippled by unrest from 1905, which continued spasmodically until the overthrow of the Tsarist autocracy in 1917. Given the tumultuous events and the birth of the Soviet Union, it is of no surprise her boats were unimpressive, her new masters consumed by more cataclysmic affairs. By 1914, the start of the war and the final chapter of tsarism, Russia had forty-one boats. They were of shabby quality and only suitable for inshore work. The service lacked men, materials and know-how. By 1917 and the October Revolution, the Bolsheviks were looking for a way out of Russia's involvement in the Great War. Internal strife was threatening the grip asserted by Lenin and his cohorts; it could hardly cope with its own problems let alone be involved in a wider European war. At this point, three years into the war, some twenty-three new Russian boats had been built with a better range but still bereft of quality and firepower. Beyond a handful of sinkings in the Black Sea and Baltic – steamers and sail boats, not the most formidable of targets – the Russian submarine presence in the war would be largely distinguished by courage and an iron determination rather than effectiveness.

Italy

Protecting Italy's long coastline posed problems of protection for its surface and submarine fleet. In 1914 the Italian Navy had twenty-five coastal submarines, as a crippling dearth of materials ruled out a construction programme. Italy deployed its submarines of limited range and speed in largely fruitless attacks on warships in the Adriatic; a costly strategy which incurred relatively heavy casualties and the loss of seven boats.

Austria-Hungary

The Austro-Hungarian Empire had only seven inshore craft; two were deemed inappropriate for action and used for training. In 1914 the Austro-Hungarian Navy was building six more submarines when their construction was taken over by Germany. Components of German boats were dispatched to Pola, Austria's main naval base on the Adriatic, where they were assembled and manned by Austro-Hungarian crews.

France

France had 123 boats in 1914.[4] However, a lack of standardisation and an inability to maintain them meant that only a handful were fit for service. She built twenty-eight boats in the war, a meagre tally if compared to the construction programmes undertaken in Britain and Germany. The French lead in building had vaporised, in part because of her inability to resist the lure of the novel, turning out new models with a bewildering assortment of gadgets. The love of the new cost her dear: by precluding standardisation, boat maintenance became difficult and expensive; the opposite policy was pursued successfully in Britain and Germany. France had been slow in adopting petrol let alone diesel engines. Many of her submarines were still steam-driven, especially long-range boats. Steam would always be dangerous and inefficient, whereas petrol engines were perilous but a marked advance on steam. Steam slowed dive time, making boats vulnerable to surface attack while crews struggled to close apertures and quell boilers. The handicap of boats becoming intolerably hot and fume-ridden remained largely unsolved. While France fiddled with steam, competitor nations had moved on by two stages: diesel was beginning to usurp petrol and in rare instances adopted. It seemed almost inconceivable that France had fallen behind in the submarine race as she had previously constructed a range of highly capable craft and, at one time, her lead had appeared insurmountable.

Japan

A curiosity of the period is the absence of Japan in submarine technology. Today Japan is in the technological vanguard. By the outbreak of the Second World War in 1939, she had the most formidable navy in the world and a submarine fleet of impressive scale and diversity. But ninety years prior, during the opening years of the 1850s, when Britain and others were molten with engineering breakthroughs and invention, Japan barely featured in the progress being witnessed elsewhere. Yet, even by 1920, after Britain and America, the Imperial Japanese Navy had become the third largest in the world. It was also one of the most accomplished: it won victories against all odds in the Sino-Japanese War (1894–95), in which it fought with China for control of Korea, and the Russo-Japanese War (1904–5) in which it fought Russia over the imperial prizes of Manchuria and Korea. Its submarines at this time were imported *Hollands* which were assembled in Japan, but which had arrived too late for the Russo-Japanese conflict. Japan's first home-built submarines were produced by the Kawasaki company in 1904 and were, effectively, copies of the *Holland*-class, though they were lighter and marginally more powerful. With her impressive presence today on the industrial and economic stage, it is easy to overlook that as late as the opening years of the 1850s Japan was still a technological backwater; after 1854 she underwent a frantic programme of development and industrialisation, which included the building of her mighty navy.

Notes

1 Hutchinson, *Jane's Submarines*, pp.39–40

2 Pope, Wheal and Robbins, *The Macmillan Dictionary of The First World War*, pp.453–55

3 Pope, Wheal and Robbins, *Macmillan Dictionary of The First World War*, p.484

4 Pope, Wheal and Robbins, *Macmillan Dictionary of The First World War*

Appendix L

The Dardanelles Campaign

Submarine endeavour represented one of the few bright spots in the infamous Dardanelles Campaign, a joint British and French action to capture Istanbul, the Ottoman capital. On 18 February 1915 the navy bombarded the Strait at its narrowest point, a mile or so wide. But it was well protected by forts and shore-based mobile artillery. Admiral Sir Sackville Hamilton Carden (1857–1930), the Irish-born commander of the British Squadron in the Mediterranean, had hatched the plan, having been instructed by the Admiralty to find a way of opening up the Strait. He led a formidable force – eighteen battleships, destroyers, cruisers and minesweepers – and had been optimistic with Intelligence assuring him that the Turks were running short of ammunition. Once the Ottoman guns had been quelled his minesweepers would clear the Turkish mines, allowing his squadron to progress through the Strait. In theory, Istanbul would be in Allied hands in less than a fortnight.

However, the resistance was unexpectedly severe and Carden's confidence short-lived; he fell ill, a victim of stress. Turkish mines damaged or sank five Allied warships: the 12,000-ton French battleship *Bouvet* (1893) was sunk; the French pre-*dreadnought* battleship *Gaulois* (1896) and the *Suffren* (1899) were damaged. The Royal Navy battlecruiser the *Inflexible* (1908) was damaged by shore batteries and a mine. The 16,000-ton battleship HMS *Irresistible* and the 13,000-ton battleship HMS *Ocean* were lost; *Ocean* went down after striking a mine while attempting to rescue survivors from the *Irresistible*. Carden's duties were assumed by his second-in-command, Admiral John de Robeck (1862–1928), also Irish-born, and one of the navy's most able commanders. The rout led to an inquiry. The fleet had been assailed by torpedoes, mines and artillery; communications were a fiasco and the warships outdated, chosen in the belief that forcing the Straits and taking Istanbul would be so easy it could be achieved by obsolete ships. It was not the finest hour for the British or French navies, nor is it difficult to imagine the fireworks in the Admiralty where Fisher and Churchill held sway.

Appendix M

Fessenden, Rutherford: Communications

The inventive Reginald Aubrey Fessenden (1866–1932), a naturalised American born in Quebec, Canada, was a radio pioneer, the inventor of the oscillator which bore his name. It was a useful if limited contraption, which enabled submarines to send signals to one another while underwater. At the start of the war he had worked in England, helping to develop devices which could identify the presence of a submarine. Sonar – Sound Navigation and Ranging – allows a submarine to navigate while submerged. The system is based on sound waves being transmitted and reflected to detect underwater objects or to measure underwater distances. A sound wave is transmitted beneath the water and the sonar operator in the ship or submarine listens for returning echoes which are relayed by loudspeaker or displayed on a monitor. The *Titanic* calamity of 1912 had given impetus to the research; it was hoped that navigation by echo sounding might be possible and that, if realised, it could warn about an iceberg such as that responsible for the catastrophe of the *Titanic*.

Lewis Nixon, a foremost shipbuilder who ran the Crescent Shipyard in New York, had been conducting sonar experiments since 1906; much of his work had been concerned with trying to devise a system to warn surface ships about drifting icebergs, unmarked on charts, and which at night or in fog represented a common hazard. The start of the Great War and the need to locate submarines brought urgency to the research. Eminent scientists, including the French physicist Paul Langevin (1872–1946) had sought a diversity of solutions. Another Canadian, the physicist Robert Boyle (1883–1995) worked with the British scientist Albert Beaumont Wood (1890–1964) to produce ASDIC for the British Board of Inventions in 1916; its acronym is said to mean Anti-Submarine Detection Investigation Committee, but no such body seems to have existed. The search to find a way of tracking submarines involved the finest minds: Wood and Boyle, as two examples – there were others – were former pupils of the Nobel Prize-winning Sir Ernest (later Lord) Rutherford (1871–1937), the great New Zealand-born scientist, celebrated as the first to split the atom, and who in the Great War had worked on devising ways of tracking submarines.[1] In around 1900 Rutherford had been detecting 'Hertzian' waves and sending radio signals the length of the Cavendish laboratory in Cambridge, England, the world famous institution he later led. Hertzian is a form of telegraphy by wireless, taking its name from the German physicist Heinrich Hertz (1857–1894) whose instruments included an oscillator for producing waves and a resonator to detect them. Different experiments and the scientific and intellectual input saw submarine tracking prototypes being produced before the end of the war. Further refinement and real practicality came later.

Notes

1 Hackmann, *Seek & Strike*

Appendix N

The Mine and Depth Charge

While indisputably deadly, it was the *perception* of a mine which could further erode morale and chew at already frayed nerves. Mines had been used for generations: In 1900 they were deployed in the Boxer Uprising in China; Russia and Japan lost ships to them in the 1904–5 Russo-Japanese conflict; in the North Sea 70,000 were laid by Britain and its allies to block the northern exits of the North Sea; in excess of 230,000 mines were laid in all during the four years of the Great War, and it took fleets of minesweepers six months to decontaminate the oceans.

Alongside the mine the depth charge would become another submarine hazard. There had been earlier designs, but the first truly effective device came in 1916 from the Royal Navy Mine and Torpedo School at HMS *Vernon*. Originally, depth charges were large metal canisters, similar to an oil drum, packed with explosive. They were pitched over the transom, or the side of a warship, or released through a chute. They were supposed to detonate at a pre-determined depth by the use of a hydrostatic valve. Some did, many did not. Like all else to do with submarine and anti-submarine technology, in their initial guise they were as dangerous to the hunter as the prey. Early ones exploded unintentionally, sooner or later than expected. It was a hit or miss business, literally. With warships trying to guess where and at what depth a submarine might lurk, few depth charges hit their targets. To have achieved that would have been beyond luck. The potency of the depth charge lay in the enormity of its blast. If detonated in close vicinity to a submarine it could shake ger to pieces, loosening joints, causing leaks to burst forth, its violence making instruments malfunction and forcing the vessel to the surface; she could then be rammed by a warship or decimated by guns. It was not especially effective in the Great War, though towards its conclusion depth charges were modified and could be fired in multiples by cannon. Its real potency would be refined during the Second World War.

Appendix O

Godfrey Herbert and *Q-boats*

In a previous role Godfrey Herbert had been the commanding officer of the early British submarine *D-5*, built by Vickers at Barrow and commissioned in February 1911. The *D*-class were used to protect Britain's east coast in the early stages of the Great War. Herbert's *D-5* was the first submarine to fire a torpedo in the war. She fired two at the new German light cruiser *Rostock* in the Heligoland Bight. They missed, passing beneath her – the *Rostock* was later sunk at Jutland in 1916. It is feasible the early problem of warheads being heavier than mock versions caused Herbert's torpedoes to miss. On 3 November 1914, *D-5* joined other *D*-class boats to attack German warships bombarding Great Yarmouth on the Norfolk coast, today famed primarily as a holiday resort but formerly a significant port – it still has extensive oil, gas and wind farm servicing activities – with a thriving fishing industry. *D-5* struck a mine while off Great Yarmouth and sank; out of twenty-five only five survived, including Herbert.

A year later Herbert was embroiled in a *Q-boat* episode which became known as the *Baralong* incident. *Q-boats* represented another type of subterfuge. A supposedly unarmed ship disguised as a 'soft target' would tempt a U-boat to the surface. The ship would then reveal itself as heavily armed and out-gun her assailant. It was another tactic like that of the 'tethered goat', which would be made obsolete by a growing familiarity; once the trick had lost its surprise, and German submarine commanders had become wise to it, it was inevitable that the number of U-boats tempted to come to the surface would decrease. There had, however, been a number of instances in which British decoy vessels or *Q-boats* – named after their home port at Queenstown, Ireland – had succeeded in sinking unsuspecting German U-boats. By 1915 the U-boat peril had increased and the British Admiralty was determined to combat them: The *Q-boat* experiment was part of its response.

On 19 August 1915 Herbert was in command of the *Q-ship* HMS *Baralong* when it sank *U-27*, which had attacked a merchant steamer, the *Nicosian*, of the Leyland Line, carrying a cargo of mules from America. *U-27*, under the command of *Kapitanleutnant* Bernd Wegener, had shelled the *Nicosian*, forcing her to halt. *U-27* had a formidable record. She had already achieved glory in an especially rare encounter, being the first U-boat to sink another submarine, the British *E-13*, which she had torpedoed on 18 October 1914. When Godfrey Herbert's *Baralong* arrived at the point where the U-boat had stopped the *Nicosian*, his ship was disguised in American colours, the US still being neutral at this stage of the war. The *Baralong* made the international signal to *U-27* that she would approach the scene of the intervention to rescue the *Nicosian's* crew. However, when hidden from *U-27's* gaze, disguising herself behind the *Nicosian*, she swiftly raised the white ensign and suddenly opened fire, repeatedly hitting the U-boat, which began to sink. It is alleged that Herbert then opened fire on some twelve German submariners who had survived his assault and begun to swim towards the *Nicosian* in what Herbert interpreted as an attempt to scuttle or set it ablaze; he also, it is alleged, ordered a party of marines to board the *Nicosian* and shoot six German submariners who had managed to board her. Whatever the truth, all thirty-seven hands died. It is believed that after the incident when they were safely back in port, the mule-handlers who had been on the *Nicosian* spread rumours of an atrocity by the British.

It was as difficult then, as it still remains, to decipher the truth; it happened at an especially fevered time in the conflict. U-boats were beginning their campaign against unarmed merchant craft, and Herbert and his crew were aware that on the same day, 19 August 1915, a date which would take on its own maritime infamy, another German submarine, *U-24*, had without warning torpedoed and sunk, south of the Irish coast, the White Star liner *Arabic* (15,801 tons) which had been making for the United States. A total of forty-four people had been killed, a handful being Americans. The attack was in direct violation of assurances given on a regular basis by Germany to the United States. Germany claimed the sinking of the *Arabic* had been unintentional; that it had been difficult to recognise her as a passenger liner; that she had turned threateningly towards *U-24*, which had caused her commander, *Kapitanleutnant* Rudolf Schneider, to think that her intention was to ram his craft. The German protests were naive: the single-funnel *Arabic* was not the largest passenger vessel afloat, but at 600ft and clearly marked, it should have been obvious to a captain as seasoned as Schneider that she was a passenger liner. Schneider was 33; at that age, and given his experience, he was something of a veteran. He had been in the navy fourteen years and had already sunk the pre-dreadnought HMS *Formidable* (1898) on 1 January 1915 in the English Channel. Godfrey Herbert, for his part, before intercepting *U-27*, had picked up wireless calls from the stricken *Arabic*; it was in his mind, and that of his crew, that Germany had committed an outrage. The *Baralong* incident was used as German propaganda. Germany would reap worldwide opprobrium for its U-boat attacks on unarmed shipping. The *Baralong* incident provided it with her own atrocity charge which she could level against the British.

While acting as a *Q-ship* the *Baralong* was dogged by dispute. Originally a tramp steamer, built in 1901, her original name had been the *Wyandra*. Prior to the Great War she had served uneventfully as a vessel in the Ellerman & Bucknall Line, part of the Ellerman group founded by the shipping magnate Sir John Reeves Ellerman (1862–1933). At the outbreak of the Great War a variety of different ships in Ellerman's fleet were acquired by the government and converted for use in the conflict, the little *Wyandra* (4,192 tons) being one. She had been converted and disguised as a decoy ship at Barry Docks, Wales, the world's largest coal exporting base. Cunningly reconfigured to look like an innocent merchantman, a juicy target to whet the appetite of marauding U-boats, her hidden armaments included a trio of 12-pounder guns, offering sufficient muscularity to cripple any unsuspecting U-boat that might venture to the surface.

A month after the *Wyandra*, renamed the *Baralong*, had destroyed *U-27* she was on patrol again under a new commander, Lieutenant Commander A. Wilmot-Smith. Herbert had by then returned to the submarine service. Wilmot-Smith came upon a merchant vessel, the cargo steamer *Urbino* (6,651 tons), owned by the extensive Wilson Line of Hull, on Britain's north-east coast, and making passage from New York to Hull. Built by Earles Shipbuilding and Engineering, a leading constructor based in Hull, she was being attacked by the German submarine *U-41*. Accounts differ as to the precise detail of what followed. The *Baralong* was flying an American flag, as she had been doing when Herbert had made his attack on *U-27*. It appears *U-41* dived when the *Baralong* approached. Wilmot-Smith put down a small boat to rescue crewmen from the *Urbino*, in advance of the German submarine destroying the ship. The U-boat rose to the surface once more and the *Baralong* opened fire, destroying the conning tower and killing the U-boat commander. The submarine crash dived but had to quickly resurface. Two submariners leaped into the water to save themselves, while the rest of their compatriots were drowned as the submarine went down. The crew of the *Urbino* and the two surviving submariners were rescued; one, an officer, was badly wounded and repatriated. He subsequently told stories of a second *Baralong* atrocity, which triggered German disgust and became more fodder for the Kaiser's (not particularly effective) propaganda machine. The allegations were dismissed by the British Admiralty, though what actually happened has been lost in the fog of war. The events hinged on interpretation of the convoluted rules of war, which covered such occurrences as flying a false flag – allowed as long as it was struck before a *Q-ship* began hostilities – and putting captured crew members into a lifeboat, which was illegal, as a lifeboat was not considered a safe refuge. The latter is what the U-boat is said to have been doing with the *Urbino* crew when the *Baralong* intervened. The *Baralong* incidents – the second in terms of international diplomacy being judged far less onerous – and, in addition, the sinking of the *Arabic*, worsened the already deteriorating German–American relationship.

Bibliography

Appleyard, Rollo, *Charles Parsons: His Life and Work* (Constable, 1933)

Arnold-Forster, Rear Admiral D., *The Ways of the Navy* (Ward, Lock & Co., 1931)

Ashmead-Bartlett, Ellis, *The Uncensored Dardanelles* (Hutchinson, 1928)

Aspinall-Oglander, Brigadier General Cecil F., *Roger Keyes: Being the Biography of Admiral of the Fleet Lord Keyes of Zeebrugge and Dover* (Hogarth Press, 1951)

Bacon, Admiral Sir Reginald, *The Dover Patrol, 1915–1917*, 2 vols (Hutchinson, 1919)

— *The Life of Lord Fisher of Kilverstone*, 2 vols (Hodder & Stoughton, 1929)

Barnes, Eleanor C. (Lady Yarrow), *Alfred Yarrow: His Life and Work* (Arnold, 1923)

Batchelor, John and Chant, Christopher, *The Complete Encyclopaedia of Submarines* (Rebo International, 2009)

Bauer, Admiral Hermann, *Reichsleitung and U-Bootseinsatz, 1914–1918* (Klosterhaus, 1956)

Beresford, Admiral Lord Charles, *The Betrayal* (P.S. King, London, 1912)

Birnbaum, Karl E., *Peace Moves and U-Boat Warfare* (Almqvist & Wiksell, 1958)

Brice, Martin H., *M-Class Submarines* (Outline Publications, 1983)

Brodie, Bernard, *Sea Power in the Machine Age* (Oxford University Press, 1943)

Brodie, C.G., *Forlorn Hope 1915: The Submarine Passage of the Dardanelles* (W.J. Bryce, 1958)

Brown, D.K., *The Grand Fleet: Warship Design and Development 1906–1922* (Seaforth Publishing, 2010)

Carr, Lieutenant William G., in the *By Guess and By God: The Story of the British Submarines War* (Hutchinson, London, *c.* 1930)

Chalmers, Rear Admiral, William S., *Max Horton and the Western Approaches* (Hodder & Stoughton, 1954)

Chatterton, E. Keble, *Beating the U-boats* (Hurst & Blackett, 1942)

— *Fighting the U-boats* (Hurst & Blackett, 1943)

— *Q-ships and their Story* (Ayer Publishing, 1980)

Churchill, Winston S., *The World Crisis*, 6 vols (Butterworth, 1923–1931)

Compton-Hall, Richard, *Submarine Boats* (Conway Maritime, 1983)

— *The Submarine Pioneers* (Sutton Publishing, 1999)

Corbett, Julian S., *Some Principles of Maritime Strategy* (Longmans, 1911)

Cowie, Capt. J.S., *Mines, Minelayers and Minelaying* (Oxford University Press, 1949)

Dewar, Vice Admiral, K.G.B, *The Navy from Within* (Gollancz, 1939)

Dewey, George, *Autobiography of George Dewey* (Naval Institute Press, 1987; originally published in 1913 by Charles Scribner's Sons)

Dickinson, H.W., *Roger Fulton, Engineer and Artist* (The Bodley Head, 1913)

Edwards, Lieutenant Commander Kenneth, *We Dive at Dawn* (Rich & Cowan, 1939)

Evans, A.S., *Beneath the Waves: A History of HM Submarine Losses* (William Kimber, 1986)

Everitt, Don, *The K-Boats* (Harrap, 1963)

Fisher, Admiral of the Fleet, *Memories* (Hodder & Stoughton, 1919)

— *Records* (Hodder & Stoughton, 1919)

Frank, Wolfgang, *The Sea Wolves* (Weidenfeld & Nicolson, 1955)

Gayer, Lieutenant Commander Albert, *Die deutschen U-Boote in ihrer Kriegführung 1914–1918* (Mittler, 1930)

Gibson, R.H., Prendergast, M., *The German Submarine War, 1914–1918* (Constable, 1931).

Grant, Robert M., *U-Boats Destroyed* (Putnam, 1964)

— *U-Boat Intelligence, 1914–1918* (Putnam, 1969)

Gray, Edwyn, *A Damned Un-English Weapon* (Seeley, Service & Co. Ltd, 1971)

— *British Submarines in the Great War* (Charles Scribner's Sons, 1971)

— *The Devil's Device* (Seeley, Service & Co. Ltd, 1975)

— *Few Survived: A History of Submarine Disasters* (Pen & Sword, 1996)

Halpern, Paul G., *The Mediterranean Naval Situation, 1908–1914* (Harvard University Press, 1970)

Halpern, Paul G. (ed.), *The Keyes Papers, Selections from Private and Official Correspondence of Admiral of the Fleet Baron Keyes of Zeebrugge*, 3 vols (Allen & Unwin for the Navy Records Society, 1972–81)

— *A Naval History of World War 1* (Routledge, 1994)

Hankey, Lord, *Government Control in War* (Cambridge University Press, 1945)

— *The Supreme Command*, 2 vols (Allen & Unwin, 1961)

Hashagen, Commander Ernst, *The Log of a U-Boat Commander* (Putnam, 1931)

Hezlet,Vice Admiral Sir Arthur, *The Submarine and Sea Power* (Peter Davies, 1967)

High, Robin, *The British Rigid Airship, 1908–1921* (Foulis, London, 1961)

Hislam, Percival A., *The North Sea Problem* (Holden & Hardingham, 1914)

Horton, Edward, *The Illustrated History of the Submarine* (Sidgwick & Jackson, 1974)

Hough, Richard, *Dreadnought: A History of the Modern Battleship* (Michael Joseph, 1965)

— *First Sea Lord: An Authorized Biography of Admiral Lord Fisher* (Allen & Unwin, 1969)

Hubatsch, Professor Walther, *Die Ara Tirpitz: Studien zur deutschen Marinepolitik 1890–1918* (Musterschmidt, 1955)

Humble, Richard, *Naval Warfare* (Little, Brown, 2002)

Hurd, Sir Archibald, *Who Goes There?* (Hutchinson, 1942)

Hutchinson, Robert, *Jane's Submarines* (Harper Collins, 2001)

Ireland, Bernard and Parker, John, *The Illustrated Encyclopaedia of Destroyers, Frigates & Submarines* (Hermes House, an imprint of Anness Publishing, 2011)

James, Robert Rhodes, *Gallipoli* (Batsford, 1965)

James, Admiral Sir William, *The Eyes of the Navy: A Biographical Study of Admiral Sir Reginald Hall* (Methuen, 1955)

Jameson, Rear Admiral Sir William, *The Most Formidable Thing* (Hart-Davis, 1965)

— *Submariners VC* (Hart-Davis, 1962)

Jellicoe, Admiral of the Fleet, Earl, *The Crisis of the Naval War* (Cassell, 1920)

— *The Submarine Peril* (Cassell, 1934)

Kemp, Lieutenant Commander P.K., *HM Submarines* (Jenkins, 1952)

Keyes, Admiral Sir Roger, *The Naval Memoirs of Admiral of the Fleet Sir Roger Keyes: The Narrow Seas to the Dardanelles, 1910–1915, vol. 1; Scapa Flow to the Dover Straits, 1916–1918, vol. 2* (Thornton Butterworth, 1934–35)

— *Adventures Ashore and Afloat* (Harrap, 1939)

King-Hall, Commander Stephen, *A North Sea Diary, 1914–1918* (Newnes, 1936)

Lambert, Nicholas (ed.), *The Submarine Service, 1900–1918* (Ashgate for the Navy Records Society, 2001)

Laughton, J.K., *Studies in Naval History: Biographies* (Adamant Media, 2001; facsimile reprint of 1887 edition Longmans, Green & Co.)

Lavery, Brian, *Ship* (National Maritime Museum / Dorling Kindersley, 2004)

Lewis, Michael, *The Navy of Britain* (Allen & Unwin, 1948)

Mackay, Richard, *A Precarious Existence* (Periscope Publishing, 2003)

Mahan, Alfred T., *Influence of Seapower upon History* (Farrar Straus & Giroux, 1957)

March, Edgar, J., *British Destroyers, 1892–1953* (Seeley Service, 1966)

Marder, Arthur J., *British Naval Policy, 1880–1905: The Anatomy of British Sea Power* (Putnam, 1941)

— *Fear God and Dread Nought: The Correspondence of Admiral of the Fleet Lord Fisher of Kilverstone*, 3 vols (Cape, 1952–59)

— *From the Dreadnought to Scapa Flow: The Royal Navy in the Fisher Era, 1904–1919*, 5 vols (Oxford University Press, 1961–70)

— *From the Dreadnought to Scapa Flow*, vol. 5 (Oxford University Press, 1970)

Marshall, P.J., *The Cambridge Illustrated History of the British Empire* (Cambridge University Press, 1996)

Massie, Robert K., *Dreadnought: Britain, Germany and the Coming of the Great War* (Jonathan Cape, 1992; Pimlico edition, 1993)

— *Castles of Steel: Britain, Germany and the Winning of the Great War at Sea* (Random House, 2003)

Michelsen, Vice Admiral Andreas, *Der U-Bootskrieg, 1914–1918* (Koehler, 1925)

Miller, David and Jordan, John, *Modern Submarine Warfare* (Salamander, 1987)

Morison, Elting E., *Admiral Sims and the Modern American Navy* (Houghton Mifflin, 1942)

Parkes, Oscar, *British Battleships* (Seeley Service, 1966)

Pope, Stephen, Wheal, Anne and Robbins Keith, *The Macmillan Dictionary of the First World War* (Macmillan, 1995)

Preston, Anthony, *World's Great Submarines* (Blitz Editions, 1998)

— *World's Worst Warships* (Conway Maritime Press, 2002)

Raeder, Grand Admiral Erich, *My Life* (US Naval Institute, 1960)

Robinson, Douglas H., *The Zeppelin in Combat: A History of the German Naval Airship Division, 1912–1918* (Foulis, 1966)

Roskill, Captain S.W., *Naval Policy between the Wars* (Collins, 1968)

— *Hankey: Man of Secrets* (Collins, 1970)

Scott, J.D., *Vickers: A History* (Weidenfeld & Nicolson, 1962)

Shankland, Peter and Hunter, Anthony, *Dardanelles Patrol* (Collins, 1964)

Sprout, Harold and Sprout, Margaret, *Toward a New Order of Sea Power: American Naval Policy and the World Scene, 1918–1922*, 2nd edition (The University Press, 1943)

Sueter, Rear Admiral Murray F., *Airmen or Noahs* (Pitman, 1928)

— *The Evolution of the Submarine Boat, Mine, and Torpedo: From the 16th Century to the Present Time (1907)* (Kessinger Publishing, 2009; facsimile reprint)

Swinfield, John, G., *Airship: Design, Development and Disaster* (Conway Maritime; US Naval Institute Press, 2012)

Sykes, Major General Sir Frederick, *From Many Angles: An Autobiography* (Harrap, 1942)

Talbot, Frederick A., *Submarine* (William Heinemann, 1915)

Thompson, Julian, *The Imperial War Museum Book of the War at Sea, 1914–1918* (Sidgwick & Jackson, 2005)

Tirpitz, Grand Admiral. Alfred von, *My Memoirs*, 2 vols (Hurst & Blackett, 1919)

Treadwell, Terry C., *Strike from Beneath the Sea: A History of Aircraft-carrying Submarines* (Tempus Publishing, 1999)

Index